Healthy Teachers, Happy Classrooms

Twelve Brain-Based Principles
to Avoid Burnout, Increase Optimism,
and Support Physical Well-Being

MARCIA L. TATE

Solution Tree | Press

a division of

Solution Tree

555 North Morton Street
Bloomington, IN 47404
800.733.6786 (toll free) / 812.336.7700
FAX: 812.336.7790

email: info@SolutionTree.com
SolutionTree.com

Visit **go.SolutionTree.com/teacherefficacy** to download the free reproducibles in this book.

Printed in the United States of America

Library of Congress Cataloging-in-Publication Data

Names: Tate, Marcia L., author.
Title: Healthy teachers, happy classrooms : twelve brain-based principles
  to avoid burnout, increase optimism, and support physical well-being /
  Marcia L. Tate.
Other titles: 12 brain based principles to avoid burnout, increase
  optimism, and support physical well being
Description: Bloomington, IN : Solution Tree Press, [2022] | Includes
  bibliographical references and index.
Identifiers: LCCN 2021053473 (print) | LCCN 2021053474 (ebook) | ISBN
  9781952812972 (Paperback) | ISBN 9781952812989 (eBook)
Subjects: LCSH: Teachers--Job stress. | Burn out (Psychology)--Prevention.
  | Teaching--Psychological aspects. | Stress management.
Classification: LCC LB2840.2 .T38 2022 (print) | LCC LB2840.2 (ebook) |
  DDC 371.1--dc23/eng/20211213
LC record available at https://lccn.loc.gov/2021053473
LC ebook record available at https://lccn.loc.gov/2021053474

Solution Tree
Jeffrey C. Jones, CEO
Edmund M. Ackerman, President

Solution Tree Press
President and Publisher: Douglas M. Rife
Associate Publisher: Sarah Payne-Mills
Managing Production Editor: Kendra Slayton
Editorial Director: Todd Brakke
Art Director: Rian Anderson
Copy Chief: Jessi Finn
Senior Production Editor: Suzanne Kraszewski
Content Development Specialist: Amy Rubenstein
Acquisitions Editor: Sarah Jubar
Proofreader: Elisabeth Abrams
Cover and Text Designer: Laura Cox
Editorial Assistants: Sarah Ludwig and Elijah Oates

Acknowledgments

The early 2020s have been an unprecedented time in education. In addition to the multitude of typical responsibilities inherent in the teaching profession, educators were being asked to deliver quality instruction in either a tenuous in-person format or virtually, and even in both ways simultaneously. Teachers and administrators rose to the occasion daily. This book is dedicated to you!

Just as health-care professionals and service workers deserve our gratitude, so do you, our educators. Thank you, teachers and administrators, for everything you did and continue to do on a daily basis to grow the dendrites (brain cells) of the students in your charge. This book is my attempt to keep you healthier as you perform an essential service.

Teaching was already challenging, prior to the pandemic, and is still now. Yet, you are meeting the needs of students daily while simultaneously delivering quality instruction, often under less than desirable circumstances. Know that you are appreciated! Continue to do what you do since you are making such a difference!

I am always grateful to my family members for their support of my professional endeavors. Thanks to my husband, Tyrone, of over forty years, and my children, Jennifer, Jessica, and Christopher, whose love undergirds me daily. Jennifer, a building principal, deals firsthand with helping to ensure that her teachers and students are both healthy and happy daily. To our nine grandchildren, I am happiest when I am spending quality time with you.

To my administrative assistant and dear friend, Carol Purviance, for over thirty years that we have worked together. I owe you a debt of gratitude for continuing to improve the quality of my work and for ensuring that the company that Tyrone and I founded, Developing Minds, Inc., continues to thrive.

Thank you, my friend, Douglas Rife, for providing me an opportunity to share my writings with Solution Tree. I am looking forward to another bestseller!

Visit **go.SolutionTree.com/teacherefficacy** to download the free reproducibles in this book.

Table of Contents

Reproducible pages are in italics.

About the Author

 **Marcia L. Tate, EdD,** is the former executive director of professional development for the DeKalb County School System in Decatur, Georgia. During her thirty-year career with the district, she has been a classroom teacher, reading specialist, language arts coordinator, and staff development executive director.

Marcia is currently an educational consultant and has taught over 500,000 administrators, teachers, parents, and business and community leaders throughout the world. She is the author of the eight books in the best-selling *Worksheets Don't Grow Dendrites* series and *Formative Assessment in a Brain-Compatible Classroom: How Do We Really Know They're Learning?* Her latest two books are *100 Brain-Friendly Lessons for Unforgettable Teaching and Learning K–8* and *100 Brain-Friendly Lessons for Unforgettable Teaching and Learning 9–12.* Participants in her workshops refer to them as some of the best ones they have ever experienced since Marcia uses the strategies outlined in her books to actively engage her audiences.

Marcia received her bachelor's degree in psychology and elementary education from Spelman College in Atlanta, Georgia. She earned her master's degree in remedial reading from the University of Michigan in Ann Arbor, her specialist degree in educational leadership from Georgia State University, and her doctorate in educational leadership from Clark Atlanta University.

Marcia is married to Tyrone Tate and is the proud mother of three children: Jennifer, Jessica, and Christopher, and nine grandchildren: Christian, Aidan, Maxwell, Aaron, Roman, Shiloh, Aya, Noah, and Alyssa.

Marcia and her husband own the company Developing Minds, Inc. Visit her website at www.developingmindsinc.com. You can also follow her on Twitter and Instagram at @drmarciatate.

To book Marcia L. Tate for professional development, contact pd@SolutionTree.com.

Introduction

Julia Sanders rises at 5:30 a.m. She rushes to get ready for her day, first preparing breakfast for her three school-aged children. Following breakfast, and under normal circumstances, she would make sure that each child had on a clean and neat uniform, had their school bags packed, and got safely on the school bus. However, thanks to the COVID-19 pandemic, Julia's children don't need uniforms, backpacks, or a school bus since they receive virtual instruction at home. Julia cannot remain at home with them, though; once her aunt arrives to spend the day with the Sanders children, Julia leaves for her job as an eighth-grade teacher where she teaches using a concurrent model: teaching eleven socially-distanced students face to face in her classroom while delivering virtual instruction to the sixteen remaining students whose parents have chosen online learning.

Julia must keep all her students engaged as they all wear masks and socially distance. Some virtual instruction students have little support at home while online and find it difficult to remain on task. They are failing to submit many of their assignments. Julia is constantly reminding her in-person students to remain apart from one another, even during engaging tasks. She is disheartened by her inability to provide those reassuring physical touches that so many of her students need. She consistently sanitizes the classroom for her own safety and the safety of the students she loves.

When school ends at 3:20 p.m., Julia heads home, but she isn't done teaching for the day. She must be sure that her own children have learned their lessons and completed their daily assignments. Aunt Peggie is a tremendous help, but she doesn't have the skills or ability to keep up with the children's work.

Julia then receives a call informing her that a close contact of one of her students has tested positive for COVID-19. She discovers that the parents have emailed her, upset that their child must remain at home until he receives a negative COVID test. The student's parents indicated that they live paycheck to paycheck and need to be at work. They don't have the resources to arrange care at home for their child. Life is further complicated for Julia as she is trying to figure out ways to teach concepts that could easily be understood in an in-person setting, but not as easily virtually. She has also had to redesign assignments since it becomes difficult for her students to acquire the necessary materials to complete some projects. Other students have simply disengaged, so she has to contemplate how to regain their attention by redesigning her lesson delivery.

Before she retires for the evening around 10:00 p.m. absolutely exhausted, Julia places a grocery order (after wrestling with computer problems for a half hour) that she will pick up on her way home from work the next day, throws another load of laundry in the dryer, and looks at her children's schedules for the week to determine how she will get them to their after-school appointments with all her other commitments.

She goes to bed knowing she must replicate this day again tomorrow and for the remainder of the week and beyond. She feels overwhelmed, overworked, and hopeless. She works hard to fight back the tears!

A Challenging Profession

This is my forty-eighth year in education. I would venture to say that teaching is more challenging today than ever before. Even without the challenges of COVID-19, many teachers are describing themselves as simply burnt out. In other words, the fire and passion they once had for teaching have simply been extinguished. According to Richard Ingersoll, Lisa Merrill, and Daniel Stuckey (2018), experts on teacher burnout, 40 to 50 percent of those who enter teaching decide to depart the profession within the first five years. What, then, can cause burnout? Lou Whitaker (2018), in his article "Stress: What Happens to a Teacher's Brain When It Reaches Burnout?", lists five reasons why so many teachers burn out:

1. Loss of control over what happens in the classroom due to increased district, state, and national mandates

2. *Cognitive dissonance* between what should be going on in the workplace and what is actually happening

3. Increasing complex workload with timelines that are not realistic

4. Lack of recognition for a job well done

5. Feelings of intense isolation once the classroom door closes

The chronic stress caused by burnout can overload cognitive skills and neuroendocrine systems resulting in diminished cognitive function in the areas of creativity, short-term memory, and problem-solving (Michel, 2016).

In my work with educators, I have collected more than two thousand emails from teachers, many of which reflect the challenges they face. Here is a part of one such email from a beginning teacher in New York prior to COVID-19.

> I am in my first year of teaching (social studies, eighth grade). I have felt overwhelmed by the duties that come with being a teacher. I have felt discouraged and disheartened more often than I anticipated. I've continued to compare myself to other teachers and felt very small because of it. It has been a tough year! As teachers, we are pulled into so many different directions. One moment we're focused on literacy and text evidence, the next we're all about integrating technology, the next is project-based learning, on and on. As a new teacher, I don't know where to even start! (Eighth-grade social studies teacher, personal communication, April 10, 2017)

Then there are the challenges that veteran educators have always faced, such as how to meet the physical, social, and emotional needs of students whose needs are not being met in their home environments. In fact, according to Don Colbert (2009), this generation may be the first in two hundred years whose life expectancy will not exceed that of their parents. Surprisingly, it has nothing to do with COVID-19. It has to do with the nutritional deficits, lack of movement, and high-stress lifestyles of many of today's children.

Teachers are dealing with so much, yet the research is clear: the single most important impact on student achievement does not come from the curriculum, textbooks, or technology. *The biggest impact is from you, the classroom teacher.* According to John Hattie's Visible Learning (n.d.) website, with an effect size of 1.57, Collective Teacher Efficacy (CTE) is very strongly correlated with student achievement. *CTE* is defined as "the collective belief of teachers in their ability to positively affect students" (Visible Learning, n.d.). Therefore, it stands to reason that if we can provide teachers with specific ways to remain healthy and satisfied with their work, we give students the best chance of staying happy in the classroom and becoming successful at school.

The Brain Research

Since the late 1990s, I have studied the brain and its implications for teaching and learning. Even though there is still so much about the brain that remains a mystery, we know more today than ever before. In this book, I have attempted to examine neuroscientific research and make practical recommendations of its applications for educators. After all, teachers interact with and instruct brains daily. I have often said that the only people who should know more about the brain than a teacher are a neurosurgeon or neuroscientist.

Much of the brain research I studied appears in the bestselling series *Worksheets Don't Grow Dendrites: 20 Instructional Strategies That Engage the Brain* (Tate, 2016). This series, with some books focusing on specific subjects and others cross curricular, delineates twenty brain-based strategies that every teacher, regardless of grade level or subject matter, should use to deliver instruction. These include the common-sense strategies of cooperative learning, games, graphic organizers, metaphor, movement, music, storytelling, and technology, to name only a few. This book shifts the focus from classroom strategies for use with students to positively impact learning to principles based on brain research for teacher health and happiness.

The Purpose of This Book

There are a multitude of books that address teacher health and happiness; there are very few, however, that synthesize the principles that correlate with improved health and longevity and also provide the brain research that supports why these principles work for both the brain and body. It is my hope that this book will instruct and support you about how you can remain mentally and physically healthier throughout your educational career, avoiding burnout and increasing your optimism.

For those of you who are beginning teachers, this book may assist you in initially identifying those essential components of a healthy lifestyle and provide you with specific suggestions for classroom application. For those who are veteran teachers, this book enables you to stop and assess where you are in your personal and professional journey and can add some tools to your toolbox. For those of you who are nearing the end of your career in education, you will find information that can increase your longevity and help you maintain the passion you felt when you entered the profession. This book is also for administrators, teacher leaders, instructional coaches, counselors, or anyone else who devotes their professional career to improving the lives of teachers and students.

About This Book

This book is divided into twelve chapters. Each chapter defines a longevity principle, explores the brain rationale for why that practice leads to improved health and longevity, and provides examples of how to operationalize the principle into daily living. The twelve principles for longevity are as follows.

1. Passion for your purpose
2. Laughter
3. Optimism
4. Games
5. Movement
6. Music
7. Calm surroundings
8. Close personal relationships
9. Nutrition
10. Sleep
11. Spirituality
12. Purpose

In the 1980s, Robert Fulghum wrote the bestselling book *All I Really Need to Know I Learned in Kindergarten,* which reminds us that it is the simple things that make a positive difference in the quality of our lives and the quantity of our years (Goodreads, n.d.). That book is currently in its fifteenth-anniversary edition, which indicates how long-lasting its guiding principles are. Those things that make little children happy (such as laughter, movement, close personal relationships, games, and so on) are the same things that keep older people thriving. These principles may seem simple—and they are—but we often overlook their importance or cast them aside in the midst of our busy lives. Teachers, especially, are some of the busiest people I know. (After all, I come from a family of educators.) However, if teachers fail to balance their numerous professional duties with their abilities to take care of themselves, they will not be healthy teachers for long. This book will assist teachers and other educators with this effort.

Chapter Overview

Each chapter of this book describes one of the twelve principles teachers should practice if they are to maintain good mental and physical health and increase longevity, both in the profession and in life in general. Since music is a brain-compatible strategy and one of the principles that is correlated with with longevity (see chapter 6, page 60), I begin each chapter by describing a song that has lyrics depicting the principle. After all, music helps us remember. Most of us have experienced hearing a song we haven't heard for years and still being able to sing along. Alzheimer's patients who may no longer remember people's names or recognize their faces can often recall the lyrics to a favorite song. These songs are some of my favorites, and getting to know their lyrics may help you recall the principles contained in each chapter.

Each chapter is divided into three major sections: Healthy Teachers, Happy Classrooms, and Action Plan. The Healthy Teachers section constitutes the majority of each chapter since the major goal of the book is to assist you in improving your mental and physical health. The Healthy Teachers section is divided into three parts: (1) *Principle for Longevity: What Should I Do?*, which introduces the principle; (2) *What the Brain Research Says: Why Should I Do It?*, which provides neuroscientific research to support why that principle is worth pursuing; and (3) *Action Steps: How Should I Do It?*, which delineates specific activities you can undertake to operationalize the principle. These activities are not meant to be an exhaustive list; rather, they represent some recommendations for getting started. By the time you finish this book, you will have learned more than sixty ways to practice the principles contained in the chapters. The Action Plan sections provide reproducible templates to guide you in planning for each of the twelve principles.

The Happy Classrooms section in each chapter tells you how you can take that same principle for longevity and apply it to the students in your classroom. At the conclusion of each chapter is a reproducible action plan you can use as a tool for incorporating the principle into your daily life. It takes the brain from 18 to 254 days to develop a new habit, so be sure to practice the new action steps often enough so the principles become a way of life for you personally and professionally (Frothingham, 2019).

Conclusion

Julia, like most teachers, is a conscientious professional; however, she realizes that she cannot continue at her current pace if she is to be successful within her professional and personal life and rekindle the passion that she once felt for her chosen career. If she is not to become a statistic, she must focus on taking care of herself. Only then can she be a healthy teacher with a happy classroom.

Passion

*A strong feeling of enthusiasm or excitement
for something or about doing something
(Passion, n.d.)*

When Donna Summer (1983) cowrote and sang the song "She Works Hard for the Money" with Michael Omartian, she is telling the story of a hard-working blue-collar woman by the name of Onetta Johnson (Smith, 1998). Summer met Johnson, an exhausted restroom attendant, at a Los Angeles restaurant and decided to write a song about her. Summer even featured a photo of Johnson on the back cover of the album.

Like Onetta Johnson, the majority of teachers are working hard, but it is not for the money. They work hard because they are passionate about the difference they can make in the lives of the students they serve. Knowing that the job has a positive impact gives them purpose and the ability to get through the challenging times.

Passion for Your Purpose

Part 1: Healthy Teachers

Passion for Your Purpose: What Should I Do?

I have been in the business of educating students and teachers for almost half a century, and I never regretted one day of my choice. I knew when I was six years old that I wanted to be a teacher. I would line up dolls in my bedroom and teach them for hours. Dad bought me a chalkboard so I would have somewhere to write. Funny, I never had a single behavior problem! In my class, students wouldn't talk unless I wanted them to.

My sister is a retired teacher. In fact, she was my professor of French at Spelman College. My niece is a teacher. I have a daughter, Jennifer, who is an elementary principal. We are truly a family of educators, and we love what we do.

I began my career forty-eight years ago as a classroom teacher at Gresham Park Elementary School with the DeKalb County School System in Decatur, Georgia. My first fourth-grade class consisted of thirty-four students. Need I say more? Although my first year was challenging, I knew I was destined to teach. I was not the best classroom manager that first year. Thankfully, a seventh-grade teacher named Mrs. Stewart took me under her wing and showed me the ropes. In those days we did not have the peer coaching or mentoring programs that are invaluable to teachers today.

Each year, I became better at what I was doing and soon discovered that my true calling was helping students to become better readers. I became a reading specialist and then a reading consultant. As language arts coordinator for the same school district, I was now in a position to work with language arts teachers and help them improve their practice. The difference I was making with a classroom of children now became exponential.

I knew that I had found my true calling when I was placed in the department of staff development and would have an opportunity to broaden my horizons beyond language arts. I eventually was appointed as executive director of the department and began working with a phenomenal staff. My colleagues and I became fascinated with brain research and began attending workshops and reading everything we could get our hands on regarding how the brain learns. We developed courses for DeKalb educators based on the knowledge we were acquiring.

While sitting in my office one day, it dawned on me that regardless of the age or grade level of the student or the curriculum to be taught, there were twenty brain-based ways to deliver instruction, but they weren't published together all in one book. This was when I decided to become an author. Since then, I have been blessed with a career that has enabled me to present on five continents and in forty-seven U.S. states. I hope I have positively influenced the over half a million educators I have taught over the last thirty years with my passion for the content.

Being passionate about your career not only makes work more enjoyable, but it also helps you do your job better (Rosengren, 2011).

I share this description of my career to illustrate how passion for a purpose can transform and focus your job and take you in new directions. This is what happens when you love what you do! In all my career, I have never had a job I didn't love. I always felt that I was making a major contribution to the people I served. The saying goes, *If you love your job, you will never work a day in your life.*

In a 2005 commencement address at Stanford University, Steve Jobs unveiled his work philosophy. He related that if a person hasn't found that job he or she loves yet, they need to keep looking and not choose to settle. He says they'll know when they have found it (Chowdhry, 2013).

According to Steve Jobs, "Your work is going to fill a large part of your life, and the only way to be truly satisfied is to do what you believe is great work. And the only way to do great work is to love what you do" (Chowdhry, 2013).

There are educators who simply no longer love what they do. They are not experiencing a passion for their purpose. There are many reasons for this feeling, including the overwhelming responsibilities that are inherent in the job itself, the lack of support from peers and superiors, or the loss of autonomy and decision-making abilities due to local, state, and national mandates. One of the purposes of this book is to help you rekindle that passion while improving the quality of your personal life. Read on and uncover some specific plans for doing just that.

What the Brain Research Says: Why Should I Do It?

Not counting the time a person spends sleeping, which should be approximately eight hours a night, 63 percent of a person's available time is spent working. This is a large chunk of a person's life. If that much time is devoted to anything, it needs to be something that the person loves. How can one tell if they truly enjoy their work? Noam Lightstone (2021), founder of Light Way of Thinking and best-selling author, has written twenty self-help books to improve people's lives in all aspects and enable them to conquer anxiety and depression. Lightstone (2021) provides the following ten signs to look for that indicate you are enjoying what you do.

1. **You enter a state of flow where time flies by and you lose yourself.** When a person is in a flow state, the only thing that matters is what they are doing at the time while other worries and tasks appear to slip away.

2. **You feel fulfilled because you are doing something that is of value.** You become grateful that, regardless of the job, you can help and serve others.

3. **You get up in the morning with excitement about your day.** Although there may be days when you feel off, you should not continuously dread having to go to work.

4. **You work side by side with coworkers and superiors with whom you can accomplish great things.** You love that you get to work and struggle to make something you truly believe in reality.

5. **You are not complaining.** If you are, it may mean that you need to be more thankful for what you have, or it can mean that you need to find a different job that would be more to your liking.

6. **Even if you must struggle, you don't mind!** The ultimate goal of producing something worthwhile is worth the challenge.

7. **Talking about what you do energizes you.** When asked, "What do you do?" you want everyone else to know the answer, and you will tell them in detail.

8. **Work is more than just work or a means to an end.** It is an extension of you and your personality.

9. **You are always interested in learning more about the job.** It may even involve things for which you are not directly responsible.

10. **You feel tired at the end of a challenging day.** It is because you produced something valuable and feel accomplished and satisfied doing it.

Speaker, author, and life coach Curt Rosengren (2011) lists the positive effects of loving your job.

- **You have more energy**. When doing work you love, you are energized which, in turn, enables you to do more work. When work is not enjoyable, energy is dissipated, which leaves you feeling depleted and drained.

- **You have more confidence.** When doing work that is not enjoyable, the work does not come naturally. When doing work you love, the work comes more naturally and you feel more secure about what you're doing.

Lissa Rankin (Live Your Legend, 2020), a mind-body medicine physician and *New York Times* bestselling author, spent more than twelve years seeing patients as part of her clinical practice. Out of frustration, she abandoned her practice realizing that her work with patients was not really helping them. She sought to determine why some patients were experiencing miraculous recoveries from illnesses that seemed incurable while others remained sick, even with the best medical care. After perusing journals from reputable institutions like Johns Hopkins and Stanford, she found something remarkable. While diet and exercise were important, of more importance to long life are other elements, such as spending time with close friends, having a healthy marriage, laughter, and doing work that excites and fulfills you (Live Your Legend, 2021). So finding a passion for your purpose is not only good for your mental health; it is also good for your physical health.

Be aware, however, that finding a balance is critical. In Japan, there is a word, *karoshi*, that means "death by overwork" (Karoshi, n.d.). Karoshi usually affects people who are relatively young but overworking in a less-than-desirable work environment. Officials estimate that approximately ten thousand cases of karoshi occur annually. The deaths appear to be caused by the stress-induced physiological changes of a fight-or-flight repetitive response. The impact on the body results in high blood pressure, increased heart rate, and an overstressed cardiovascular system (Live Your Legend, 2021).

A study of the U.S. workplace finds that one in five Americans comes to work when ill or injured, with one-third failing to use accumulated vacation time, which has actually been proven to predispose to an early death (Gump & Matthews, 2000).

 One study in the journal *Psychosomatic Medicine* examined twelve thousand men over a nine-year period and found that those who chose not to take annual vacation had a 21 percent higher risk of dying regardless of the cause and were 32 percent more likely to die from a heart attack (Gump & Matthews, 2000).

Following are specific action steps to help you regain your passion for what you do. Determine which steps are most applicable for you. It may be that a change in the area of education in which you are working could be the answer. This might include moving to a different content area or grade level or finding a different area of specialization, such as counselor, school psychologist, instructional coach, administrator, and so on. For example, I loved teaching students, but when I began providing professional development for teachers and administrators, I realized that I had truly found my niche.

Action Steps: How Should I Do It?

Do What You Love

I once heard someone say that you will know you are in the right profession if you are willing to do the job to the best of your ability even if you are not being paid one dime. There may be times when you have to take a job in the short term to make ends meet that will not necessarily be one you would choose as your life's calling. However, never lose sight of that calling.

Recall Lightstone's (2021) ten criteria presented on page 11. Based on the ten conditions, consider whether you are already in a profession that you truly love or whether you might select a different profession that would allow you to have passion for your purpose. Here are some reflection questions to guide your thinking.

- Do you ever end the day thinking, "Where did the time go?"

- Are you satisfied that you can be of service to improve the lives of others?

- Are you excited and energized to start each day?

- Are you happy to work side by side with coworkers who share your beliefs?

- Even when facing challenging tasks, do you feel that the effort is worth it?

- Even though you are weary at the end of a long day, do you know that you have been productive and accomplished great things?

Set Healthy Boundaries for Work Time

No matter how much you enjoy what you do, doing too much of it is not a good thing. The older I become, the more I realize that everything in life is supposed to be in balance. When there ceases to be balance, something suffers.

Allow me to relate a personal story. When I retired from the DeKalb County School System and my husband and I founded our company, Developing Minds, Inc., I didn't turn down any requests for workshop bookings. After all, I was building a new business—the more clients, the better. There was one week when I boarded ten flights in five days. Every day, Monday through Friday, I presented in a different state. At the end of that week, I said, "Enough!" I realized that one of the things I loved most—sharing knowledge with other educators through my work-shops—was becoming a liability. From that point forward, I began scheduling workshops in a way that allowed me to live a life that kept my mental, physical, social-emotional, and spiritual life in balance.

Renew Yourself With Downtime

You fill so many roles: teacher, administrator, mother, father, grandparent, aunt, uncle, friend, community member, and so on. With each role, there are specific responsibilities. Be sure you are building in time to renew yourself along the way. After all, when I fly, the flight attendant during the initial safety instructions always asks the passengers to put on their masks before helping others with their masks. In other words, if you do not take care of yourself, you will be hard-pressed to continue being the best teacher, administrator, parent, or friend that you can possibly be. Stephen Covey (2020) refers to this same concept as habit 7, "Sharpen the saw." This is the habit—self-care—that allows you to focus on the other six.

Plan a few minutes of downtime each day just for personal renewal. It can be as simple as taking a warm bath, listening to a few minutes of calming music, or doing some yoga exercises or some other enjoyable activity.

Make Vacations Part of Your Schedule

Make self-care a priority by scheduling some much-needed vacation time. Visit places you have always wanted to see. Vacations don't have to be expensive. Travel by car and stay in a place that isn't cost prohibitive. Whether you choose to go to a beach, the mountains, or just do some sightseeing in a city, enjoy the change of scenery. Build in time for relaxation so you can focus on your passion and purpose with clarity and energy.

Part 2: Happy Classrooms

Hopefully, you have chosen well and are in a career that you are passionate about—and a career in education is truly your calling. Never forget that teaching is the only profession that directly influences every other profession. Every doctor, lawyer, electrician, plumber, or technician came by way of a teacher who made it possible for them to learn the content inherent in their profession. I cannot count the number of educators in my workshops who have related that they are in education because of a teacher who made a discernible difference in their lives. Those were the teachers who developed a relationship with them, had a passion for their content, and used instructional strategies that engaged their brains, with the highest of expectations for student success (Tate, 2014). And the research is clear—within the classroom, it is the teacher who makes the biggest difference in student learning.

If you believe in the magnitude of the impact you have on students, then you will teach with passion. I always say that the day I instruct teachers or students without passion will be the last day I teach. Think about it. How can a mathematics teacher get students excited about learning mathematics if he or she is not excited about teaching mathematics?

It is never too soon for students to begin to think about what they are passionate about. I knew I wanted to teach when I was six years old. Find out what interests your students have and engage them in conversations based on those interests. A good time to engage them is when they are entering or leaving class. Discuss with them the prerequisites for entering the profession that they ultimately visualize themselves occupying.

My granddaughter Christian would like to be a pediatrician. When her mother, Amanda, was in the hospital giving birth to her baby brother, Maxwell, I sat in the waiting room with Christian. As the intercom announced the names of various doctors and in what part of the hospital they were requested, I reminded Christian that one day her name would be called over the loudspeaker. We also discussed the years of schooling that would be required for the goal of a doctor to become a reality and how she would have to make good grades all along the way to achieve that goal. After all, she needed to understand that she would not wake up one morning as a doctor without achieving the necessary prerequisites to become one.

Teachers will learn a great deal about their students as they develop relationships with them. If students are old enough, administer an Interest Inventory to understand their likes, dislikes, and career goals. Much of the conversation regarding those interests can occur as teachers are standing at the door at the beginning or end of class. Teachers can also work student interests into class discussions if those interests relate to the content being taught.

Part 3: Action Plan

Recall at the beginning of the chapter the discussion of Donna Summer's hit song "She Works Hard for the Money." As a teacher, you too work hard for the money. But it isn't the money that attracted you to the profession in the first place, nor is it the money that will sustain you throughout your career. It is, instead, a passion for the job you are doing. It is the knowledge that you are making a major difference in the lives of those students who are fortunate enough to be in your class. Complete the following action plan (page 16) to determine if you are finding the passion for your purpose.

Action Plan for Finding Passion for Your Purpose

What are my plans for becoming more passionate about my job?		
Recommendations	Presently Doing	Strive to Do
Find what I love and seek a job doing it.		
Use Lightstone's (2021) ten indicators to determine if I truly love what I am doing: 1. Do I enter a state of flow where time flies by and I lose myself? 2. Do I feel fulfilled because I am doing something that is of value? 3. Do I get up in the morning with excitement about my day? 4. Do I work side by side with coworkers and superiors with whom I can accomplish great things? 5. Do I complain? 6. Do I mind when I must struggle? 7. Does talking about what I do energize me? 8. Is my work more than just work, or is it a means to an end? 9. Am I always interested in learning more about my job? 10. Do I feel tired at the end of a challenging day?		
Set healthy boundaries for my work time.		
Renew myself with downtime.		
Make downtime and vacations an integral part of my schedule.		
Communicate my passion for my content to students as I teach.		
Encourage students to explore their passions.		
Goals and Notes:		

Source for ten indicators: Lightstone, N. (2021, February 11). 10 signs you are enjoying your work. *Accessed at www.lifehack.org /articles/work/10-signs-you-are-enjoying-your-work.html on July 20, 2021.*

Laughter

*To show emotion with a chuckle or
explosive vocal sound that inspires joy
(Laugh, n.d.)*

You are probably familiar with Pharrell Williams's 2013 song "Happy." This song became so popular that it was *Billboard*'s number-one single for 2014, and the accompanying video also won the Grammy Award for Best Music Video at the fifty-seventh annual Grammy Awards (Bauer, n.d.). In the song, Williams expresses that he's so happy that nothing can bring him down from that feeling and calls for listeners to find what makes them happy. This upbeat tune exudes happiness with its lyrics; its cheerful, optimistic melody; and a music video that features people of all ages from all backgrounds dressed in bright colors, dancing and smiling. "Happy" represents the second principle for longevity: laughter.

Laughter

Part 1: Healthy Teachers

Laughter: What Should I Do?

Allow me to begin with a joke: Eighty-two-year-old Joe goes to the doctor's office. He has been feeling poorly for some time. The doctor examines Joe and tells him that there is so much wrong that it is difficult to know where to begin treatment. Not the least of Joe's problems is that he is hard of hearing. The doctor gives Joe medication to correct some immediate health issues and asks him to return in a few days to discuss more long-term intervention. Joe returns home exhausted and goes to bed immediately.

Several days later, the doctor sees Joe walking down the street. He is stepping spryly and looks as if he doesn't have a care in the world. Holding onto Joe's arm is a beautiful young woman. In amazement, the doctor stops Joe and asks how he could have improved his health with very little intervention in such a short amount of time. Joe responds, "Doctor, I did exactly what you instructed me to do!" Perplexed, the doctor asks Joe what he means. Joe replies, "You told me to be cheerful and get a hot momma!" Appalled, the doctor exclaims, "I told you to be careful! You've got a heart murmur!"

If this joke about Joe made you chuckle—even just a little—you just added minutes to your life. The impact of humor or laughter on the brain and body is astounding. So astounding, in fact, that part of the holistic treatment at Cancer Treatment Centers of America (2019) is laughter therapy. This just may be the reason that clowns can be found in the children's wards of hospitals. Laughter also relieves physical tension and stress, boosts our immune system, improves our moods, and prevents heart disease (McGauran, 2015).

Some people's personalities may predispose them to be happier; however, we're all born happy people. Researchers have observed that little children laugh an average of three hundred times a day. By the time we reach adulthood, however, we are lucky to laugh seventeen times a day (U.S. Preventive Medicine, 2017). According to University Hospitals Connor Integrative Health Network's blog (University Hospitals, 2015), there are five major contributors of stress to our lives. Before I share them with you, close your eyes and see if you can visualize what may be on the list. You can probably come up with many more.

The top five stressors are as follows:

1. Death of a loved one
2. Divorce
3. Moving
4. Major illness or injury
5. Job loss

While this blog was published prior to COVID-19, the pandemic is definitely impacting every one of these major contributors to stress, making it so easy to live each day with our brains in a state of perpetual negativity. Dr. Françoise Adan (University Hospitals, 2015), medical director of this health network, cautions about living in this negative state of being since the body responds to these and other perceived threats by switching into fight or flight mode, thereby releasing the stress hormones of cortisol and adrenaline. This stress, if stored up, can contribute to a variety of health issues, including increased inflammation and negative effects on the immune system, digestive health, bone density, sexual health, anxiety, and sleep (University Hospitals, 2015).

High stress is the number-one cause of aging. Time and again, we have watched people who have publicly gone through a prolonged, highly stressful experience grow older before our eyes. Former U.S. presidents often look twenty years older after leaving office than they did while taking office four or eight years prior. This chapter will delineate the profound benefits of humor and laughter on the quantity and quality of life.

One note of caution: Be sure to differentiate laughter from sarcasm. Anything that demeans or puts down another human being is not humor, it is sarcasm and at the very least, it can place the brain under threat, which shuts down the frontal lobe. When the brain perceives a threat, a fear response is triggered in the amygdala, which activates the motor functions involved in a fight-or-flight response (Javanbakht & Saab, 2017). Emphasis then shifts from the cognitive to the affective part of the brain, making memory more difficult.

How, then, do we go from laughing three hundred times a day to just seventeen? Is it possible to recover the other two hundred eighty-three missed moments of joy?

Since the early 2000s, I have been paying special attention to how long many comedians live. Of course, there are exceptions. In some instances, comedians' lifestyles and stress levels may have contributed to their early demise. However, I have noticed that more comedians than not are examples of the rule, supporting the finding that a sense of humor lowers mortality rates, especially for women (Rodriguez, 2016).

What the Brain Research Says: Why Should I Do It?

As far back as the 13th century, surgeons are reported to have used humor to take patients' attention away from pain. Now, according to Cancer Treatment Centers of America (2020), three sixty-minute laughter therapy sessions are sufficient to improve the mood and self-esteem of patients undergoing radiation. This is due to the brain's release of endorphins that laughter triggers (Cancer Treatment Centers of America, 2020). Laughter has so many medicinal benefits. It actually reduces blood pressure, relaxes tense muscles, and stimulates the immune system (Sousa, 2012).

 "The risk of psychological and social factors such as depression, anxiety, stress, and hostility has almost as great an impact on the medical markers for cardiovascular disease as do obesity, smoking, and hypertension" (Rodriguez, 2016; Underwood, 2005).

The Mayo Clinic staff (2019) delineate the following short-term physical benefits of laughter.

- In addition to increasing the level of oxygen-rich air and increasing the endorphin level, laughter stimulates the body's heart, lungs, and muscles.

- A hearty laugh can also produce the relaxed feeling that occurs when the heart rate is increased and then decreased and the stress response is fired up and then cooled down.

- Physical symptoms of stress can be relieved when circulation is stimulated and the muscles relax due to laughter.

Laughter is also beneficial in the long term in the following ways (Mayo Clinic Staff, 2019).

- Laughter releases neuropeptides that over time help fight stress and more serious illnesses. Negative thoughts, on the other hand, can change into chemical reactions that can bring more stress into the body and decrease immunity.

- Pain can be eased when, through laughter, the body produces its own natural painkillers, called *endorphins*.

- Laughter enables you to connect with others and can make it easier to cope in difficult situations.

- Laughter can lessen depression and make one feel generally happier.

In India, people participate in what is often referred to as *laughter yoga* in clubs like the Central India Laughter Club, founded by physician Madan Kataria. Members in these clubs practice forced laughter during a series of relaxation and breathing techniques. Laughter, even when forced, is extremely beneficial. Forced laughter can improve heart rate, strengthen the immune system, lower blood pressure, reduce the production of stress hormones, and elevate one's tolerance for pain (Manohar, 2020).

It has been said that "what we learn with pleasure, we never forget" (Allen, 2008, p. 99). There are many reasons why this statement rings true. Oxygen is to a brain what gasoline is to a car: fuel. When a person laughs, additional oxygen enters the bloodstream so the brain is better fueled, enabling more efficient thought processes. Humor has been shown to free an individual's creativity and foster the higher-level thinking skills of perceiving and anticipating novel situations, creating visual images, and forming analogies (Costa, 2008).

 Laughter can improve the mental attitude of both teachers and students, enabling us to take our work seriously and ourselves lightly (Sousa, 2017).

The endorphins, or feel-good chemicals, that are produced when one laughs stimulate the frontal lobes of the brain, thereby increasing levels of attention and the degree of focus (Sousa, 2011). So since emotions enhance the retention of information, the positive emotions that result when people laugh increase the probability that we will remember content and recall that content later.

The next section looks at strategies to increase laughter to achieve these body and brain benefits.

Action Steps: How Should I Do It?

Smile

It's not just that happiness makes you smile; smiling can also make you happier. It only takes thirteen facial muscles to smile. It takes more than forty-seven muscles to frown. People have to work much harder to frown! Yet, as I travel throughout the world, for every one person I see with a seemingly positive disposition or a smile on his or her face, there seem to be many more who are scowling, frowning, or in a state of perpetual negativity. Forming a smile—genuine or not—actually boosts feelings of well-being over time (Stibich, 2021). A simple smile can not only improve your disposition, but it can make those around you glad to be there. I encourage teachers to greet their students and colleagues with a smile. It helps to think of the word *SMILE* as an acronym that stands for <u>S</u>how <u>M</u>e <u>I</u>'m <u>L</u>oved <u>E</u>very day.

Force Laughter

Your body does not know the difference between simulated laughter and spontaneous laughter. People who teach laughter yoga know this. They encourage their participants to practice laughter as a group. Initially, it is forced, but it can soon turn into a more natural humorous experience. In India, there are over 1,800 laughing clubs where people get together and laugh for the benefit of their health. For example, when a student is acting silly just to get some attention from you or their peers, try using forced laughter. Chances are you will look back on the episode and laugh later, so just go ahead and fake it now.

Buy a Smile

When you simply don't feel like smiling, use a Smile on a Stick® (www.smile onastick.com) instead. This fun prop is a color picture of a smile on a wooden stick that you can hold up in front of your mouth. Smiles come in a variety of skin tones with a variety of expressions and in some fun holiday styles. The prop is perfect to use virtually or in person when greeting your students.

Surround Yourself With Funny Visuals

Locate a few simple items, such as greeting cards, cartoons, or photos that make you laugh. Post them at home, in your classroom, or in your office. As you see these day after day, your mood can improve. Even when you take them down from the wall, your brain can still visualize what was there. When I am in someone else's office, like a doctor's office, I often laugh at humorous cartoons on the wall while I am sitting in that uncomfortable gown waiting to be seen.

Learn to Laugh

Contrary to popular belief, laughter can be learned. When I began teaching educators, I was hesitant to tell jokes for fear that no one would laugh. When I finally mustered the courage to try a joke, to my surprise, my audience did indeed laugh. That gave me the courage to add more and more jokes and riddles to my repertoire. Laughter is now an integral part of my work with educators.

Keep funny movies, books, magazines, or videos on hand for when you need a boost of laughter. Seek out jokes and riddles online and visit humor websites. I am always in pursuit of riddles that I can use in my workshops. For example, here's one to use when working with English teachers: What is the difference between a cat and a comma? A cat has claws at the end of its paws. A comma is a pause at the end of a clause. Remember if you don't like this riddle, just fake the laughter.

Share a Laugh

The Mayo Clinic staff (2019) suggest that you seek out those people who make you laugh and make it a habit to spend time with them. Share your jokes and funny stories with this group.

- Do you have people in your life who always have a smile on their faces?

- Is there someone who never fails to make you laugh?

- Are there people whom you need to avoid because they take away your joy and bring down your mood?

Form grade-level or departmental laughing clubs and take turns bringing in and sharing jokes or riddles for the start of the school day. Remember, if the jokes are not funny, simply fake it. Forced laughter has benefits as well.

Watch Shows That Engender Laughter

As I was growing up, television was filled with comedy and variety shows. One of my favorites was the *Carol Burnett Show*. On Saturday night, we would spend an hour doubled over laughing at the antics of Carol, Harvey Korman, Tim Conway, Lyle Waggoner, and Vicki Lawrence. Another favorite is *Seinfeld*. I find most episodes as funny as I did the first time I watched them, and when the half-hour is over, I feel so much better for having spent quality time producing endorphins.

Avoid Sarcasm

Some people confuse humor with sarcasm. Any comment that belittles a person or makes them feel uncomfortable is not humor. It is sarcasm. Avoid sarcasm at all costs. Although the person that a sarcastic comment is directed at may smile or laugh, the remark might still negatively affect them. Indeed, if the person perceives the comment as a threat, it can erode your relationship with them and shut down the frontal lobe of the recipient's brain.

Part 2: Happy Classrooms

Laughing together is the best way to create a sense of community. When there is high stress in an environment, there is often a loss of humor.

Greet students daily with a smile. Don't forget the acronym SMILE: Show me I'm loved every day. On the days when smiling is difficult, use a Smile on a Stick that you have purchased or made yourself. Your students will love it! Provide students with popsicle sticks and poster board and have them design their own smiles. Students can use these throughout the day when they would like to agree with another student's answer or make a positive comment.

If you don't think you are funny, use a joke or riddle book or search online to select jokes or riddles that would be appropriate for the age and grade level of your students. Starting your lesson with a humorous story, joke, riddle, or pun gets the attention of your learners. Open your virtual or in-person lessons with daily jokes or riddles. Your students will look forward to being in your class.

Many students in the primary grades have difficulty understanding the subtle humor in a good joke, but they love riddles. Share riddles with students and then have them submit their own riddles virtually or in person. Be sure to read over them in advance to ensure that they are appropriate for school.

By the time students reach middle and high school, some of them have developed reputations for being class clowns. Take advantage of that talent by appointing a class clown for the week who will share a joke or riddle either before or after class. (Be sure to monitor what students plan to share.) Give all students the opportunity to assume the role of class clown for the week.

Humor can be more than a strategy to start a class, however. Since humor is such a good strategy for getting students' attention and for retention of information, Sousa (2017) suggests using humor throughout lessons within the context of the learning objective. Don't use sarcasm—be careful to stick to humor.

Part 3: Action Plan

Recall at the beginning of the chapter the discussion of Pharrell Williams's 2013 song "Happy." I cannot hear that song without feeling upbeat and joyful. Music can have a very positive effect on our lives, and so can laughter. Use the following Action Plan (page 26) to decide which steps you will take to incorporate laughter into your routine to strengthen your immunity and improve your overall health.

Action Plan for Incorporating Laughter

What are my plans for incorporating more humor and enjoyment into my life?		
Recommendations	**Presently Doing**	**Strive to Do**
Smile more than I frown.		
Practice laughter yoga.		
Surround myself with funny visuals.		
Practice laughing.		
Share laughter with others.		
Watch visuals that engender laughter.		
SMILE (show me I'm loved every day) with students.		
Integrate humorous cartoons, jokes, and riddles into my lessons.		
Avoid sarcasm at all costs.		
Appoint class clowns to share jokes and riddles with the class.		
Use Smile on a Stick props with students or have them create their own.		

Goals and Notes:

3

Optimism

Derived from the Latin word optimus *meaning "best"; a "belief in and expectation of positive outcomes, even in the face of difficulty, challenge, or crisis" (Ventrella, 2001)*

It's hard not to smile when listening to the song "Don't Worry, Be Happy," by musician Bobby McFerrin (1988). The first a cappella song to reach number one on the *Billboard* Hot 100 (*Billboard*, n.d.), "Don't Worry, Be Happy" calls on listeners to not focus on the negative. The song's lyrics could even be considered a formula for facing the challenges of life. It's not surprising this extremely catchy song won the Grammy Award for Song of the Year in 1988 (Recording Academy, n.d.). The video featuring comedians Robin Williams and Bill Irwin doing silly dances while wearing crazy outfits reminds us of the principle for longevity that is the focus of this chapter: optimism.

PRINCIPLE 3
Optimism

Part 1: Healthy Teachers

Optimism: What Should I Do?

In his book, *The Power of Positive Thinking in Business,* Scott Ventrella (2001), a disciple of Norman Vincent Peale, delineates ten traits of a positive thinker. One of those ten traits is optimism. However, it is simpler to live life in a pessimistic state. Why? It all has to do with the way we are designed. Our brains are hardwired to focus on threats. This survival mechanism served us well thousands of years ago when we were hunters and gatherers, living each day with the threat of being eaten or starving to death. Anything we saw as a threat triggered a fight-or-flight survival instinct within us that increased our breathing, blood pressure, and heart rate. Since this physical reaction is still so powerful even today, negative events have a much larger impact on our moods than do positive events. Even when we simply visualize future events that we perceive to be negative, we can become miserable in the present (Cherry, 2020).

This biological mechanism breeds negativity. When we imagine a threat, we spend months convinced that the project we're undertaking will flop, the students we're teaching will develop behavior problems, and the lessons we've planned will not be successful. We become wary of any situation that may lead to failure or cause us embarrassment. We perceive simple mistakes as major blunders.

Identifying your negative thoughts is the first step toward releasing them. The following list presents categories of pessimism or negative thinking (Ferguson, 2019; Star, 2020).

- **All-or-nothing thinking:** I have to do things perfectly because anything less than perfection constitutes a failure.

- **Forgetting the positives**: Life feels like one disappointment after another.

- **Catastrophizing:** If I fail, the outcome will be the worst-case scenario.

- **Negative self-labeling:** I feel like a failure. I'm flawed. If people really knew me, they wouldn't like me.

Try this experiment with a member of your family or a friend to discover the body's reaction to negative thinking. Stand and have the other person stand behind you.

Hold your dominant arm out to the side of your body, creating a right angle with your body. Think about something positive—something that makes you happy. Ask the family member or friend to put their hands on your shoulder and attempt to push down your arm. While thinking positive thoughts, keep your arm rigid and do not let the other person pull it down. Then repeat the process but this time while thinking negative thoughts—perhaps think about a situation that makes you unhappy or creates stress. Ask your family member or friend to attempt to pull your arm down again. Is there a difference in what happens to your arm?

When I conduct this exercise in my workshops with volunteers from the audience, the person whose arm is outstretched manages to keep the arm up when thinking positive thoughts. Conversely, when thinking negative thoughts, their arm is easily pushed down. I then ask every educator to pair with someone else in the workshop and try the experiment. This activity is a powerful example of the impact of positive and negative thinking on the brain and body.

The effects of positive and negative thinking are easy to see in sports. As an avid sports fan, I have noticed that a baseball player who hits a home run will often come back to the plate later in the same game and hit another home run. A football player who kicks a field goal through the uprights stands a better chance of kicking the next field goal through as well. Success breeds success! The same is true of negative thinking. A baseball player who commits an error will often commit another error. A field-goal kicker who misses one field goal will often miss the next field goal.

The next time you are watching any type of sporting event, take note of the number of times the announcer mentions the word *confidence*. It will likely be an integral part of the broadcast. When the level of confidence is high, the brain is more optimistic regarding a successful outcome, and the body simply performs better. This is the reason that tennis players who win the first set have a decided advantage for the remainder of the match. Football and baseball teams that score first have a similar advantage. This doesn't mean that a team cannot come from behind to win. It happens all the time, but it is much more difficult and requires a higher level of confidence. When the confidence level changes from player to player or team to team, that is referred to as a momentum shift and can even result in a change in the score.

What the Brain Research Says: Why Should I Do It?

According to Ventrella (2001), a person demonstrates optimism when he or she does the following:

- Sees the positive opportunities and benefits of a crisis, difficulty, or problem

- Expects success, achievement, or satisfaction in any undertaking

- Identifies the limitless possibilities to achieve the desired life
- Feels in control when addressing a new opportunity or meeting a challenge
- Diminishes or eliminates the impact of both internal and external fears, concerns, and doubts
- Keeps spirits up regardless of the circumstances
- Tackles problems with a mindset of how they can be accomplished

Why is optimism so important? Pervasive pessimism is detrimental to both the brain and body. Studies show that pessimism decreases immunity, slowing down the body's ability to heal itself (HealthyPlace.com Staff Writer, 2016). It fosters anxiety and poor physical health. When dealing with setbacks, pessimism can promote passivity and depression.

"To the pessimist, setbacks become disasters and then catastrophes create a self-fulfilling prophecy" (Ventrella, 2001, p. 109).

Optimism, then, does the opposite. It increases immunity, aids us in being resilient when setbacks happen, and prevents us from giving up when things get in our way. Pessimists see a setback as a sign that things will never be the same. Optimists see setbacks as challenges to be overcome. When something goes wrong, pessimists see it as an innate character flaw. Optimists blame the wrong on temporary, external forces that are within their control.

"The tough-minded optimist views any problem as a challenge to his intelligence, ingenuity, and faith. He knows there is a solution, and so he finally finds it" (Peale, 1993).

Researchers from the Boston University School of Medicine, National Center for PTSD at VA Boston Healthcare System, and Harvard T. H. Chan School of Public Health found that people with a greater degree of optimism were more likely to achieve what they call exceptional longevity, which they defined as living to age eighty-five or older (Centre for Optimism, 2019).

You can change your outlook from a pessimistic one to an optimistic one. Harvard professor Amy Edmondson (2003) studied the success rate of four hospitals, all attempting to adopt a less invasive, yet more successful, process for open-heart surgery. Adopting the new technology turned out to be more difficult than anticipated, with two hospitals succeeding and two failing. The difference between the successful hospitals and those that failed had nothing to do with resources, management support, expertise, or even the hospital's history of prior innovation. Rather, success was determined by how the new surgical process was framed. The hospitals that succeeded framed the new surgical procedure as a learning opportunity that would yield great benefits to patients. In the hospitals that failed, the new process was negatively framed as a time-consuming, difficult process that management required. In other words, by framing the challenge of implementing new technology optimistically, successful surgical teams were capable of overcoming the challenges.

According to the Mayo Clinic (2020b), *optimism* is defined as "looking for solutions and silver linings in times of hardship and stress" (p. 83). People who are optimistic consider the disappointments they encounter, but they view them as temporary roadblocks. In other words, optimists don't allow a setback in a specific event to negatively influence every other area of their lives.

Optimism can be contagious because of what neurologists call *mirror neurons*. Mirroring happens when one person mimics another person's gestures and expressions during a conversation (Pentland, 2010). Listeners may smile or frown along with the speaker or imitate the speaker's body posture or attitude. This behavior establishes a brain connection between people, thereby increasing empathy and enhancing support. This behavior can help lower feelings of risk within groups. According to Sandy Pentland (2010) of the Massachusetts Institute of Technology, negotiations that include a lot of mirroring tend to be more successful, regardless of which party copies the gestures of the other.

So how can we approach life and work with an optimistic outlook even when we are facing challenging times?

Action Steps: How Should I Do It?

Monitor Your Moods

If you find yourself immersed in an upsetting or stressful situation, try and view it for what it is—a temporary negative event with which you must deal. Deal with it, and then consciously change your brain activity by switching your thoughts to something else. Switch your focus outward away from the stressful situation and toward other concerns that are not your own. Once you've monitored your mood and recognize feelings of negativity, you can then decide to focus on something else that you feel positive about. When immersed in a challenging situation, I often monitor my mood by reminding myself that *it could always be worse.* When you consider the challenge from this perspective, it is possible to see that the situation is not as dire as it appears to be.

Don't Fear Optimism

According to Ventrella (2001), many people are afraid of being optimistic for fear that they will experience disappointment. People often rationalize that if they don't expect great things, then they will not be disappointed when great things fail to materialize. But without the hope for great things, we are not likely to accomplish much. Think of the popular saying, *Reach for the moon*. If you miss the moon, then you stand a good chance of landing on a star.

Overcome Negative Thinking

The good news is that negative thoughts and behaviors, which develop from the time we're exposed to language and broader negativity, are soft wired. They are learned behaviors that can be changed. The key to positive thinking is to recognize when you are having the types of negative thinking outlined in the first part of this chapter (all-or-nothing thinking, forgetting the positives, catastrophizing, and negative self-labeling) and reflect on how to shift your thinking to realize that not every challenge is a threat or a crisis. Every single day brings moments of relaxation, reflection, and laughter if we just look for them. Spend time doing just that!

Visualize a Positive Outcome

In his bestseller, *The 7 Habits of Highly Effective People* (2020), Covey discusses the power of visualization or seeing in your mind what you expect to happen. Covey states that everything happens twice—once in the mind and once in reality. This is the reason many athletes visualize a positive performance before achieving it and why patients receiving medical treatment like chemotherapy may be advised to visualize the treatment working in their body.

According to Judy Willis (2007), a board-certified neurologist and middle school teacher, what the brain is actually smelling, hearing, and seeing, and what the brain imagines when it visualizes those same smells, sounds, and sights, stimulate the same neural circuits of the brain. Visualization increases the probability that one will be successful because it is "priming the neural circuits that will be used during the activity" (Willis, 2007, p. 83).

When the brain visualizes a positive outcome, it stands a better chance of achieving it. Before you begin any challenging task, imagine yourself being successful at it. You have probably heard the saying, "Fake it until you make it." When I began teaching teachers, I was very nervous. It was a good thing I was standing behind a podium since my legs were weak and shaky. Then at one workshop I was presenting, a teacher approached me afterward and complimented me on my performance. She had no idea how much confidence she gave me in that moment and beyond. Twenty-five years later and after teaching more than half a million educators, I have developed the confidence to believe I will be successful at every opportunity. But to be on the safe side, I still visualize myself doing so each time I present.

Write a Positive Affirmation

When faced with a specific obstacle, write down a positive affirmation accepting and acknowledging the fact that you are capable of handling anything that you have to face. Then write down as many viable options as you can for dealing with the obstacle. Writing a list is important since the brain stands a better chance of remembering and following through on what it puts in writing (Locke, n.d.). No doubt, there will be some negative options on your list, but there will also be positive ones. Focus on the positive.

Gain Confidence

If success breeds success, then one positive outcome gives the brain the confidence to believe that it can have another successful outcome. Outline specific plans for experiencing success. Here is a personal example. When traveling to my next keynote, seminar, or workshop, I always make sure that I arrive the day before. On several occasions, due to cancelled or delayed flights, it has appeared as if I would miss my connection or not arrive at all. Since I pride myself on my work ethic, it is very important to me that I exceed the expectations of my client. Therefore, as I sit in the airport, watching the time between flights diminish, I am visualizing myself presenting the following day for my client while simultaneously looking for an alternative way to get to my destination. Perhaps there is a later flight for making the connection, or I could purchase a ticket on another airline. I never lose my optimistic attitude that I will find a way to get there. I am fortunate to say that in the twenty-five years I have been teaching teachers, during more than one hundred bookings per year, there have been less than five times when I was not presenting on the scheduled day.

Reframe Pessimistic Situations

In attempting to be optimistic about a challenging situation, try *reframing*, or adopting a positive set of assumptions or beliefs to replace the pessimistic ones. For example, when driving around a parking lot, if you can't find a parking space close to the store, you might feel pessimistic about the fact that it will take more time to accomplish what you came to do. Instead, reframe the situation. Having to park so far away may take a little additional time, but it also means you will get more exercise from the extra steps. You might even decide to park farther away on purpose. As a teacher, when you receive a student whose records indicate that they have had discipline problems in years past due to their efforts to gain attention in negative ways, reframe the situation by thinking of ways you can give attention to this student for the positive things he or she will do for you this year.

Stay Within Your Circle of Influence

The Circle of Influence and Circle of Concern is a principle in Covey's (2020) *The 7 Habits of Highly Effective People*. It is such a life-changing concept that I not only teach it, but I also practice it in my daily life. The concept is based on the two circles we all have in our lives. There is a larger circle called the *Circle of Concern*. That circle contains all of the things we are concerned about but can do very little to directly impact. Within that larger circle is a smaller circle called the *Circle of Influence*. In this circle are all of the things we are concerned about and can directly impact. For example, our health is within our Circle of Influence. We can eat healthier, exercise, get sufficient amounts of sleep, and so on.

People who are positive and live life optimistically spend more time in their Circle of Influence changing the things that they are capable of changing, which gives them very little time to worry about the things that are only within their Circle of Concern. Pessimistic people spend more time complaining about those things they can do nothing about. Their complaints only serve to make them feel worse while having no effect on challenges they face.

Think about personal situations that are within your Circle of Influence. Do what you can do to change those situations for the better. For other situations that are only within your Circle of Concern and that you can do nothing about, you must learn to let go. Simply worrying about them accomplishes nothing except negatively impacting your health and well-being. This concept is also expressed in "The Serenity Prayer," attributed to theologian Reinhold Niebuhr. This well-known prayer that is often a staple in twelve-step recovery programs, asks for God to grant serenity, courage, and wisdom.

Share Your Optimism With Others

Thanks to mirror neurons, if you start acting positively—smiling, laughing, giving compliments—others will mirror those same behaviors. They'll start smiling, nodding, laughing, or adding a *yeah* or *right* into the conversation. Then, soon, others will follow along and the entire group will feel better.

Part 2: Happy Classrooms

Make a point to wake up every morning thinking, What is going to be good about this day? Admittedly, some days this will be harder to do than other days. However, research shows that it is humanly impossible for the brain to be negative and thankful at the same time (Young, n.d.). Begin the day by thinking about all the things for which you are grateful.

 "Choosing to become a teacher is a telling vote for optimism" (Silver, Berckemeyer, & Baenen, 2015, p. 5).

Maintain optimism and high expectations about what your students are capable of achieving. Often, teachers look at the permanent records of the students they teach, and if those records are not positive, they might make a predetermined conclusion that this year will be no different. However, as we all know, it is the teacher who makes the difference! Students who have not experienced previous success can still accomplish great things in your classroom if you build up their confidence by beginning where they can be successful. Since success breeds success, each positive experience a student has increases his or her confidence, leading to greater accomplishments or higher achievement.

Use the strategy of reframing in your classroom. For example, for a student who exhibits challenging behaviors, consider the reason for the inappropriate behavior. This reframing of the challenging behavior allows you to address the root cause so the student can improve the behavior. After all, a teacher's expectations are the greatest predictors of what happens in the classroom (Allen & Currie, 2012). Consider students who are well-behaved in one classroom but demonstrate what could be described as terroristic behavior in another. What produces this difference? The students are the same; the difference lies with the teacher. When teachers expect negative results from their students, they will expend their energy getting negative results from students. However, when teachers reframe and expect positive results, they will spend just as much energy making those positive results happen (Wong & Wong, 1998).

As you work with students and their parents or guardians, operate within your Circle of Influence—understand where you can have an impact and focus your energy there. I cannot count the number of teachers in my workshops who tell me that they are educators today because of the influence of a teacher who took a personal interest in them when they were in school. You can have a similar impact on your students and their families if you are optimistic about your ability to work together with them.

Part 3: Action Plan

Recall at the beginning of the chapter the discussion of the song "Don't Worry, Be Happy" by musician Bobby McFerrin (1988). Although desirable, it is often more easily said than done. We have a tendency to worry, even about those things that may not ever happen. After all, it is in our nature. Use the Action Plan (page 38) to enable you to live your life with a more optimistic outlook rather than a pessimistic one. This practice alone will reap big dividends.

Action Plan for Becoming More Optimistic and Positive

What are my plans for becoming more optimistic and positive?		
Recommendations	Presently Doing	Strive to Do
Become aware of and monitor my moods.		
Expect great things to occur.		
Shift negative thinking to more positive thoughts.		
Visualize a positive outcome.		
Write positive affirmations.		
Use personal successes to build confidence.		
Reframe pessimistic situations.		
Remain within my Circle of Influence at home and school.		
Maintain high expectations for student success.		
Build confidence in the brains of students.		

Goals and Notes:

4

Games

Activities engaged in for diversion or amusement (Game, n.d.)

Singer Cyndi Lauper's first single as a solo artist, "Girls Just Want to Have Fun" (Hazzard, 1983), made her famous and became a hallmark of 1980s pop culture, inspiring fashion trends and becoming an anthem for female empowerment. The video for the song, which won the MTV Video Music Award for Best Female Video in 1984, follows a group of young women as they dance through town (IMDb, n.d.). The video ends with the women dancing at a party full of people, women and men, young and old. According to William Glasser (1999), fun is one of the five critical needs for motivation. One of the best ways to have that fun is by playing games, the principle this chapter explores.

PRINCIPLE 4

Games

Part 1: Healthy Teachers

Games: What Should I Do?

Little children love games. Most of us grew up playing Candy Land, Chutes and Ladders, Monopoly, and UNO. Game shows like *Wheel of Fortune, Jeopardy!,* and *Family Feud* are some of the longest-running syndicated shows in American television history.

I grew up playing Scrabble. As a very young girl, I would lay out tiles with the help of my sisters. As I grew older, the game became much more meaningful. I have played Scrabble my whole life. Many a family gathering has been spent around the dining room table in a competitive game of Scrabble.

As time passed and my travel schedule increased, I had to find an alternative to face-to-face game playing. I discovered Scopely and Words With Friends—two different forms of Scrabble—which my sister, Eleanor, and I now play. Eleanor makes longer and more complex words than I do, so her final scores are usually higher than mine. When she is unavailable, I play the computer game Practice, which tends to match the caliber of the person it is playing. I can usually beat Practice. However, it is not nearly as much fun as playing with my sister! The brain loves a challenge, and Eleanor fulfills that role for me. Although I am likely to lose, my scores are always higher when I play her, and if I win—that's quite an accomplishment!

Video game developers are aware of the brain's need for a challenge. Most video games start at an easy level where the probability of success is very high. This builds a player's confidence. Then as soon as that confidence is established, the difficulty level of the game increases. Why does the player continue to play? Because he or she believes he or she can play at a more challenging level and still be successful. Thus the popularity of video gaming.

I also play an individual game called Word Calm. While listening to calming music, I can earn coins by taking six or seven letters and arranging them into words in something similar to a crossword puzzle. I set personal goals of earning coins that I can use when I need clues to solve difficult puzzles. However, I only use clues as a last resort. I challenge my brain by solving the puzzles without help. Word Calm keeps my brain active.

Somewhere between childhood and adulthood, many people stop playing games. Remember, the simple things that little children love are the same things that keep older people thriving. One of those things is game playing. According to George Bernard Shaw, "You don't stop playing because you grow old. You grow old because you stop playing!" (BrainyQuote, n.d.).

What the Brain Research Says: Why Should I Do It?

According to Glasser (1999), there are five critical needs that must be satisfied if people are to be effectively motivated: the need for (1) survival, (2) belonging and love, (3) power, (4) freedom, and (5) fun. The need for fun can be satisfied with game play, which is not only perfect for increasing the level of the brain's feel-good chemicals, but in proper amounts, game playing can also increase working memory and cognition (Jensen, 2007). The following sections suggest four types of gaming—video games, brain games, indoor and outdoor games, and playtime at work—to fulfill these needs.

Video Games

According to Kenneth Terrell (2019), an American Association of Retired Persons (AARP) survey reported that the number of video game players over the age of fifty grew from 40.2 million gamers in 2016 to 50.6 million gamers in 2019. The survey found that older adults are using gaming approximately five hours per week to connect with others socially, to stay mentally healthy, reduce stress, or just to have fun. The largest spike was within the age range of fifty to fifty-nine, with women choosing to play more often than men. The most popular games were logic and puzzle games, with tile and card games (without the gambling) coming in at a close second.

Experiments with elderly participants are showing that video gaming can result in improvements in the brain areas of working memory, attention, abstract reasoning, and cognitive flexibility, all of which tend to decline with age (Basak, Boot, Voss, & Kramer, 2008). According to neurologist and educator Judy Willis (Paturel, 2014), for youth, video games can get information to the brain in ways that maximize learning, since they can improve visual perception, the processing of information, and the ability to switch from one task to another.

Brain Games

Brain games are games that stimulate your thinking, such as crossword puzzles, Scrabble, and traditional games like chess, Sudoku, and bridge. According to Harvard Men's Health Watch (2019), some studies find that brain games can have long-term benefits such as delaying the progression of dementia. Playing card and board games can improve our ability to retrieve information as well as enhance the mental skills of sequencing, visualization, and memory (Harvard Health Publishing, 2021).

 When one plays, body and mind are fully integrated since certain pathways connecting the frontal lobe of the brain and the limbic system are formed (Hannaford, 2005).

Indoor and Outdoor Games

According to Rick Warren, Daniel Amen, and Mark Hyman (2020), authors of the bestseller *The Daniel Plan: 40 Days to a Healthier Life*, there is an overwhelming amount of scientific evidence supporting the beneficial effects of playing active indoor and outdoor games for your body and health. These benefits include the following (Warren et al., 2020):

- Increasing the capacity of the lungs, blood flow, and muscle tone
- Stimulating the brain by improving problem-solving and listening skills
- Delaying the memory loss associated with age
- Creating friendships and social relationships
- Reducing the risk of diabetes, heart disease, cancer, and osteoporosis
- Strengthening immunity
- Lowering levels of depression and stress
- Sleeping better
- Increasing energy

 Active games are not only beneficial to your physical heart but also your mental, social, and spiritual heart (Warren et al., 2020).

In addition to physical activity, games can help the brain build up what is known as *cognitive reserve*. This reserve is similar to a savings account in the brain that can be squirreled away and used when quick thinking is needed.

Playtime at Work

Employers should know that even scheduling playtime at work has the following benefits:

- Enables you to be functional while under stress
- Encourages teamwork
- Prevents burnout and increases the ability to work as a team
- Helps you to see problems in innovative ways
- Triggers motivation and creativity (Robinson, Smith, Segal, & Shubin, 2021)

According to Harvard Men's Health Watch (2019), novelty is the key to brain development. It is recommended that you mix up the game playing. If you are already good at bridge or crossword puzzles, those games may not adequately stimulate the brain. Instead, do something different that forces your brain to learn differently and work harder.

 Play is beneficial for all ages since it relieves stress, improves brain function, boosts creativity, improves relationships, and enables you to feel young and energetic (Robinson et al., 2021).

Action Steps: How Should I Do It?

Play With Your Children

Playing with kids, grandkids, nephews, nieces, or other young people in your life will allow you to experience the joy of gameplay from a different perspective. Robinson and colleagues (2021) recommend setting a scheduled playtime when you can give the child or children in your life your full attention without the distractions of cell phones, television, or computers. Select games that are age-appropriate and safe, and allow the child to take the lead. If your playdates are very young, then you might have to sit on the floor or get on your knees so that you are matching the level of the child. It is even beneficial to play the same game over and over since the brain learns through repetition.

When my three children were growing up, we set aside Friday night as the game night in our house. This was the one night when there were no scheduled meetings or sports activities and any homework could wait until the weekend. When I began to work on my doctorate, I began to spend some Friday nights at the library or writing my dissertation, and eventually, the game night went by the wayside. I did not even realize what had happened until one day our son, Chris, asked me, "Mom, why are we not playing games anymore?" It was then that I realized how important that time was—not just for game playing, but for building the relationships within our family, so game night returned!

Host a Game Night With Friends

Find a game that you really enjoy playing such as bridge, gin rummy, Spades, Mahjong, pool, and so on, and schedule a night to get together with friends or relatives to play and have fun. Set a consistent time when the group can get together and rotate hosting responsibilities. That way the group always has something fun to look forward to in the middle of a busy work week.

Participate in Active Games

Instead of dreading the physical exertion that comes along with a workout, add active games to your routine. It is recommended (Warren, 2020) that you participate in active games at least three to five days a week for twenty to sixty minutes per session. Warren and coauthors (2020) suggest the following active games: badminton, baseball or softball, basketball, bowling, dodgeball, fencing, flag football, Frisbee golf, handball, hula hooping, jumping rope, pogo stick, racquetball, soccer, table tennis, tag, tennis, trampoline jumping, Ultimate Frisbee, volleyball, and Wii Fit.

Attend Sporting Events

Being involved in the action of playing a game is best for the brain and body, but watching a game also has benefits. I am an avid sports fan and, regardless of my busy schedule, over the years I have found time to watch many tennis matches and football and baseball games. Before the COVID-19 pandemic, one of the ways we built close family relationships with our daughter, Jennifer, and her family was with our trips to the Atlanta Falcons football games or the Atlanta Braves baseball games. These memorable experiences produced serotonin in our brains and bonded us together, whether our team won or lost.

Play With a Pet

The majority of households in the United States has at least one pet (Centers for Disease Control and Prevention, 2019). Pets can be wonderful companions, and they offer additional health benefits as well. Pets can increase your opportunities to get outdoors, exercise, and socialize. Consistent walking or playing with pets can decrease cholesterol and triglyceride levels, as well as blood pressure. Make some time to play with your pet. The health benefits can be numerous (Centers for Disease Control and Prevention, 2019).

Take Up Video Gaming

Video games are not just for teenagers. Adults play them as well. According to a study by the Entertainment Software Association (ESA, 2020), 64 percent of U.S. adults play video games on a regular basis and the average age range of an American gamer is thirty-five to forty-four years old. ESA also finds that six percent of gamers are over sixty-five years old.

Video games can be beneficial. Action video games improve eye-hand coordination and spatial visualization skills as well as other areas of brain function listed in the aforementioned research. Select video games that you personally enjoy and engage in them regularly.

Learn a New Word Daily

Make a game out of learning a new word every day. Learning new words not only enriches one's understanding of the world, but it also enhances the brain's language centers and the prefrontal cortex (Marchal, n.d.). Examples of advantageous word games include crossword puzzles, word jumbles, anagrams, Boggle, and Scrabble. I myself have acquired so many new words simply by playing the games Words With Friends and Word Calm. Challenge a friend, family member, or roommate to learn new words along with you.

Put a Puzzle Together

Select puzzles to solve or put together. Different types of puzzles exercise different parts of the brain. Crossword puzzles challenge the language and memory areas, while jigsaw puzzles provide exercise for the parietal lobes. Putting the pieces of a puzzle together can improve problem-solving skills and enhance short-term memory as well as increase productivity and creativity (Baylor College of Medicine, 2020).

Part 2: Happy Classrooms

As I travel across the United States doing my work with educators, I have come to realize that the fun has simply gone out of teaching and learning in so many classrooms. With increased emphasis on standardized testing and accountability, school in many places is just not fun anymore. Prior to the COVID-19 pandemic, in the name of increased time on task, some school systems were even removing recess from the school day of students. Removing play is dangerous as the benefits of play for children are significant. While their stress levels decrease with play, student motivation usually increases. In addition, it's amazing the amount of content a teacher can teach or review within the context of a game.

One idea is to use a ball-toss game to review content. When teaching my class Worksheets Don't Grow Dendrites, I use a ball-toss game to review the characteristics of a brain-compatible classroom. Here are the rules of the game: One person in each cooperative group stands and participates in the game. That person must catch the ball and state one characteristic. Then he or she must throw the ball to another person who is standing and then sit down. Here is the challenge: They cannot toss the ball to anyone standing near them. They must toss it at a distance. Another rule of the game is that if anyone misses catching the ball, everyone who previously sat down stands up again and the game starts all over. The more participants miss the ball, the funnier and more challenging the game becomes. The greatest number of times that we have started over in any class is eleven. The benefit of this game is the number of repetitions of content that students are exposed to when the game finally ends.

 A ball-toss game not only enables students to think and act quickly while operating in a safe environment, but the game also encourages cooperation, physical movement, and problem-solving (Jensen, 2007).

Simply tossing a softball or a Frisbee to students as you call on them to respond to your questions adds a motivational element to the classroom. *Jeopardy!* makes a wonderful review game, and *Family Feud* is a perfect structure for having one part of the class compete against the other.

One teacher turned her classroom of five rows of desks into a BINGO board. She labeled the rows LEARN instead of BINGO. Therefore, if you were sitting in the first row, third seat, you were in seat L3. At the front of the room, the teacher turned a canister filled with chips representing each seat in the room. When she needed a student to respond to a question, she would reach into the canister and pull out a chip and call on that student.

Whether you are teaching virtually or in person, look for games that you can use to engage the brains of your students. Many students are motivated by the competition of a friendly game that encourages students to cooperate with one another and enables them to pay attention (Algozzine, Campbell, & Wang, 2009). Refer to Strategy 4: Games in *Worksheets Don't Grow Dendrites: 20 Instructional Strategies That Engage the Brain* (Tate, 2016) for research on the beneficial effects of games on students' brains and over fifteen additional games you can utilize in the classroom.

Part 3: Action Plan

Recall at the beginning of the chapter the discussion of Cyndi Lauper's (1983) song "Girls Just Want to Have Fun." In fact, girls and boys, young and old, should all want to have fun. We all benefit when we play games, from Candy Land to Words With Friends, from board games to video games. The brain benefits during game playing are numerous. Use the following Action Plan (page 48) to determine how you will infuse more fun into your life.

Action Plan for Playing Games

What are my plans for incorporating more games into my life?		
Recommendations	**Presently Doing**	**Strive to Do**
Experience the joy of playing with children.		
Participate in active games on a consistent basis.		
Host a game night with friends and relatives.		
Attend sporting events.		
Play with a pet.		
Take up video gaming.		
Play word games that increase vocabulary.		
Put puzzles together.		
Incorporate games like ball toss and BINGO into instruction to motivate students.		

Goals and Notes:

5

Movement

The act or process of moving, especially a change of place or position or posture (Movement, n.d.)

"The Way You Move," recorded by Big Boi (2003) of the hip hop duo OutKast, peaked at number one on the *Billboard* Hot 100 and won a BET Award for Video of the Year in 2004 (*Billboard*, n.d.; IMDb, n.d.). It was named the twenty-second most successful song of the 2000s on the *Billboard* Hot 100 Songs of the Decade (*Billboard*, n.d.). The song's instantly recognizable and appealing chorus repeats the word *move* fourteen times. The song is back on the airwaves again in the 2020s; the instrumental version is featured in a commercial encouraging people to move after they've been treated with a remedy for arthritis. "The Way You Move" represents the fifth principle for longevity: movement.

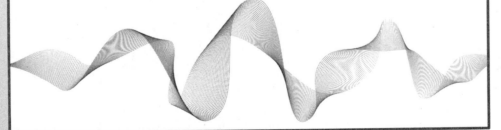

PRINCIPLE 5

Movement

Part 1: Healthy Teachers

Movement: What Should I Do?

In 2014, we learned that my husband, Tyrone's, kidneys were failing and that he would need a transplant. Fortunately, our oldest daughter, Jennifer, was a perfect match for her father. One of the most important post-operative instructions Tyrone's surgeon gave to us was to be sure that he moved, that he walked and exercised during and after the recuperative period. Now, several years later, his doctor still reminds him at every appointment to move. I had always known about the correlation between good health and exercise, but it was during that post-operative conference and subsequent appointments that I came to truly understand the positive power of exercise on the brain and body.

According to the *American Journal of Public Health*, researchers from Canada, Australia, and the United States find that more than eight hours of sitting a day increases the risk of premature death and certain chronic diseases (ScienceDaily, 2018). New devices like VariDesks and VersaDesks raise the flat surface of desks for standing while working to encourage movement, while business leaders now consider how to make exercise an integral part of the workday. Teachers move more than people in many other professions. In fact, I coined a motto, *Teach on your feet, not in a seat*. However, the motion that occurs as teachers are circulating around the classroom may not be enough to exercise those crucial muscles and make those brain-body connections that are essential.

Allow me to share two stories regarding movement shared with me by two teachers who attended my workshops. One shared that her mother who has Alzheimer's disease no longer recognizes her children or grandchildren; her mother, however, is a pianist and can still go to the piano and play all the songs she once played.

A second teacher shared a story from when her grandmother was in the hospital near death. The family had gathered around her bedside to bid their final goodbyes. Her grandmother had knitted her entire life and made many beautiful hats, sweaters, scarves, and blankets for her family. Now, as her grandmother was lying in a hospital bed unconscious, she was still knitting. Obviously, there was no needle and yarn in her hands, but her hands were still going through the motions of knitting.

These two stories lead to one point: Memories that are embedded into long-term, or procedural, memory are those that appear to remain with us longer. Why? Because the way they entered that memory system is through movement.

What the Brain Research Says: Why Should I Do It?

What, then, is the positive impact of exercise and movement on longevity? We are designed for motion. In fact, in his bestseller *Brain Rules*, molecular biologist John Medina (2014) states that "one of the greatest predictors of successful aging was the presence or absence for a sedentary lifestyle" (p. 23). According to Medina (2014), an active lifestyle increases the likelihood that you will make it to your nineties. David Sousa (2012), an international consultant in educational neuroscience, shares that human beings are mentally and physically designed to be in constant motion, and evolution has provided us with the appendages and cerebral networks to enable that to happen (Sousa, 2012).

 Without the propensity for movement, one can have lethargy and the deterioration of cognitive, psychological, and physical functions (Sousa, 2012).

Medina (2014) recalls the story of one day watching a documentary on television where wheelchair-bound people in their eighties lined the halls of dimly-lit nursing homes. Many looked lonely or downcast with vacant stares and appeared to be sitting and waiting to die. Their brains, Medina noted, appeared to be withering right before his eyes. Then he changed to a channel where the journalist Mike Wallace (1957) was interviewing the architect Frank Lloyd Wright who was then in his late eighties. In the interview, Wright demonstrated his clarity of thinking, vision, and ability to think out of the box. Medina was not surprised when he learned that Wright had completed designs for the Guggenheim Museum at the age of ninety.

Movement or exercise appears not only essential for lengthening life, but it also facilitates our mental proficiency while we are living. In fact, the more they study the cerebellum, the more researchers realize that movement is inescapably linked to learning and memory (Sousa, 2017).

The nerve fibers of the cerebellum, once thought to only coordinate the performance of learned motor skills, such as walking, driving, golfing, or tying a shoe, also communicate with other areas of the brain (Sousa, 2017). Research shows that the cerebellum also plays a crucial role in attention, social interactions, and long-term memory, as well as the cognitive function of the frontal lobe: areas that are associated with learning (Sousa, 2017; Van Overwalle & Mariën, 2016). According to brain researcher and consultant Eric Jensen (2008), probably the only known cognitive activity that uses 100 percent of the brain is physical performance.

Physical activity increases blood flow and the delivery of nutrients and oxygen to hardworking brain cells (Sousa, 2012).

Physical exercise facilitates blood transport by increasing the number of brain capillaries and increasing the amount of oxygen in the blood. This rise in oxygen significantly enhances cognitive performance.

"Exercisers outperform couch potatoes in tests that measure long-term memory, reasoning, attention, problem-solving, even so-called fluid intelligence tasks" (Medina, 2008, p. 14). These tasks require a person to think abstractly and reason quickly and to use material previously learned in order to solve new problems.

This is the reason that classroom teachers need to incorporate methods for correlating movement with curricula so that students not only recall content for tests but also for learning in general. This begs the question, why are schools eliminating recess and physical education classes in an effort to increase academic achievement? What's wrong with this picture?

In his article "Covering Ground With These Benefits of Walking," Jeff Hayward (2020) provides the following seven reasons the simple act of walking can lead to a healthier life.

1. Decreasing the chance of developing cardiovascular disease

2. Decreasing the chance of developing other chronic diseases, such as type 2 diabetes and certain forms of cancer

3. Controlling anxiety and improving one's mood due to increased serotonin

4. Losing weight (getting into the walking habit can enable one to lose one pound per week)

5. Supplying joints with oxygen and nutrients that they would not receive with inactivity

6. Supplying the brain with the oxygen and fresh air that an outdoor walk can provide

7. Increasing the brain's creativity

Sousa (2011) relates that complex problems can often be solved simply by taking a walk since the cerebellum, mid-brain, and motor cortex that coordinate movement also coordinate the flow of thoughts.

Action Steps: How Should I Do It?

Move

It is easy in this day and age for human beings to become sedentary. Allow me to relate this story. When I was growing up, if my father wanted to build a fire in our living room fireplace, he would have to journey across the street to a vacant lot, cut down and gather wood and twigs, and bring them back up the steep driveway to our house. Now, all I have to do to have a fire in the fireplace in my den is flip a switch. What once required a great deal of work now can come so easily. Everything we want is at our fingertips. To avoid the dangers of being sedentary, we must find ways to move our bodies during daily living.

My daughters, a principal and a chef, both have hiring responsibilities in their professions. Both complain about the lack of work ethic in many of the prospective employees they interview. I truly believe that part of the reason is the ease at which many tasks can be completed today. Many young people are just not accustomed to completing jobs that require expending a great deal of energy or that challenge them mentally.

Find ways to add movement or exercise into your ordinary daily tasks. Take the stairs instead of the elevator or escalator. Park at a distance from the front door of a mall or store and walk. Clean your house rather than having someone else do it. Go outside and actually run, jump, and play with children and grandchildren. Think of specific ways to add years to your life by adding movement to each day.

Walk

When people hear the word *exercise*, they most often visualize countless hours at the gym or intense involvement in one or more sports. However, the benefits of regular exercise, like walking, can pay large dividends even though 40 percent of adults don't participate in this form of exercise at all (Rettner, 2017). Unfortunately, with the time we spend using technology, this percentage is increasing, not decreasing.

Walking is the most natural physical activity in which we can engage. It is easily accessible and, if capable, human beings do it easily all the time. It also places less stress on the body than some other forms of physical activity.

Researchers in multiple studies found that walking reduces the risk of cardiovascular events by 31 percent and the risk of dying of a cardiac event by 32 percent in both men and women (Harvard Men's Health Watch, 2020).

So how much walking should we do? According to Harvard Men's Health Watch (2020), for good health, people should walk thirty to forty-five minutes almost every day. It can be done all at once or in segments of five to ten minutes. Walkers should aim for a brisk walk of three to four miles an hour, but strolling at a slower pace can be beneficial if the walker is consistent (Harvard Men's Health Watch, 2020).

Walking is one form of exercise I feel fully capable of practicing. Even during the COVID-19 pandemic, my daughter, Jessica, and I push the grandchildren in their respective strollers while walking and talking at least three to five times each week. I have personally experienced several of the benefits of walking: an improved disposition, a lessening of the arthritic pain in my left hip, and the maintenance of a more consistent weight.

I have always admired the ability of my administrative assistant, Carol, and her husband, Don, to make a habit of walking. For more than forty years, they have been walking together. In the past, they were accustomed to walking five miles per day. Currently, even with some of Don's health challenges, they are still walking two to three miles per day or every other day at seventy-nine and eighty-three years old.

Run or Jog

Like walking, regular running or jogging has the health benefits of building strong bones, strengthening muscles, burning a large number of kilojoules (nutritional calories), improving cardiovascular fitness, and assisting in maintaining a healthy weight (Better Health, n.d.).

Exercise

M. Andrew Garrison and Sally K. Severino (2016), authors of *Wellness in Mind* and founders of BodyFacts Wellness Services, outline the following four major components of exercise.

- **Cardiorespiratory fitness:** "Aerobic exercise consists of rhythmic, continuous, and repetitive movements with major muscle groups" (p. 20). It enables the body to deliver oxygen to its working muscles and improves cardiovascular fitness. Muscles devoid of oxygen can become easily tired and susceptible to injury or illness.

- **Muscle strength:** Another name for muscle strength is absolute strength. Free weights, machines, or calisthenics can maintain or increase muscle strength. Every major muscle group (arms, legs, chest, back, stomach, and hips) should be strengthened. The American Council on Exercise (ACE) recommends beginning with eight repetitions of a weight that feels comfortable to handle and adding more weight or repetitions (in sets of eight to twelve) as it becomes easy (Garrison & Severino, 2016).

- **Muscle endurance:** Muscle endurance, on the other hand, is the capability of the muscles to consistently perform for long periods of time. As in the case with muscle strength, when exercising, include every muscle group using free weights, machines, and calisthenics. Add repetitions gradually until twelve reps become easy to accomplish. Weight can then be increased.

- **Flexibility:** One maintains flexibility by engaging in two forms of stretching. Both forms should be relaxing and not painful. Dynamic stretching is a pre-warm-up activity and involves moving body parts from rest to activity. Alternatively, static stretching does not involve movement and is generally practiced after a workout. During static stretching, a person should breathe deeply while slowly holding the muscle being stretched at the furthest range of motion for twenty to thirty seconds.

Yoga

Yoga, meaning *union*, is the practice of incorporating body postures, meditation, and breathing control. It is an ancient Hindu ritual that has been in existence for more than 5,000 years (Yoga, 2018). While there are varying types of training, all consistently involve breathing exercises, simple meditation, and postures and poses that flex and stretch various muscle groups.

Yoga has obvious benefits not only for this chapter on movement but also for spirituality. Some of those benefits include: (1) strengthening of the muscles in the core, arms, back, and legs by managing the control necessary for holding various poses; (2) enhanced flexibility due to stretched and elongated muscles; (3) increased levels of the hormone cortisol, which in low levels can cause fatigue and oxygen deprivation; (4) built-up respiratory stamina due to breathing practices; (5) weight loss due to a combination of low impact yoga and a balanced diet; (6) benefits to the cardiovascular system due to breathing techniques, muscle targeting exercises, and controlled positioning; (7) less chance of injury and workouts for areas of the body *untouched by other training*; and (8) development of skills to manage stress levels due to meditation and breathing techniques (Charmaine, 2018).

My personal experience with yoga has been limited to one afternoon several years ago that I shall never forget. I had been observing teachers at Saint Benedict at Auburndale High School in Cordova, Tennessee, looking for the use of brain-compatible strategies in a number of classrooms during the school day. I saw many excellent, engaging lessons! I was also impressed with the school's emphasis on teacher wellness and was, therefore, invited to participate in an after-school yoga class with members of the faculty. The yoga teacher was very proficient, but I learned firsthand what it was like to be a remedial student in a class of high achievers. I left that class with a new regard for the amount of muscle strength and flexibility it took to pull off those moves and a realization of the many benefits of this ancient Hindu ritual.

Add Fun Activities to Your Day

Rather than dreading a workout, Warren and colleagues (2020) suggest that you make aerobic activities an integral part of your life. These can include backpacking, bicycling, dancing, horseback riding, hula hooping, jumping rope, mountain climbing, roller or ice skating, rollerblading, rowing, skateboarding, skiing, surfing, swimming, tag, trampoline jumping, and Zumba. See chapter 4: Games (page 40) for additional fun activities that include exercise.

Begin to think of specific ways to incorporate the principle of movement into your daily life if you are not already doing so. You will reap great rewards!

Part 2: Happy Classrooms

In my class titled "Worksheets Don't Grow Dendrites," we talk about the necessity to get students moving while learning. During one class, a teacher shared the following ironic anecdote: We spend the first three years of children's lives teaching them to walk and talk and the next fifteen years telling them to sit down and shut up!

If the goal of schooling is to prepare students to be successful in the world of work, then why do we not encourage more movement during the school day? What appears to happen naturally at the kindergarten level so diminishes in classrooms as students get older that by the time they get to high school, the only movement that may occur is when they are changing classes.

According to Sousa (2011), when students sit for twenty minutes or longer, the blood pools in two parts of the body, the seat and the feet. Within a minute after getting up and moving, the blood recirculates with 15 percent of the recirculated blood going to the brain. Students then become more alert and are capable of improved thinking.

To encourage movement, consider flexible alternative forms of seating for your students. These might include tables and chairs, stools, exercise balls, couches, bean bag chairs, standing desks, or simply working on the floor with a clipboard. Give students an opportunity to select the form of seating they would prefer and then rotate so that students can experience more than one form.

Think of ways to integrate movement into your lessons. It could be as simple as telling students to stand if they agree with an answer and remain seated if they disagree. Have them make appointments with other students who sit at a distance in the room. Then, at an appropriate time, have students stand and keep their appointments while discussing or reviewing content you have taught.

Some teachers take brain breaks so that students can experience the joy of movement. This is a worthwhile activity. However, if the movement is related to the concept being taught, then the benefits are twofold. Students are active while increasing the likelihood that the content they are learning will end up in procedural, or muscle, memory. Content-related movement could involve solving a mathematics problem on the dry-erase board, forming a living timeline, or role-playing the definition of a vocabulary word. Consult *Worksheets Don't Grow Dendrites: 20 Instructional Strategies That Engage the Brain* (Tate, 2016), Strategy 10: Movement, for additional ways to integrate this principle into your lessons.

Part 3: Action Plan

Recall at the beginning of the chapter the discussion of "The Way You Move," recorded by Big Boi (2003) of the hip hop duo OutKast. You can't listen to that song without wanting to move to the music. In fact, music with beats of 110 to 160 per minute make us move our feet, swing our arms, and snap our fingers. Use the Action Plan to delineate specific additional ways to merge movement into your daily life.

Action Plan for Incorporating Movement

What are my plans for incorporating more movement into my daily life?		
Recommendations	**Presently Doing**	**Strive to Do**
Find ways to add movement to each day.		
Walk thirty-five to forty minutes daily at three to four miles per hour.		
Establish a running or jogging ritual.		
Exercise major muscle groups daily.		
Practice yoga.		
Integrate aerobic activities into my life.		
Incorporate student movement into my lessons.		
Allow students to use flexible seating in class.		
Goals and Notes:		

6

Music

Sounds that are sung by voices or played on musical instruments (Music, n.d.)

The Doobie Brothers' first hit, "Listen to the Music," was written by the band's lead vocalist, Tom Johnston (1972). The lyrics are based on his Utopian idea that on a sunny day, if world leaders were all able to sit down together on a grassy knoll and listen to music, they would realize that people have more in common than they do not have in common (Mastropolo, 2012). He believed that music would make everything better. I truly believe that also. In fact, according to Eric Jensen (2005), a leader in the mind/brain movement, the musical arts have the ability to engage all people since music can break down barriers between cultures, religions, races, geographic distinctions, and socioeconomic status. Music is the sixth principle for longevity.

Music

Part 1: Healthy Teachers

Music: What Should I Do?

Close your eyes for a moment and imagine a world without music. It plays a large part in daily life for most people. Music connects us to meaningful time periods and events in our lives. Music evokes memories. It represents personal style and tastes. It is part of both celebration and mourning. And, importantly, music has a great impact on our brains and learning. Many of us experience music from a young age, whether we would describe ourselves as musical or not.

In elementary school, I had a music teacher, Mrs. Theodora James, who introduced me to varying genres of music. She is the reason that, to this day, I love classical music as much as I love rhythm and blues. I sang in the chorus during elementary and high schools and took piano lessons for a number of years, never realizing the profound effects music was having on my brain. Even in the elementary chorus, we were expected to sing in three-part harmony, and we did!

It is my exposure to the work of Eric Jensen (2008, 2019), an authority on brain-based teaching and learning, that prompted me to incorporate music into my workshops. I started changing the brains of my adult learners with music twenty-five years ago. The results have been significant. Educators who have been a part of my workshops, even virtually, often comment about the effects of music on their brains. When educators enter my workshops in the morning, I usually have piano music playing—songs most people recognize played on a classical piano. The music is calming and readies the brain to learn. In the afternoons, I turn to more high-energy music since energy levels typically decline after lunch. The energy level remains high until the end of the day when we are moving left and right to Kool and the Gang's song, "Celebration," as we celebrate all the new learning that has occurred. I've even had teachers tell me they love my playlist.

Glen Campbell, one of my favorite country singers, suffered from Alzheimer's disease during the final years of his life. My favorite song by Campbell will always be "Wichita Lineman." In 2011, he embarked on his farewell tour, Ghost on the Canvas. His family traveled with him and would assist when and if he forgot the lyrics to one of his songs. Glen's wife, Kimberly, commented that his brain would have declined much faster had it not been for his music.

Music can intellectually and emotionally affect the brain by altering the heart rate, blood pressure, breathing, pain threshold, and muscle movements (Sousa, 2017).

What the Brain Research Says: Why Should I Do It?

According to Jensen (2008), music's powerful effects on the mind and body include the following:

- An increase in molecular and muscular energy
- A decrease in heartbeat
- An altered state of metabolism
- A reduction in stress and pain
- An increase in the speed of healing and recovery in surgical patients
- Relief for fatigue
- Helps the body release emotion
- Stimulates sensitivity, thinking, and creativity
- Assists in building and strengthening connections between brain cells in the cortex

Baroque music has been known to calm and soothe while pop music can raise endorphin levels and increase concentration (Gregory & Chapman, 2013). Calming music at 40 to 45 beats per minute can aid in relaxation, while fast music with 100 to 140 beats per minute can be energizing (Jensen, 2005).

Music and Mathematics

Mathematics appears to be the content area most closely aligned to music. Why? According to Sousa (2017), music, like mathematics, relies on the following:

- Fractions for tempo
- Patterns for notes, chords, and key changes
- Counting of beats, rests, and holding notes
- Geometry for remembering finger positions for notes and chords
- Ratios, proportions, and equivalent fractions for holding notes
- Sequences or intervals

An analysis of six experimental studies involving 300,000 secondary students found a strong association between music instruction and mathematical achievement (Vaughn, 2000).

Music and Memory

According to Jensen (2005), people easily learn words to new songs because the patterns, contrasts, and rhythms of music enable the brain to encode new information. The brain's subcortical region and the body's limbic system are involved in engaging emotional and musical responses and mediating long-term memory; therefore, when information is combined with music, there is a greater possibility of the information being encoded (Jensen, 2008). This all points to one fact: if the brain can continue to reap the beneficial effects of music throughout one's life, quality of life is improved.

Musical Training

Passively listening to music has some therapeutic and educational benefits; however, when people make music, it seems to be more advantageous (Sousa, 2017).

Learning to play an instrument, even as a child, can protect the brain against dementia (Rampton, 2017).

Numerous studies are showing that musical training improves the ability of the left temporal lobe of the brain to handle those things learned verbally (Sousa, 2017). Those memory benefits appear to last. In another study, musicians outperformed nonmusicians in phonological, visual, and executive memory tests (George & Coch, 2011).

Learning to play a musical instrument provides new challenges for the brain. The brain not only discerns different groupings and patterns, but it must also learn and coordinate new motor skills. This new learning appears to cause permanent changes in the brain structures of the motor cortex, auditory cortex, cerebellum, and corpus callosum. These structures appear to be larger in musicians than nonmusicians (Schlaug, 2015).

Musical training strengthens the brain's executive functioning such as processing and retaining information, making decisions, controlling behavior, and boosting our ability to learn (Rampton, 2017).

Playing an instrument, a rich and complex experience, is beneficial to the adult brain in the following ways (Rampton, 2017).

- Enhances verbal memory, spatial reasoning, and literacy skills
- Increases resilience for any age-related decline in hearing
- Can improve long-term memory
- Increases mental alertness
- Improves auditory, tactile, and audiotactile reaction times
- Increases blood flow to the left hemisphere of the brain
- Lowers levels of depression and anxiety
- Integrates multisensory information (like vision, hearing, touch, and fine movements)

 Older adults who had four to fourteen years of musical training at a young age appear to be able to process speech sounds faster than those who did not, even if they hadn't played an instrument in forty years (Bhanoo, 2013).

Action Steps: How Should I Do It?

Surround Yourself With Calming Music

I was presenting in Baltimore, Maryland, on a Saturday to a group of administrators. We were discussing the profound effects of calming music on the brain. One principal's husband, who also attended the workshop, was the chief of police. He shared the following story with the class. Barbers from a shop in downtown Baltimore appealed to the police department to get rid of the drug dealers who had set up shop outside of their establishment. The barbers related that they might have to close since their clients did not want to walk past the drug dealers to get their hair cut. The police chief, realizing the power of music, decided to play classical music in the barbershop loud enough to be heard on the sidewalk. Within two days, the drug dealers had disappeared. They simply did not appreciate the calming effects that classical music was having on their brains. The police chief told me that he was going to write a book. Instead of being called, *Stop, or I'll Shoot!* it would be called *Stop, or I'll Play Vivaldi!*

Certain types of music have the ability to calm the brain. These include classical (particularly from the Baroque period), new age, slow Celtic, Native American, and smooth jazz. Find a genre you prefer and surround yourself with it. Play it at home or in the car. You can even ask Alexa or Siri to play music that would prove inspirational to you. My favorite music by Emile Pandolfi, a classical pianist, is

By Request and *Days of Wine and Roses*. I play his songs as teachers wait to begin my virtual or in-person workshops. It puts their brains in a great state for learning.

Enjoy High-Energy Music

When a song with a faster tempo like the theme from the movie *Rocky* or the song "Happy" is played, our fingers start popping, our bodies move, and our toes start tapping. This is the effect of high-energy music on our brains and bodies. The genres of music in this category might include salsa, rock and roll, rhythm and blues, positive rap, or fast-paced country.

One parent related to me that she was having a difficult time getting her children to clean their rooms on Saturdays. They perceived it as a chore in which they did not want to be involved. She came up with the great idea to turn the chore into a game. She put on some high-energy music and challenged her children to be finished with their rooms before the songs played three times. What began as a dreaded day turned into a fun, challenging Saturday morning, and as a bonus, the rooms got cleaned.

Incorporate Music Into Professional Learning

I know that I can change the state of educators' brains with the type of music I play in my workshops. Television and movie producers also know this fact. How many times have you been watching a movie and shed tears just as the emotional music begins to play? Maybe in another movie, you moved to the beat of a fast-paced song. One music teacher asked that the next time I watch *Cast Away* with Tom Hanks to notice that from the time he lands on the island until the time the volleyball, Wilson, floats away in the ocean, there is absolutely no soundtrack. This makes the character seem more alone than he would be if there was music. I watched, and she was correct! If you conduct any type of professional learning or a faculty meeting for adults, be sure to incorporate appropriate music. Your teachers will be the beneficiaries.

Learn to Play a New Musical Instrument

It is never too late to grow new neurons (memory cells). One way to do that is to learn to play a new musical instrument, particularly later in life (Sousa, 2017). This learning permanently changes the brain's structure by enabling it to discern different groupings and tone patterns. It also assists the brain and body in learning and coordinating new motor skills. Whenever you perform an activity requiring finger dexterity, your brain is enhanced. Knitting and woodworking are fine, but taking up a musical instrument is even better. Retracing memories of things we have mastered over the years, such as playing piano or the guitar, is not a bad thing. However, it is even better to learn to play an instrument never before attempted.

Part 2: Happy Classrooms

Incorporate both calming and high-energy music into your work with students. Use calming music as students are assembling for class, during creative writing assignments, or as students are meeting in cooperative groups. If you are asking students to engage their brains, then it is probably best to use calming music without lyrics. High-energy music is motivational. Use it for class celebrations or when you need students to move.

When providing direct instruction, it is desirable not to use music at all. Since the brain can only pay conscious attention to one thing at a time, students should not have to decide whether to listen to you or sing along with the catchy lyrics they are hearing. However, when teaching content students must commit to memory, it is beneficial for younger students to find songs that will help them recall content. Older students may be able to create original songs. Students who have difficulty memorizing content long enough to pass a test may have no difficulty remembering the lyrics to the songs they love. Capitalize on this propensity to recall song lyrics by supplying students with songs that teach content.

Following are some resources for using music to teach content across the curriculum.

- Dr. Jean (Feldman) (primary grades; www.drjean.org)
- Jack Hartmann (primary grades; https://jackhartmann.com)
- Rock n' Learn (all levels; www.rocknlearn.com)
- *The Green Book of Songs by Subject* (5th ed.) by Jeff Green (all levels; www.greenbookofsongs.com)
- Flocabulary (all levels; www.flocabulary.com)
- Mr. Betts (social studies, all levels; www.mrbettsclass.com)
- Warren Phillips (science, all levels; www.wphillips.com)
- Mr. Parr (science, all levels; www.youtube.com/user/ParrMr/videos)

By the time students get to the upper elementary, middle, or high school grades, they may be capable of creating their own songs. Provide the content that students need to remember and allow them to write original songs, rhymes, or raps, which they can perform for the class if desired.

Incorporate music into your lessons. When studying a particular culture or time period in history, play music appropriate for the culture or time period. Have multicultural students share samples of the music from their lives with other students in class.

Encourage students who are interested in learning to play a musical instrument to do so. In elementary school, I had the opportunity to play the recorder, flute, ukulele, and xylophone, all major contributors to my love of music. The school band and orchestra as well as the chorus offer students many opportunities to express their musical talents and abilities and will likely positively affect their academic achievement.

Part 3: Action Plan

Recall at the beginning of the chapter the discussion of the Doobie Brothers' (1972) "Listen to the Music." For me, music is about more than just listening—I incorporate it into my teaching, training, and daily life. The type of music I listen to depends on the state I want to create in my brain—do I need to relax or boost my energy? Use the following Action Plan (page 68) to determine which steps you will use to make music an integral part of your life.

Action Plan for Incorporating Music

What are my plans for incorporating more music into my life?		
Recommendations	**Presently Doing**	**Strive to Do**
Surround myself with calming music during relaxation activities.		
Enjoy high-energy music to motivate and energize myself.		
Use music with adults in professional learning to change the states of their brains.		
Learn to play a new musical instrument.		
Incorporate music in the classroom to calm and energize students.		
Use prerecorded or student-created songs to enable students to remember content.		
Encourage students to select a musical instrument of interest and learn to play it.		
Integrate music representing various cultures or periods of history into your lessons.		

Goals and Notes:

Calm

A quiet and peaceful state or condition
(Calm, n.d.)

In an interview, John Denver (BBC, n.d.) tells the story of writing "Annie's Song" ("You Fill Up My Senses"; Denver, 1974) while on a ski lift in Aspen, Colorado, surrounded by the beauty and serenity of nature. This isn't surprising since everything about "Annie's Song" exudes calm: the simple and soft folk melody, the intimate lyrics, and John Denver's placid voice. The song has the ability to transport you to a place of peace, calming the mind and body. It is one of my very favorite songs, and it represents the seventh principle: calm surroundings.

PRINCIPLE 7

Calm Surroundings

Part 1: Healthy Teachers

Calm Surroundings: What Should I Do?

Our bodies are directly affected by what is happening around us. A calming environment can lessen stress, decrease anxiety, and help increase positive feelings (Bratman, Hamilton, Hahn, Daily, & Gross, 2015). Surrounding yourself with calm when you feel stressed or have negative thoughts can help relieve the pressure and help you feel more peaceful and positive. Color, music, lighting, and aroma all contribute to a calming environment. A calming environment increases our levels of serotonin (Premier Health, 2018). Serotonin, a chemical that relays signals from one part of the brain to another, contributes to feelings of well-being and happiness through endorphin production. Many successful antidepressants work by increasing concentrations of serotonin in the brain.

The colors, sights, and sounds of nature are very satisfying to the human brain. Nature appears to restore mental functioning in the same way that food and water restore our physical bodies. Therefore, the environment can be a natural antidepressant. According to Gregory Bratman and his colleagues (2015) at Stanford University, neurological factors for *brooding*, or what they call *morbid rumination*, can be positively affected by spending time in nature. People who spent time walking near a highway had no changes in mood or brain function, but those who walked near a park had meaningful improvements in their mood.

Many mental and physical health offices incorporate environmental elements like earth-tone walls, trickling waterfalls, live plants, aquariums, and gentle music into their design. In stressful situations, these features help people remain calmer with a more positive attitude. Think about the environment of some of the doctor's offices you frequent. My dentist's office, for example, has a waterfall in the waiting room and plays smooth jazz. The staff are well aware of the need for these calming influences on nervous patients.

As I progressed in my brain studies, I decided to include what I was learning about calming external factors in two of my books, *Preparing Children for Success in School and Life* (Tate, 2011) and *Shouting Won't Grow Dendrites* (Tate, 2014). From those works, I settled on four elements of a calming environment: (1) color, (2), music, (3) lighting, and (4) aroma, which this chapter explores.

As you read about each one, visualize which are already part of your surroundings and which you might take action to incorporate.

What the Brain Research Says: Why Should I Do It?

The research indicates several strategies you can use to create calm surroundings: incorporating calming color, music, lighting, aroma, and nature.

Color

Research (Reynolds, 2016) shows that different colors have different effects on us psychologically, emotionally, and physically. The colors of nature are calming: the blue sky, green grass, brown earth, and the soft colors of a rainbow. The most calming colors for the brain tend to be blues, greens, earth tones, and pastels.

In a *New York Times Magazine* blog post, Gretchen Reynolds (2016) writes about a Stanford University study demonstrating that just by looking at green images, people tended to lower their heart rates and recovered much more quickly from stress.

 Research indicates that the colors of green, blue, and the earth tone color of brown can facilitate memory, while reds, oranges, and yellows can be used for emphasis (Cooper & Garner, 2012).

New neuroscience research suggests that just looking at green roof gardens—urban roofs covered with greenery like flowers, plants, and grasses—through a window for just forty seconds is beneficial (Augustin, 2018). The findings show that such a brief break restores attention enough to improve focus and reduce errors. According to research, nature can provide cognitive benefits in much shorter time frames, and in smaller amounts than previously demonstrated.

Studies in hospitals have also shown that patients who look out at trees recover faster, are less depressed, and experience less pain than those who look at a wall, curtain, or door (Consult QD, 2017). In a separate study, children who sat indoors but had a natural view of the outdoors were calmer, more focused, and performed better on cognitive tests. The next time you dine at an expensive restaurant, pay particular attention to the color of the walls. They are more likely to be either earth tone colors or dark green, blue, or pastels so that patrons will want to stay and relax and are inclined to be happier and indulge in more food and drink.

Music

Music has such a profound effect on the brain that this book devoted the entirety of chapter 6 (page 60) to it. This chapter, however, addresses music's contribution to a calming environment.

Music can change the state, or mood, in our brains. It can make us joyous, sad, calm, or agitated. The sheer volume of positive research on the beneficial effects of music attests to its therapeutic effects. For example, music has been known to relieve stress (Trappe, 2010), and improve the performance of those with even severe disabilities such as mental retardation, Alzheimer's disease, and hearing and visual impairments (Sousa, 2017). Music (singing, dancing, and creative movement) has been shown to improve the social skills of people on the autism spectrum (Eren, 2015). Premature babies who are exposed to lullabies in the hospital leave the hospital earlier and have fewer stress-related problems than their counterparts who are not exposed to music (Gooding, 2010).

While studies on the so-called "Mozart effect" (the theory that simply listening to Mozart's music can increase scores on a portion of an IQ test) are inconclusive, the majority of researchers is in agreement that passive listening to music seems to stimulate spatial thinking and enhance recall, attention, concentration, and dexterity (Sousa, 2017).

Research has shown that music may assist in building and strengthening connections between brain cells in the cortex. Doctors are finding that stroke patients who have lost their ability to speak still sing. Therefore, by having patients sing what they want to say, therapists are improving fluency and retraining the speech centers of the brain (Norton, Zipse, Marchina, & Schlaug, 2009).

Even listening to background music can improve visual imagery, concentration, dexterity, and the brain's ability to recall information (Sousa, 2017).

My husband's favorite type of calming music is smooth jazz. In my home, I frequently hear him asking Alexa to play some Boney James, the Jazz Masters, or the Crusaders. I appreciate many different genres of music, depending on which state I want to create in my brain. For calming, I often choose piano music by my favorite classical pianist Emile Pandolfi. If you attend one of my workshops, you'll hear Pandolfi playing as you enter, as I mention in chapter 6.

Making music has even more cerebral advantages than simply listening to it. Chapter 6 explores these advantages.

Lighting

We are not only positively influenced by the colors of nature, but we are also impacted by the lighting in nature. There are certain places, such as Alaska and Antarctica, that have six months of light and six months of darkness annually. During the time of darkness, alcoholism, depression, and suicide rates increase, all impacted by the absence of light (Torres, 2020).

Sunlight and other types of natural light are the best sources of light for the brain and body. There are many benefits of natural light, including the following (Garone, 2020).

- It boosts vitamin D.
- It can ward off seasonal depression.
- It improves sleep.
- It reduces the detrimental effects of fluorescent lighting.

Other types of healthful and calming light include the light from a fireplace or candle. Visualize that expensive restaurant once again and consider the light source. Usually, the lights are so low that you can just barely read the menu. Candlelight might be a source of natural lighting on your table. Lamp light, candlelight, or the light from a fireplace all have the propensity to relax the brain and put it in a more creative state of mind.

 Strong natural lighting can have a dramatic and lasting positive effect on the learning environment (Jensen, 2008).

The worst possible light source for the brain is fluorescent lighting. The consistent buzz and constant glare of fluorescent lights can increase the incidence of migraines, cause epileptic seizures in those who experience them, and make hyperactive children more hyperactive (Bullock, 2018). If we know this, then why do we continue to build new schools with fluorescent lights? Halogen and incandescent light bulbs are often recommended in lieu of fluorescent lights, but they both have undesirable effects as well (Leonette, 2018).

Aroma

Aromatherapy is a big business. It's not surprising given the impact scent has on the brain. Natural aroma has been used for spiritual, mental, and physical healing for centuries. Many ancient civilizations, including India, China, and Egypt, used essential oils and fragrance compounds to treat psychological and physical disorders such as pain, headaches, insomnia, eczema, depression, and digestive disorders (Sowndhararajan & Kim, 2016). In fact, of all the senses, our sense of smell is the one most closely tied to memory. It is directly connected to the frontal lobe of the brain that controls the limbic system and willpower, where emotions and memories are housed (Van Toller, 1988). That is why real estate agents recommend baking bread or cookies during an open house so that prospective buyers are influenced by the enticing smell.

Lavender, vanilla, sandalwood, eucalyptus, and chamomile tend to be calming fragrances for most brains. Citrus, such as lemon or orange, peppermint, and cinnamon tend to be more energizing aromas. Those who work in air traffic control towers have been known to spritz peppermint to keep the controllers more alert (Scott, 2020a).

 Scientists have known about the Proust effect, which states that smells can bring back long-term memories, for more than one hundred years (Medina, 2014).

It is best to proceed with caution when using aroma in surroundings in which other people are present. Colleagues or students might have allergies or be otherwise aggravated by fragrances. Essential oils tend to be less detrimental to those who suffer from such allergies since they are concentrated extractions that come directly from plants (Brennan, 2020).

 The sense of smell enjoys unfiltered, undisturbed access to the brain; therefore, the brain processes this sense unlike any of the other physical senses (Jensen, 2007).

Nature

Research shows that nature is more calming because of a psychological concept called *attention restoration theory* proposed by Rachel and Stephen Kaplan (1989, 1995; Berman, Jonides, & Kaplan, 2008). This theory posits that when we are in an urban environment, we are forced to direct our attention to obstacles like traffic, curbs, stoplights, doors, and steps. These features can be draining since they force us to continuously make decisions to successfully navigate them. Otherwise, we could get hit by a car or break an ankle, as I did when stepping off a curb and not realizing that the street was much lower.

Forests, streams, rivers, lakes, and oceans demand very little attention from us. They enable us to think as much or as little as we want without forcing us to make any other decisions. Therefore, natural colors, sights, smells, and sounds replenish our exhausted mental resources, enable us to become happier and healthier, and improve our total well-being.

Action Steps: How Should I Do It?

Paint the Walls

Now that you realize the impact of color on the brain, be cognizant of the colors you use within your home. Painting the walls blue, green, or other pastels as well as earth tones will provide a more relaxed atmosphere.

Red, orange, and deep yellow tend to be high-energy colors. If you don't believe that to be true, just look at the colors of most fast-food restaurant signs—McDonald's, Burger King, KFC, or Sonic. It's common for these places to be decorated in high-energy colors; they want you to come in, quickly get your hamburger or chicken, and leave. This makes sense for the fast food industry, but painting an infant's room red may present some challenges. For those spaces in your home where you want stimulation, use more vibrant, high-energy colors.

Incorporate Calming Music

Music that contains beats within the range of 50 to 70 per minute tends to be more calming for the brain since the beats simulate those of a heart. It is not necessary to count beats to determine which music to use. Classical, new age, smooth jazz, Native American, slow Celtic music, and nature sounds usually fit the bill.

Music with beats in the range of 110–160 per minute tends to get the body moving. These types of music would include rhythm and blues, rock and roll, positive rap, or fast-paced country.

Seek Calmer Light Sources

Since research shows that fluorescent lights can be detrimental, it is beneficial to limit their use. If you must use them and have more than one light switch, turning off half or more of the lights may create a calmer atmosphere. Eliminating ceiling lights and utilizing lamps make for a warmer and cozier room.

The light from a fireplace can be hypnotic. Reflect for a moment on the following scenario: You've been traveling all day, and you finally make it to your hotel. There is snow piling up outside, and you feel like your limbs are frozen. As you enter your hotel, frazzled from the busy day and bad weather, you are drawn in by the light of the fire in the hotel lobby. How does it make you feel? Have you had a similar experience where light had a calming influence?

Introduce Aromatherapy

Explore aromatherapy options for both your home and other places where you spend large amounts of time. There are so many options—pots that spritz fragrance into the air, candles, or plug-in diffusers that emit scent. Take a few moments to think about your favorite fragrances. Which fragrances are the most calming to you? My favorite fragrances appear only twice a year: at Thanksgiving, I love the fragrance of autumn leaves, and at Christmas, my choice is balsam and cedar, so I stock up on enough to last throughout the year.

Build an Aquarium

Watching the colorful fish in an aquarium is another way to bring calm to the brain and body. Aquariums have several calming sensory attributes. They have filters that produce the sound of a babbling brook, they are filled with plants and scenery to mimic nature, and the motion of the fish swimming can have a calming effect. My husband's hobby is his 250-gallon saltwater aquarium in our den. I have spent many days mesmerized by the sounds and movement from the tank.

Spend Time in a Sunroom or Porch

If you are lucky enough to have a porch, sunroom, or Florida room as part of the house or apartment in which you live, take advantage of it whenever possible. These spaces allow the outside in and are very brain-compatible with their colors, lighting, sounds, and connection to nature. Even if the weather outside is poor, you can enjoy the calming sights and sounds of nature from a protected space.

Part 2: Happy Classrooms

You can apply these elements discussed in part 1 of this chapter to change the state of your environment at school to make it calmer and more peaceful.

Pay attention to the color of the walls in your classroom. If you have any say-so in the matter, consider repainting with calming colors on at least three of four walls. The fourth wall could be a high-energy color.

Whether teaching virtually or in person, have calming music playing prior to the beginning of a lesson or during creative writing. Then use energizing music to motivate and stimulate. Try not to play music, however, when delivering direct instruction. Students shouldn't have to decide whether to pay attention to the music or to what you are saying.

If you are fortunate enough to have windows, let the sunshine in. If fluorescent lights are your only option and you have two light switches, turn off half the lights and bring in lamps, if permitted.

Aromatherapy can be a bit trickier to incorporate into your classroom since not everyone likes or can tolerate the same scents. If you do wish to use scents, essential oils may work better than other types of aromatherapy. Fragrances such as lavender, vanilla, sandalwood, chamomile, and eucalyptus have a calming effect, whereas citrus scents are energizing.

Take your students outdoors for instruction from time to time if possible. This change of scenery into nature can be calming, and it also adds some novelty to your lessons.

Part 3: Action Plan

Recall at the beginning of the chapter the discussion of John Denver's "Annie's Song." We can actually fill up our senses with the environment in which we find ourselves. When that environment is calming and beneficial to both brain and body, our lives are enriched. Use the following Action Plan to determine how to create calm and uplifting surroundings.

Action Plan for Creating Calm Surroundings

What are my plans for creating a calming atmosphere?		
Recommendations	**Presently Doing**	**Strive to Do**
Allot time to spend in nature for its calming effect.		
Consider the wall colors of the rooms in my home and classroom.		
Incorporate calming music while relaxing.		
Limit fluorescent lighting use in my home and classroom.		
Seek sources of natural light.		
Select essential oils that can provide aromatherapy.		
Build an aquarium or use an aquarium screen saver at school.		
Spend time in a sunroom or porch.		
Convene class outdoors from time to time to provide students with a calming, novel environment in which to learn.		
Goals and Notes:		

8

Relationships

Emotional or other connections between people (Relationship, n.d.)

One of my favorite rhythm and blues musical groups is Sister Sledge, known for their hit disco anthem "We Are Family" (Edward & Rogers, 1974). The song was so popular the Pittsburgh Pirates baseball team chose it as their motto and theme song when they clinched the 1979 World Series, a nod to the song's theme of togetherness, optimism, and faith in one another (Flaherty, n.d.). Close personal relationships, such as the ones Sister Sledge sings about, improve the quality and quantity of our lives. This chapter explores this eighth principle.

Close Personal Relationships

Part 1: Healthy Teachers

Close Personal Relationships: What Should I Do?

In my classroom management book, *Shouting Won't Grow Dendrites* (Tate, 2014), the first chapter is "Develop a Relationship With Each Student." Without positive relationships with students, classroom management is difficult at best. When teaching classroom management, I share the following motto: *Rules without relationships equal rebellion.* Students do not see the need to honor your requests if they do not feel that you truly care about them as individuals.

The same is true in a family. Spouses must continually nurture their relationships with one another. Parents must seek to understand their children through all the phases of their lives and build a relationship of trust and mutual respect. Many of today's families are blended; in these situations, family members are all establishing new relationships with one another.

Humans require positive interaction with other humans if they are to stay healthy. Family gatherings, get togethers with friends, or being part of a special workplace, religious, or community activity allow opportunities for us to exchange ideas and provide social support for one another. According to a Harvard article on the health benefits of strong relationships, these same social activities can have as positive an influence on long-term health as good nutrition, adequate sleep, and refraining from smoking (Harvard Women's Health Watch, 2019). Those who are not fortunate enough to experience these essential social ties tend to experience depression, a cognitive decline in later life, and increased mortality.

Many studies have shown that persons who have the social support of family, friends, and the larger community are healthier, happier, and live longer (Harvard Women's Health Watch, 2019).

My mother lived with us for over twenty years. During the last few years of her life, she resided in an assisted living facility since we were no longer able to care for her unique needs. My sister and I searched for the best facility to maintain Mom's high quality of life. The facility provided many opportunities for Mom to bond with others. Three times per day, meals were served in a dining room where she was assigned to a table with five other women who eventually became her close friends. Each day's schedule was replete with activities that necessitated that Mom be out of her room and in the company of others. I watched as she participated in exercise classes, had her nails painted, sang songs, and completed art projects. I believe that Mom lived to be ninety-two with a high quality of life because of those close personal relationships.

This principle of longevity—close personal relationships—may be one of the easiest to access of the twelve in this book. It requires no special equipment or resources and it can be inexpensive, yet its impact is significant.

What the Brain Research Says: Why Should I Do It?

The research is clear: positive social relationships help us live longer, while loneliness shortens our lives (Amen, 2018; Harvard Women's Health Watch, 2019). Despite this, one in five Americans is lonely, which makes the lack of close personal relationships a public health concern (Amen, 2018). Our need to belong and be loved is just as potent and essential as our need for food and water. In his landmark book *Choice Theory*, William Glasser (1999) shares that the need for belonging and love is one of the five needs that humans must satisfy (along with survival, power, freedom, and fun).

Marital problems and affairs, domestic violence, breakups, or the threatened loss of a relationship often trigger panic attacks, depression, obsessive behaviors, and emotional crises (Amen, 2018).

One study of data from more than 300,000 people found that the lack of strong relationships increased by 50 percent the possibility of dying prematurely, regardless of the cause. This effect on the risk of mortality is comparable to the effects of obesity, being physically inactive, or smoking as many as fifteen cigarettes daily. Research has also found reduced immunity in couples during marital arguments that are especially hostile (Amen, 2018).

Rejection can also trigger aggression. Broken social bonds can often result in suicide, murder, and murder-suicides. According to Amen (2018), researchers who studied fifteen school shooters in 2003 found that with the exception of two, all suffered from social rejection.

"A Swedish study of people seventy-five and over concluded that the risk of dementia was lowest in those with a variety of positive contacts with relatives and friends" (Harvard Women's Health Watch, 2019).

The health benefits of connecting with other people contribute to relieving the harmful effects of stress, which can adversely affect coronary arteries, insulin regulation, and digestive function. Additional research suggests that caring for others triggers the release of hormones that reduce stress (Ritvo, 2014). Interestingly, those who remain single are at a 42 percent higher risk of developing dementia than their married counterparts. Those who are widowed have a 20 percent higher risk (Amen, 2018).

Action Steps: How Should I Do It?

Create Effective Relationships

The following eleven relational principles (Amen, 2003) will help you maintain important social connections in your life.

1. Assume responsibility for the relationship and examine what you can personally do to improve it.

2. Do not take the relationship for granted and work daily to let the special people in your lives know that you love them.

3. Protect the relationship by building the other person up and not belittling or degrading him or her.

4. Assume the best, and not the worst, about the other person's intentions or motivation.

5. Look for new and different ways to add spice to the relationship.

6. Spend time noticing the positive, not the negative, aspects of the relationship.

7. Spend time listening and really understanding what others in the relationship are saying to you.

8. Maintain and protect a trusting relationship.

9. In a kind, but firm manner, stick up for what you know to be right during difficult times.

10. Make the relationship a priority and invest quality time in it.

11. Since touch is critical to life itself, make certain that physical touch is a part of the relationship.

Be sure to take care of the relationship you have with your spouse or partner. As you age, it is important to have the love and support of one of the most important people in your life. Relationship issues can occur if time is not spent adding spice and creating novelty (Mayo Clinic, 2020b).

Hold Hands to Relieve Pain

Researchers at the University of Haifa in Israel recently found that holding the hand of someone with whom you have a relationship who is in pain can help ease their discomfort (Malamut, 2018). Experiments have shown that when your spouse is in pain and you hold his or her hand, breathing rates, heart rates, and brain-wave patterns sync up. With increased empathy for the partner in pain, the more in tune the brain waves become and the greater the ability to relieve that pain (Malamut, 2018).

Keep in Touch With Relatives and Friends

During the COVID-19 pandemic, immediate families spent more time together than ever before. When in-person interaction is not possible, however, other forms of contact are essential. These could include phone calls, text messages, emails, Zoom chats, and FaceTime calls. During communication, focus on content that is energizing, positive, and uplifting. Remember that only 7 percent of your message will come from the words you use (Smith, 2020). The other 93 percent will come from your tone of voice, gestures, and body language—in other words, your nonverbals. I believe that this is the reason that people often misinterpret text messages and emails. While they are receiving 7 percent of the content of your message, they do not have access to the other 93 percent, which goes far in truly communicating your message.

Relate to Others

Amen (2018) uses the acronym RELATING to help his clients remember the habits of an essential relationship.

- R is for *Responsibility* (responding in a positive, helpful way).
- E is for *Empathy* (treating others as you would like to be treated).
- L is for *Listening* (practicing good communication skills).
- A is for appropriate *Assertiveness* (saying what you believe in a kind, calm, clear way).
- T is for actual, physical *Time* (spending meaningful time with others).
- I is for *Inquiry* (deciding if negative thoughts are true and correcting them if they are not).

- N is for *Noticing* (observing what you like in others more than what you don't like).

- G is for *Grace* (forgiving others whenever you can).

Practice Active Listening

Active listening is a technique used by therapists to increase effective communication, especially when the encounters are emotionally charged. The technique involves repeating back what the other person is saying to ensure that what you heard is what the speaker intended. Since 93 percent of a person's message is conveyed nonverbally (such as through gestures and tone of voice), communication can break down because of differences between what was understood and what was intended (Amen, 2018). By simply saying, "What I hear you saying is . . ." or "Let me be sure I understand what you mean . . ." you are clarifying the speaker's intent and also letting him or her know you understand and are listening.

Active listening enables you to receive more accurate messages, clears up misunderstandings, increases your ability to hear what the other person is saying rather than thinking about what to say next, and also cools down conflicts (Amen, 2018).

Make Deposits in the Emotional Bank Accounts of Others

There is a concept called the Emotional Bank Account that is a fundamental principle in *The 7 Habits of Highly Effective People* (Covey, 2020). It is a metaphor for the relationships we establish with others. As is the case with a financial bank account, we need far more deposits than withdrawals. If we make more, or larger, withdrawals than deposits, the account is soon overdrawn.

What, then, could be considered a deposit? A smile, a compliment, a kind act, keeping a promise, or making an apology are all examples of deposits. Withdrawals might include rudeness, arrogance, breaking a promise, or being disloyal. Accounts are closed when there is a divorce or other type of separation of individuals where there have been so many withdrawals that there is nothing left in the account.

If people want strong relationships with others, there must be far more deposits than withdrawals. When you know people well, you know what they would consider a deposit and a withdrawal. For example, I have one daughter who loves sports, so I make a point to watch football games with her and her family. My other daughter couldn't care less about sports but loves Broadway shows, so we enjoyed the show *Hamilton* together.

In addition to making frequent deposits with family and friends, make deposits with people you don't know personally. For example, if I have excellent service at a restaurant, I not only compliment the server, but I may also ask to pass the compliment on to the server's boss. Making a deposit is not only great for the recipient. It is also extremely beneficial to the giver. It feels good to let others know you care.

Delegate or Discard Tasks That Eat Into Time

There are only twenty-four hours in a day. It is up to us to ensure that every minute counts toward a quality life. Abandon those tasks that are not as crucial in favor of those that are. If family is important to you, then rather than spending hours watching television shows, gather the family together for quality conversation or game playing. Rather than having every family member fix a plate and retreat to a separate corner of the house at dinnertime, gather the people together around the table for a meal. It is not the meal that is nearly as important as the conversation that occurs during the meal.

Tasks inherent in everyday life often keep us from spending quality time building personal relationships. Share those duties and responsibilities with other members of the family. If your children are old enough, inform them that it is everyone's job to share in keeping the house clean or preparing and cleaning up after a meal. Even if spending quality time means foregoing a chore from time to time, it will be well worth it.

Limit the Technology

Even prior to the COVID-19 pandemic, I worried about the exorbitant amount of time many people were spending on social media—Facebooking, tweeting, Instagramming, snapping, and texting. While this is certainly a beneficial way to communicate in many ways, it can never replace the face-to-face interactions that must still be a part of our lives. How much social media is considered a healthy amount? Experts suggest thirty minutes per day as the maximum amount of time that should be spent on social media. What matters, however, is how the time is being spent (Wells, 2019).

The more often children are talked to, the more they will understand. As children listen, they begin to speak. As they speak, they begin to read (Sprenger, 2008).

I have heard from speech and language pathologists during my workshops that they have never before seen children coming to school so language deprived since many parents and caregivers are replacing face-to-face interactions with tablets and technology. There is no technology to date that can replace human interaction.

Set limits for the amount of time you and your children spend with technology. Use that extra time for relationship building.

Seek Out Healthy People

According to Amen (2015), "The best thing you can do for your brain is to spend time with healthy people" (p. 29). He relates that the fastest way to get healthy is to locate the healthiest person you can find and then spend as much time around that person as possible. As it turns out, healthy people are contagious. Separate yourself from people who are negative and unhealthy. They are contagious as well!

Part 2: Happy Classrooms

Develop a relationship with every student you teach. Greet students before class (both online and during face-to-face classes). Personally compliment students on their improved behavior or academic performance or inquire about something occurring in their personal lives. Show that you are interested in them and their welfare.

At the beginning of the school year, share personal information about yourself that you feel is appropriate for students to know. I like to play the game Three Truths and a Lie where I reveal four things about myself, three of which are true and one which is false. Students have to guess the false statement. In this way, students are more likely to perceive you as a real person, with likes, dislikes, feelings, and an actual life. I even use this game with my adult audiences.

Take a personal interest in your students and find out their likes and dislikes. Develop a relationship first with those students who provide the greatest behavioral challenge for you and then work your way through the remainder of the class. Help students realize that you care about their success in your class and that you will be there to support them in their academic efforts. Let them know that you are expecting great things from them and that you will be available to assist them in meeting the challenge.

Practice the principle of the Emotional Bank Account (Covey, 2020) with students by putting more deposits than withdrawals in the bank accounts of each student. This will help to develop a strong relationship. In addition, be sure that the first time you contact parents or guardians is for a positive reason. This will be your initial deposit. This way if you have to contact them for a negative reason later in the school year, at the very least, you will have some money in the bank.

Utilize technology when appropriate but also spend time in conversation with your students.

Part 3: Action Plan

Recall at the beginning of the chapter the discussion of Sister Sledge's song "We Are Family." If we are to remain a close family or strengthen personal friendships, then time and effort are necessary—even if it means foregoing those things in life that are not nearly as important, such as watching television or spending time on social media. It will be well worth the effort! Use the following Action Plan to determine how you will create more meaningful close personal relationships.

Action Plan for Creating Close Personal Relationships

What are my plans for creating more meaningful relationships with family, friends, and students?		
Recommendations	**Presently Doing**	**Strive to Do**
Use Amen's (2018) eleven relational principles to maintain relationships. 1. Assume responsibility for the relationship and examine what you can personally do to improve it. 2. Do not take the relationship for granted and work daily to let the special people in your lives know that you love them. 3. Protect the relationship by building the other person up and not belittling or degrading him or her. 4. Assume the best, and not the worst, about the other person's intentions or motivation. 5. Look for new and different ways to add spice to the relationship. 6. Spend time noticing the positive, not the negative, aspects of the relationship. 7. Spend time listening and really understanding what others in the relationship are saying to you. 8. Maintain and protect a trusting relationship. 9. In a kind, but firm manner, stick up for what you know to be right during difficult times. 10. Make the relationship a priority and invest quality time in it. 11. Since touch is critical to life itself, make certain that physical touch is a part of the relationship.		
Make a special effort to take care of important relationships.		
Hold hands of loved ones to relieve pain.		
Stay in touch with relatives and friends.		

page 1 of 2

Recommendations	Presently Doing	Strive to Do
Use the acronym RELATING to develop an essential relationship.		
Practice active listening.		
Make deposits in the emotional bank accounts of others.		
Delegate or discard tasks that erode time.		
Limit time spent with technology rather than people.		
Seek out positive and healthy people.		
Develop a relationship with every student I teach.		
Take a personal interest in my students.		
Goals and Notes:		

Source for the eleven relational principles: Amen, D. G. (2018). Feel better fast and make it last. Carol Stream, IL: Tyndale House Publishers.

9

Nutrition

*The act or process of nourishing or being
nourished (Nutrition, n.d.)*

In the animated Disney movie *Beauty and the Beast* (Trousdale & Wise, 1991), the beauty, Belle, is invited to dine at the Beast's castle to the tune of "Be Our Guest," written by Alan Menken and Howard Ashman (1991) and sung by Angela Lansbury and Jerry Orbach. In the scene, plates, cups, dishes, and an assortment of delicious looking foods dance and sing throughout the dining room in preparation for a feast of French cuisine for Belle and the Beast. We can see that the meal will be extravagant, but will the food offer good nutritional value for both Belle's brain and body? This chapter explores the ninth longevity principle: nutrition.

PRINCIPLE 9
Nutrition

Part 1: Healthy Teachers

Nutrition: What Should I Do?

Before the COVID-19 pandemic, for the first time in four years, life expectancy in the United States had risen, if only by one month. The average life expectancy for a female in the United States was 81.1 years compared to 76.2 years for males (Stobbe, 2020). Because of COVID-19, we have lost between one and three years of life expectancy depending on the ethnic group to which we belong.

Long before COVID-19, Don Colbert (2009), a medical doctor and author of *Eat This and Live!,* remarked that the current generation may be the first in two hundred years whose life expectancy will not exceed that of their parents. A more recent Duke University study also shows that life expectancy is decreasing for GenXers and older Millennials (Schlemmer, 2018). What caused Colbert to make this drastic prediction? Several things are responsible.

 According to the *New England Journal of Medicine,* the rise in childhood obesity could reduce the lifespan of the current generation by five years (Colbert, 2009).

First, the amount of food consumed, especially of the unhealthy variety, is increasing. According to Colbert (2009), an average American will consume five pounds of food daily, meaning that over a lifetime, seventy tons of food will pass through the digestive system and be assimilated by the body. This amount of food is the equivalent of about four mid-sized cars. He relates that over the years, many of his patients have managed to rationalize their unhealthy food choices. Some of these reasons include:

- "I grew up eating unhealthy foods."
- "It's simply more convenient."
- "The more I eat, the more I crave food."
- "Hormones at certain times of my life can make bad foods look good."
- "I eat to feel better."

Living foods, such as fruits, vegetables, whole grains, seeds, and nuts will always be healthier for the body than processed foods (Colbert, 2009).

A second reason for the shortened life expectancy of the current generation is the sedentary lifestyle many have adopted (Harvard Health Publishing, 2020b). In days past when people were not always eating their healthiest, they were working off the calories doing manual labor. Manual labor is not as abundant as it once was, and many of today's youth are sitting in front of their televisions, cell phones, computers, and tablets more often than not. (See chapter 5, page 50, to read more about lack of movement and its detrimental effects.)

"Drinking only one can of sweetened soda or fruit punch per day can result in up to five pounds of weight gain annually" (Amen, 2018, p. 209).

What the Brain Research Says: Why Should I Do It?

The research is clear that good nutrition is necessary for healthy brain development, and those foods that are best for your brain are living foods.

The Benefit of Living Foods

Living foods, that is foods housed in "divinely created wrappers called skins and peels" (Colbert, 2009, p. 4), look healthy and alive—because they are. Living foods are plucked, squeezed, and harvested, not chemically enhanced, bleached, or refined. Eating living foods causes the enzymes in the foods to interact with digestive enzymes and other natural ingredients, such as vitamins, antioxidants, minerals, and fiber. Therefore, these enzymes enter our systems in their natural state.

Dead foods, on the other hand, have had everything done to them to enable them to be as addictive as possible and last as long as possible (Colbert, 2009). They hit the body like an unrecognizable foreign invader. Chemicals like food additives, preservatives, and bleaching agents actually cause a strain on the liver. Man-made fats, which are toxic, start to form in cell membranes, are stored as fat in the body, and form plaque in the arteries. While the body does its best to get whatever nutrients are available in these foods, people end up overfed, undernourished, and overweight (Colbert, 2009).

The Brain-Gut Connection

Good nutrition is also necessary for healthy brain development. The brain is a very demanding organ. While consuming only 2 percent of the body's total weight, the brain consumes eight to ten times more glucose and oxygen than any other organ in the body. Without the capacity to store energy to be used later like the muscles or liver, if the body does not receive the needed nutrition, the brain is the first to suffer, thereby compromising both learning and memory (Markowitz & Jensen, 2007).

 The gut, or gastrointestinal tract, is one of the most important organs for the health of your brain (Amen, 2015).

Daniel Amen (2018), a clinical neuroscientist, psychiatrist, and brain imaging expert who heads the world-renowned Amen Clinics, points out that our gut is in constant communication with our brain. This is the reason that butterflies form when we get excited or gastrointestinal distress can be caused by grief, stress, or emotional pain. The gastrointestinal tract is loaded with approximately 100 trillion microorganisms, which is ten times the number of cells in the entire human body. Eighty-five percent of those microorganisms need to be "good guys" with 15 percent being "bad guys" (Amen, 2018). If a poor diet or excessive antibiotics help the good guys become deficient, one can feel stressed or depressed. These antibiotics are usually not prescribed by a doctor but are ingested from the meats and vegetables we consume. After all, 70 percent of the total antibiotic use in the United States is not for humans; it is for livestock. This makes it critical to eat meats that are hormone- and antibiotic-free if possible, and grass fed or free range. Disorders ranging from attention-deficit/hyperactivity disorder to adult mental fogginess and depression have been contributed to imbalances in intestinal bacteria (Pennisi, 2019).

According to Amen (2018), factors decreasing healthy gut bacteria include the following.

- Some medications
- Refined sugar
- Artificial sweeteners
- Water with bactericidal chemicals
- Food with pesticide residues
- Alcohol
- Emotional, environmental, and physiological stress
- Radiation
- High-intensity exercise (such as running a marathon) (Amen, 2015)

Brain-Healthy Eating

In his book, *Change Your Brain, Change Your Life,* Amen (2015) lists nine rules of brain-healthy eating and fifty-two of the best foods that adhere to those nine rules. It is recommended that these foods be organic when possible and hormone free, antibiotic free, free range, and grass fed when appropriate.

1. Consume "high-quality calories" and not too many of them. High-quality foods include unrefined, minimally processed foods such as vegetables and fruits, whole grains, and healthy fats and proteins.

2. Don't drink your calories; drink water.

3. Eat high-quality lean protein during the day.

4. Eat low-glycemic, high-fiber carbohydrates. Low-glycemic foods include most fruits and vegetables, beans, low-fat dairy foods, nuts, and grains.

5. Include healthy fats in your diet. Foods that contain fat and yet are healthy include avocados, olive oil, salmon, eggs, and nuts.

6. Eat from the rainbow (many different colors of fruits and vegetables).

7. Boost brain function by cooking with the brain-healthy herbs and spices (listed in this chapter).

8. Make sure food is as clean as possible.

9. Eliminate foods that might be causing trouble with mood, energy, memory, weight, blood pressure, blood sugar, or skin. These might include wheat and any other gluten-containing food or grain as well as dairy, soy, and corn.

In addition, incorporate the following "brain superfoods" into your diet (Amen, 2015). These are foods that enable the brain to operate at optimal levels.

- **Nuts and seeds:** Almonds, Brazil nuts, cashews, hemp, sesame seeds, and walnuts

- **Fruits:** Apples, avocados, blackberries, blueberries, cherries, grapefruit, kiwis, and pomegranates

- **Vegetables:** Asparagus, bell peppers, beets, broccoli, cabbage, garlic, kale, leeks, onions, spinach, and sweet potatoes

- **Poultry and fish:** Chicken or turkey, eggs, lamb, salmon, and sardines

- **Oils:** Coconut oil, grapeseed oil, and olive oil

- **Tea:** Green tea

Consult Amen's (2015) book *Change Your Brain, Change Your Life* for the complete list of the fifty-two brain superfoods.

The Value of Water

The brain is 80 percent water. According to Amen (2015), being dehydrated by only 2 percent is a problem since this small amount of dehydration negatively impacts the body's ability to perform tasks that require memory, attention, or physical performance. He recommends drinking eight ten-ounce glasses of water per day. Timing, however, is everything! Drinking the water thirty minutes before eating a meal enables one to eat less but still feel satiated. However, drinking water with a meal can dilute stomach acid, which slows down digestion. Liquids that dehydrate, such as alcohol, caffeine-laden coffee or tea, or other diuretics should be consumed in moderation.

Action Steps: How Should I Do It?

Eat Three Well-Balanced Meals Per Day

Eating three high-fiber, healthy, and well-balanced meals per day and a healthy snack in the midafternoon should help you conquer your cravings for other unhealthy foods. Consult the list of the brain superfoods on the opposite page for more information on which foods offer the best nutrition. Simply choosing the right foods and eating at the right times control hunger and stabilize blood sugar.

 More than 2,000 studies support the fact that a low-calorie, optimal-nutrition diet can extend life by 30 to 50 percent (Colbert, 2009).

Use Seasonings to Improve Taste

Incorporate seasonings with food to improve the quality of the taste. Amen (2018) considers the following food seasonings so valuable to both brain and body that he says they should be kept in the medicine cabinet, rather than the kitchen cabinet.

- Basil
- Black pepper
- Cayenne pepper
- Cinnamon
- Cloves
- Garlic
- Ginger
- Marjoram
- Mint
- Nutmeg
- Oregano
- Parsley
- Rosemary
- Saffron
- Sage
- Thyme
- Turmeric

Consider Healthier Alternatives

When tempted to eat unhealthy foods, think of healthier alternatives. Amen (2009) suggests eating a scoop of frozen yogurt rather than a bowl of ice cream or baked chips and fresh salsa versus potato chips and French onion dip. Some choices may feel difficult or like they are depriving you of taste or satisfaction. Keep in mind, however, that they will help to move you in the right direction toward a healthier lifestyle.

Control Portion Sizes

I have noticed that in many restaurants, portion sizes have increased and people often feel compelled to finish all the food placed on their plate. When dining out or cooking at home, place portions of the meal you plan to eat on a smaller plate and wrap up the rest as leftovers to eat at another time.

Implement the Daniel Plan

In their bestseller called *The Daniel Plan: 40 Days to a Healthier Life,* Rick Warren, a pastor, and fitness and medical experts Daniel Amen and Mark Hyman (2020) lead readers on a journey to holistic health. Their Daniel Plan includes an easy guideline to use daily for any healthy meal. It focuses on the core food groups of healthy carbohydrates, proteins, fats, healing spices, drinks, and superfoods and is proportioned as follows.

- Fifty percent non-starchy vegetables
- Twenty-five percent healthy animal or vegetable proteins
- Twenty-five percent healthy starch or whole grains
- Side of low-glycemic fruit
- Water or herbal teas

Keep Water With You

The benefits of drinking water are numerous. As I mentioned earlier in the book, my husband is the recipient of a kidney transplant. Each time we visit his doctor, the one consistent mandate that she states will be of greatest benefit to his kidney and body, in general, is the consumption of water. It is recommended that people consume between eight and ten eight-ounce glasses of water per day (Gunnars, 2020; Mayo Clinic Staff, 2020). Therefore, keep a bottle of water with you wherever you go and drink it whenever convenient. Drinking water defers hunger, filling you up without being unhealthy like high-sugar beverages. Remember that drinking water thirty minutes before a meal can help the body feel full, but drinking it during a meal may slow digestion.

Distract Yourself

When excessive stress causes you to be tempted to overeat, try other stress-relieving activities. For example, the stress-reducing neurotransmitter of serotonin can also be produced by taking a walk, which has the added benefit of burning calories. Getting in touch with a close relative or friend to talk through concerns can also go a long way in alleviating stress. Consult other chapters in this book for additional ways to increase levels of positive neurotransmitters in the brain, like serotonin, without resorting to overeating.

Part 2: Happy Classrooms

Following the guidelines in this chapter will help you have the stamina to be the best teacher possible throughout the entire day. The healthier you are and the better you feel, the happier your students will be.

Be aware of students who may be coming into your class devoid of nourishment. Maslow's hierarchy of needs shows that the physiological need for food must be satisfied before the higher-level needs of esteem or self-actualization can even be achieved (MasterClass Staff, 2020). If your school doesn't provide breakfast or healthy snacks for students, ask school administration if local merchants would be willing to donate snacks or fruit to keep on hand for students who come to class hungry.

Impress upon students the need to eat a healthy breakfast prior to coming to school and to make healthier personal choices for snacks and other meals.

Part 3: Action Plan

Recall at the beginning of the chapter the discussion of Belle's invitation to "Be Our Guest" in the animated film *Beauty and the Beast*. While we cannot be certain that Belle partook of nutritional French food choices, you can increase the likelihood that you will make better decisions regarding your personal health and equip your students with the knowledge they need to make better decisions. Use the following Action Plan (page 100) to determine your next steps. As the saying goes, *You are what you eat!*

Action Plan for Improving Nutrition

What are my plans for improving my eating habits and my students' nutrition knowledge?		
Recommendations	**Presently Doing**	**Strive to Do**
Eat three meals per day.		
Eat a healthy, well-balanced diet.		
Eliminate some sweets.		
Add high fiber to my diet.		
Enhance food flavor with seasonings.		
Control portion sizes.		
Consume more water.		
Use distractions from overeating like walking or talking to friends.		
Secure healthy snacks for students who need them.		
Teach students about healthy food choices.		

Goals and Notes:

Sleep

The natural state of rest during which your eyes are closed and you become unconscious (Sleep, n.d.)

"The Lion Sleeps Tonight" is a song originally written in Zulu and recorded in 1939 by Solomon Linda with his group The Evening Birds (Connor, 2018). An English version, sung by The Tokens and released in 1961, is the most famous version (Linda, Peretti, Creatori, Weiss, & Stanton, 1961). In the song, the speaker soothes the listener with the promise that the lions are sleeping. Lions, however, do most of their hunting at night. This is not true for human beings, who, according to the brain research, should be sleeping. Sleep is the tenth principle for longevity and is explored in this chapter.

Sleep

Part 1: Healthy Teachers

Sleep: What Should I Do?

I overhear people bragging all the time about their need for very little sleep. Although people might feel as though they do not need much sleep, the fact is that humans need a certain amount of sleep for optimal health. I pride myself on getting seven to nine hours of sleep per night, particularly when I have a major presentation to educators the following day. There have been times, however, when I have not gotten into my hotel room in time to retire at a decent hour and I had to present the following day on five or fewer hours of sleep. Although I hope my audience doesn't notice, I can tell when I do not get enough sleep. I don't have my normal level of clarity of thought. In addition, by the afternoon, I feel tired and worn down.

As we sleep, we move through a cycle of sleep stages, each cycle lasting approximately 90–110 minutes and repeating four to six times per night. When these stages are balanced, sleep is restful and restorative. According to the Mayo Clinic (2020a), the stages are as follows:

- **N1 Transitional Sleep:** This five-minute stage transitions us from being awake to falling asleep. Brain waves and muscular activity slow down, and the eyes move slowly beneath the eyelids.

- **N2 Light Sleep:** During this first stage of true sleep, eye movements cease, heart rates slow, and body temperature decreases.

- **N3 Deep Sleep:** Brain waves become extremely slow, breathing slows, and blood pressure drops, making it difficult to awaken.

- **REM Sleep:** The majority of dreaming occurs during this stage. The eyes move rapidly beneath the eyelids, and blood pressure and heart rate increase. Arm and leg muscles become paralyzed temporarily.

It was not until I began studying the brain that I was made aware of the overwhelming value of a good night's sleep. While sleep needs vary according to an individual's age, lifestyle, environment, and genetics, science relates that people who sleep seven hours a night tend to be healthier and live longer (Parker-Pope, 2020). According to the National Sleep Foundation (Parker-Pope, 2020), seven to nine hours are the amount of sleep that the average adult requires. In fact, some memories are only consolidated after the brain has experienced at least six hours of sleep. Between the ages of fifty and sixty, sleep-wake cycles begin changing. Sleep becomes less refreshing due to the fact that more time is spent in light sleep and less in deep sleep.

Sleeping less than five hours a night or over nine hours a night may be associated with an increased risk of stroke or heart disease (Mayo Clinic, 2020a).

Sleeping less than seven hours is associated with a range of health problems including obesity, heart disease, depression, and impaired immune function (Parker-Pope, 2020). Unfortunately, many adults are not getting enough sleep. According to a study of adults in the United States, about 30 percent are sleeping fewer than six hours on the majority of nights (Pullen, 2017). It is even worse for teenagers. Most teenagers require about nine hours of sleep nightly, but very few actually get this much sleep. Thanks to earlier school start times in the morning, athletic and social events, jobs, and television and video games in the afternoon and evening, sleep just simply isn't a priority for many teenagers. The average sleep time they get appears to be closer to five to six hours.

What the Brain Research Says: Why Should I Do It?

The research is clear that sleep is important for good physical health, brain functioning, and maintenance of a healthy weight.

Sleep and Physical Health

When people become sleep-deprived, parts of the aging process are accelerated. For example, in one study, thirty-year-olds getting only four hours of sleep for six consecutive days had body chemistry that resembled that of a sixty-year-old. Given time to recover, it still took about one week for their bodies to revert to their thirty-year-old systems (Medina, 2014).

"When daylight saving time begins, it is accompanied by a higher incidence of stroke or heart attack" (American Heart Association News, 2018).

When daylight saving time returns annually in the spring, internal rhythms such as blood pressure, body temperature, hormones, blood sugar metabolism, and memory consolidation are disrupted and need to be reset similar to the way a car's belts, gears, pistons, and other parts need to be regulated when disrupted (American Heart Association News, 2018).

Swedish researchers found an average 6.7 percent increase in the risk of having a heart attack in the three days following the time change. United States researchers determined that heart attack risk increased 24 percent the Monday following the switch. This percentage decreased during the remainder of the week (American Heart Association News, 2018). Conversely, the risk of a heart attack dropped 21 percent on the Tuesday after an hour of sleep is added in the fall.

While these statistics apply mainly to those persons who already have risk factors for heart attacks (such as diabetes and high blood pressure), according to Grandner (American Heart Association News, 2018), director of the Sleep and Health Research Program at the University of Arizona in Tucson, those factors in combination with the disruption to the body's circadian rhythm (or internal clock) of the time change may cause imbalance to the entire body.

A healthy immune system can help to fight off a cold. A sleep-deprived immune system cannot. It is also during sleep that the space between brain cells enlarges, enabling many of the toxins to be cleaned out of the brain. Research is suggesting that not getting enough sleep can allow toxins to accumulate and could be linked to diseases like Alzheimer's and Parkinson's disease (National Institutes of Health, 2013).

 "Sleep loss hurts attention, executive function, immediate memory, working memory, mood, quantitative skills, logical reasoning ability, and general math knowledge" (Medina, 2008, p. 163).

Sleep apnea, a potentially serious sleep disorder, can cause breathing to repeatedly stop and start during the night. Obstructive sleep apnea is the most common and occurs when throat muscles relax and block the airway during sleep. Snoring can be a noticeable sign of this type of sleep apnea. If the sleep apnea symptoms are mild, they can be treated by doing some of the following: losing weight, exercising, avoiding alcohol and specific medications, not sleeping on one's back, and keeping the nasal passages open with a saline nasal spray or rinse (Mayo Clinic, 2020a). Treatments for more severe forms can include surgery or inserting devices that keep the airway open or move the lower jaw forward.

Sleep and Cognitive Ability

According to Sousa (2012), brains are approximately 20 percent more active when people are asleep than when they are awake. Research studies suggest that the more one learns during the day, the more dreaming they need to engage in at night (Markowitz & Jensen, 2007). It is during the dream, or REM (rapid eye movement) stage that the brain processes information learned during the day. This period constitutes about 25 percent of a total night's sleep. While the brain stabilizes existing memories so that they are readily available the following day, it is also making decisions as to what deserves to end up in long-term memory. The portion of the cerebral cortex, critical for processing long-term memories, appears very active during the period of REM sleep (Markowitz & Jensen, 2007). Just as a reboot can clear computer memory of bad or obsolete data, it is during REM sleep that unnecessary information is eliminated and the proficiency of neural networks increases. In fact, the more complex and difficult the content is to be learned, the more crucial sleep is in the learning and remembering of it.

It is fascinating that if there are memories that are both emotional and unemotional, it is during sleep that the emotional memories are retained and the unemotional ones are allowed to fade away. This certainly makes the case for the need for teachers to get students emotionally involved in the learning and to model that emotion themselves. After all, how can teachers get students excited about mathematics if they are not, themselves, excited about mathematics?

 "The brain is going through the day's information, sorting, copying, and deciding what to encode into long-term memory" (Sousa, 2012, p. 115).

It is also during the last one-third of sleep time (usually between 3:00 and 6:00 a.m.) that the hippocampus rehearses the learning sent to it by the cerebral cortex. This critical time may determine which memories in the brain are strengthened and which are weakened.

Sleep and Weight Loss

During a break at one of my workshops, a teacher related this story, which I have never forgotten. Her extreme weight gain was causing significant health problems, and she and her physician working together had set a goal of a weight loss of one hundred pounds. Through a concentrated program of diet and exercise, she had lost seventy-five pounds but had reached a plateau where she seemed incapable of losing any additional pounds no matter how hard she tried. While in conversation with her doctor, he asked "How much sleep are you getting nightly?" She replied that she slept an average of five to six hours a night. She and her doctor developed a plan to increase the nightly sleep time to at least seven hours. "Marcia," she said, "I am still amazed at what a difference a few additional hours of sleep meant to my weight-loss efforts." At the time of our conversation, she had met her weight-loss goal (one hundred pounds).

Simply ensuring that you are getting adequate sleep can have a positive effect on weight loss. Studies find that people who are deprived of sleep report having an increase in appetite (Pullen, 2017; WebMD, 2020). Why is this the case? This phenomenon may be caused by the impact of sleep on two hunger hormones: ghrelin and leptin. Ghrelin is released in the stomach and signals the brain that you are hungry. Leptin is released from fat cells and signals the brain that the stomach is full. Inadequate sleep signals the body to make more ghrelin and less leptin, therefore increasing appetite.

Sleep deprivation can also dull the activity in the frontal lobe of the brain which controls decision making and stimulates the reward centers, making one more susceptible to foods high in calories, fat, and carbohydrates.

The body's resting metabolic rate (RMR), the number of calories the body burns when totally at rest, is affected by a person's age, weight, height, sex, and muscle mass. Sleep deprivation can lower RMR as well as muscle mass.

When the body is deprived of sleep, a stress hormone, called cortisol, signals the body to conserve energy as needed for fuel during waking hours. Therefore, the body is more likely to hang on to body fat. It is found that when dieters decreased their sleep time over a fourteen-day period, the amount of weight loss from fat dropped 55 percent, even when there was no decrease in the number of calories consumed (WebMD, 2020).

Poor sleep can cause cells to become resistant to insulin. This resistance can be a precursor to weight gain and type 2 diabetes (Grandner, Seixas, Shetty, & Shenoy, 2016).

When cells become resistant to insulin, sugar remains in the bloodstream, and the body produces additional insulin to compensate. This increased insulin makes a person hungrier and informs the brain to store additional calories as fat. Short sleep duration increases the likelihood of obesity by 55 percent in adults and 89 percent in children (Pullen, 2017).

Action Steps: How Should I Do It?

Keep a Sleep Diary

If you have difficulty determining how much sleep is ideal for you, Parker-Pope (2020) suggests you keep a sleep diary for one week according to the following guidelines.

- Record the time you go to bed and the time you wake up.
- Determine the total number of hours slept. Be certain to note any naps or whether you woke up during the night.
- Note your personal feelings in the morning (are you refreshed or fatigued?).

Parker-Pope (2020) also suggests this vacation experiment to determine how much sleep your body requires. Select two weeks when you do not have somewhere to be in the mornings. Turn off the alarm clock the night before. Then pick the same bedtime each night for the two weeks and record the time you wake up in the morning. As you allow yourself to wake naturally, you may see a pattern emerge of the number of hours of sleep your body requires every night. That will help you determine a bedtime that allows you enough sleep to wake up on your own without your alarm clock.

Establish a Routine

Not only do children need a bedtime routine, so do adults. Adults should establish a consistent sleep and wake schedule and stick to it even on weekends. Stopping all strenuous activity as bedtime approaches and doing the same thing to get ready for bed each night are important since this technique prepares the body to rest and conditions the brain to sleep. Before bedtime, attempt to select activities that promote rest such as reading, meditation, yoga, or journaling.

Adapt to Daylight Saving Time

Approximately a week prior to the move to daylight saving time (springing forward) it is recommended (Cleveland Clinic, 2020) that you go to bed fifteen to thirty minutes earlier than the usual bedtime to compensate for the lost hour.

Otherwise, the schedule of eating, exercising, socializing, and going to bed during the transition should remain consistent. Long daytime naps are tempting but should be avoided since it may become more difficult to get a complete night's sleep.

Make Yourself Comfortable

What you sleep on can make a distinct difference in how well you enjoy the journey. Therefore, it is important that mattresses and bedsprings be carefully selected. No matter which mattress brand or type you prefer, it is crucial that you enjoy a comfortable night's rest. Most doctors recommend a sleep temperature of between 60 and 67 degrees Fahrenheit as the most comfortable temperature for sleeping (Pacheco & Wright, 2021).

Exercise and Stay Active

Exercise and activity can help promote a good night's sleep. Try getting a minimum of thirty minutes of vigorous exercise daily, but be sure that this energetic time is at least five or six hours before bedtime. Vigorous activity too close to bedtime can keep the body awake.

Watch What You Eat and Drink Prior to Bedtime

Avoid consuming coffee and other caffeinated beverages like tea, soda, energy drinks, and chocolate four to six hours before bedtime. Also avoid alcohol late at night since it can prohibit quality sleep. Caffeine and alcohol can make it more difficult to sleep soundly. Drinking too many fluids prior to bedtime can cause sleep disruptions as well. We've all done this and spent too much time making visits to the bathroom during the night.

Do not attempt to retire on a full stomach. Complete a full meal at least two to three hours before bedtime. Eating too much late in the evening can cause indigestion and stomach problems that may keep you awake. Make sure that any bedtime snack is small.

Put Away the Technology

Many people, particularly teenagers, feel that life will end without being in close proximity to their technology. Therefore, cell phones, tablets, and computers occupy a prominent place in the bed alongside the person. The high-intensity light of electronics, however, stimulates the brain and hinders the production of melatonin, the hormone that triggers sleepiness. Blue light at night can throw off the body's biological clock and can contribute to diabetes, heart disease, cancer, and obesity (Harvard Health Publishing, 2020a). Televisions should also be turned off, and people should choose reading material that is not suspenseful before bedtime. Once you set your alarm for the morning, hide your device to avoid temptation. If you wake up during the night, don't look at the time, which can promote worry.

Eliminate Worry Before Bedtime

It is so difficult for some people to turn their brains off when they get into bed. The Mayo Clinic (2020a) suggests that people plan a time during the day when they address the things they are worried about so that those things are not weighing on the brain when it is time for bed. Breathing exercises, yoga, prayer, or a warm bath are some of the activities recommended to prepare the body for sleep.

Stop Trying to Sleep

Quit trying to sleep if you are having difficulty doing so. You will find that the harder you try, the more awake you'll become (Mayo Clinic, 2020a). Get out of the bed and listen to calming music or read until you become sleepy, and then get back in the bed.

Part 2: Happy Classrooms

Attempt to get seven to nine hours of sleep per night since that amount will give you the greatest opportunity to be the best teacher you can be daily. After all, it is the teacher in the classroom who makes the greatest difference in student academic achievement.

Encourage your students to do the same. Students, however, need more sleep than you do. Students ages six through twelve need approximately nine to twelve hours of sleep per twenty-four hours. Students ages thirteen through eighteen appear to need eight to ten hours per twenty-four hours (Centers for Disease Control and Prevention, 2020). Enlighten students on the brain rationale for why adequate sleep is so important. Tell them that they will process much of what you have taught them during the day while they are sleeping. They also need to know that it is during sleep that the body heals or restores itself. These are two of the very important reasons why sleep is so essential.

Mary Carskadon (2011) from Brown University is an expert on understanding adolescent sleep patterns. She finds that the majority of high school students is sleep deprived, which results in 20 percent falling asleep in class. When sleep deprived, it becomes more difficult for most students to learn and remember, and emotions even become harder to control (Carskadon, 2011). Complicating matters is the early start time of the majority of secondary schools. High schools should begin the school day later in the morning than elementary schools, although most school systems do not operate that way.

Have students complete the Sleep Checklist for Students (page 112) to assess their personal sleep habits. The form of this checklist is appropriate for middle and high school students. For primary students, read the items on the checklist aloud, with the students coloring in a smiling face for yes and a frowning face for no.

Since you now know that according to the research, it is during sleep that emotional memories are more likely to be retained and unemotional ones allowed to fade away, it behooves you to teach with passion and enthusiasm. Your love of your content will become contagious, and students will catch the wave. When my three children were in school, I would ask them each year which subject was their favorite. It always changed depending on which teacher they loved most. One year I noticed that my daughter, Jessica, was reading everything that Edgar Allan Poe wrote. When I asked her why, she remarked that Poe is Mrs. Williams's favorite author. You see, Mrs. Williams was Jessica's English teacher, and Jessica loved Mrs. Williams. If you want to improve academic achievement, teach with emotion so that content will be filed away into long-term memory as students sleep.

Part 3: Action Plan

Recall at the beginning of the chapter the discussion of the song "The Lion Sleeps Tonight." Members of the animal kingdom certainly value their sleep—after all, some bears can sleep for more than five months during hibernation—and so should the human population. Sleep is often something many people compromise on when they are busy, and stress can greatly impact our ability to sleep well. I did not realize how invaluable sleep is to good health and wellness until I began to delve deep into brain research. Use the following Sleep Checklist for Students and Action Plan (pages 112–114) to improve your personal sleep habits and those of your students as well.

Sleep Checklist for Students

Sleep Checklist for Students

Please respond to the following statements according to what you do daily.

At Home	Never	Sometimes	Almost Always
I do not eat or drink for several hours before bedtime.			
I go to bed at the same time each night.			
I limit light exposure during sleep.			
I do not use technology immediately before or during time designed for sleep.			
I have difficulty falling asleep.			
I get the recommended number of hours of sleep nightly. <ul><li>Ages six to twelve (nine to twelve hours recommended)</li><li>Ages thirteen to eighteen (eight to ten hours recommended)</li></ul>			
I wake up at the same time each morning (even on weekends).			
I wake up each morning on my own without being awakened.			
At School	**Never**	**Sometimes**	**Almost Always**
I feel sleepy during my morning classes.			
I feel sleepy during my afternoon classes.			
I feel alert during all of my classes.			
I go through the entire school day without feeling tired.			
I can recall much of what I learned the previous day.			

page 1 of 2

Goals I have set to improve my sleep habits:

1.

2.

3.

4.

Action Plan for Improving Sleep Habits

What are my plans for improving my sleeping habits and helping students improve theirs?		
Recommendations	**Presently Doing**	**Strive to Do**
Keep a sleep diary.		
Establish a sleep routine.		
Attempt to get seven to nine hours of sleep nightly.		
Be mindful of what I eat or drink before bedtime.		
Exercise five to six hours prior to bedtime.		
Put away the technology at bedtime.		
Address worry prior to bedtime.		
Make adaptations for daylight saving time.		
Have students complete the Sleep Checklist.		
Teach with emotion so students retain content during sleep.		
Teach students about the importance of sleep.		

Goals and Notes:

Spirituality

A life-giving force (Ventrella, 2001)

Written in 1772, the words of "Amazing Grace" were borne from the heart, mind, and experiences of John Newton, an English slave trader who lived a tumultuous life. After becoming violently ill on a sea voyage in 1754, Newton wrote the song once he renounced his role as a slave trader, converted to Christianity, and became an abolitionist (Hansen, 2002). "Amazing Grace" is one of the most recognizable songs as an immensely popular hymn, particularly in the United States, where it is used for both religious and secular purposes. The song reminds us of the power faith and spirituality have to help us overcome times of hardship. Spirituality is the eleventh principle for longevity and is explored in this chapter.

PRINCIPLE 11
Spirituality

Part 1: Healthy Teachers

Spirituality: What Should I Do?

In March of 2020, fifty-two-year-old Air Force Colonel Jason Denney used FaceTime with his family to say goodbye and called for his final visit from his parish priest. You see, Colonel Denney was a patient in the intensive care unit of Orlando's Dr. P. Phillips Hospital, and he was dying. COVID-19 had ravished his body, and his lungs were failing. He had even just learned that his sixteen-year-old son Sean had also tested positive for the disease. He blamed himself.

However, only hours after Denney's priest left, a hospital housekeeper by the name of Rosaura Quinteros came into Denney's room to clean it and sensed the gravity of the situation. It was clear to Quinteros that Denney was running out of time. She approached the bedside and encouraged him to stay positive even amid his distress. She reminded him of the high quality of his medical staff and the importance of an optimistic outlook.

Every day for the next few days, Quinteros repeated her words of encouragement each time she entered Denney's room. Days later when he was discharged from the hospital, though still sick and struggling to breathe, he attributed much of the credit for his discharge and ultimate healing to Quinteros's positive words and true interest in his well-being. He related that she had shown up just when he needed her.

Since his release from the hospital, Colonel Denney has recovered and returned to his job as an Orlando defense contractor. Quinteros, an immigrant from Guatemala, had begun work at the hospital only seven months earlier. The backgrounds of these two individuals could not have been more different, but the one thing that bound them together was their faith. Since their story was publicized (Burke, 2020; Dodd & Young, 2020), they have kept in touch by text and have plans to meet one another's families.

Quinteros formed a relationship with Denney and was, therefore, able to make a difference in his life and health. However, it was their spiritual connection that gave Denney the confidence to begin believing that he could overcome his health challenges.

Only 54 percent of American adults think of themselves as religious, while 75 percent say they are spiritual (Lipka & Gecewicz, 2017).

Many people use the terms *spirituality* and *religion* interchangeably. They actually are not the same. According to Ventrella (2001), some people are religious without necessarily being spiritual. On the other hand, other people are extremely spiritual without subscribing to any organized religion. Spirituality is universal, crossing all religions and ethnic boundaries. Spirituality comes from the Latin word, *spiritus*, meaning "breath." Despite the fact that there are countless religions in the world, science is showing us that spirituality has a powerfully positive effect on happiness, health, and relationships.

Spirituality involves the sense of belief that there is something higher and greater than oneself, and that the greater whole of which we are a part is divine in nature. Spirituality proposes that there is an ongoing existence after death and can provide answers to questions about life's meanings, the connections of people to one another, truths about the universe, and the mysteries of human existence (Ventrella, 2001).

What the Brain Research Says: Why Should I Do It?

In his book, *The Power of Positive Thinking in Business,* Ventrella (2001) shares "Belief in self, others, and a higher spiritual power to provide support and guidance when needed" (p. 85) as one of the ten traits of a positive thinker. He relates that 75 percent of Americans believe in a higher spiritual power, but most are not comfortable with mixing that spirituality with other aspects of their lives.

Elizabeth Scott (2020b), author and wellness coach, shares that the signs of spirituality can include, but are not limited to, the following:

- Asking probing questions about suffering or what happens after death
- Searching for deeper compassion and connections with others
- Experiencing empathy for others
- Feeling an interconnectedness with others
- Feeling awe or wonder about life
- Seeking purpose and meaning
- Seeking happiness beyond what one has or other external rewards
- Striving to make the world a better place

Research (Williams, 2019) shows that there are both mental and physical health benefits to spirituality. Mental benefits include the following.

- Greater happiness due to the meaning brought to your life
- Increased gratitude
- Increased compassion
- Improved connections with others
- Improved ability to cope with stress
- Ability to develop and grow more positive relationships

Physical benefits (Williams, 2019) are as follows.

- Stronger immunity
- Lower risk of depression
- Reduced stress
- Lower blood pressure
- Improved sleep

 Dedication to God or a higher power results in less reactivity to stress, greater feelings of well-being, and even a decreased fear of dying (Scott, 2020b).

The following are a few of the many findings of spirituality and its positive influence on mental and physical health (Scott, 2020b).

- Spirituality appears to help people, particularly older adults, cope with the negative effects of everyday stress.
- The greater gratitude to God that older women show enables them to receive greater stress-buffering health effects than men.
- Those people who are extrinsically motivated tend to use religion for making friends or increasing their standing in the community, while those who are intrinsically motivated tend to selflessly dedicate their lives to God or a higher power.

Prayer and spirituality appear to work for both the young and old and have been correlated to the following (Scott, 2020b).

- Improved health
- Increased psychological well-being

- Fewer instances of depression
- Less hypertension
- Less stress, even when times are difficult
- Increased positive feelings
- Superior ability to handle stress

 One study finds that spiritual experiences can enhance positive feelings and help people cope with everyday stress and negative feelings (Scott, 2020b).

Action Steps: How Should I Do It?

Seek Out Other Spiritual People

Whether in a church, synagogue, mosque, temple, parents' group, or yoga class, find a community of people who support you in your spirituality. Plan scheduled times to get together with them to talk, listen, share your stories, and deal with life's challenges.

Focus on Other People

Feeling and expressing empathy for other people, opening your heart, and extending help to others are very important aspects of spirituality. Look for specific ways you can let other people know that you rejoice with them when they are happy and that they are not alone when dealing with difficult life situations.

Try Mindfulness

Often used as a therapeutic technique, mindfulness is defined as a mental state achieved by concentrating on one's awareness of the present moment, while calmly acknowledging and accepting one's feelings, thoughts, and bodily sensations (Greater Good Science Center, n.d.). It encourages a person to be less judgmental of themselves and others and to pay attention to the current moment rather than spending time dwelling on the past or the future.

Rather than hurrying through your day, pause for just a few minutes several times during each day to reflect. In the article, "5 Simple Mindfulness Practices for Daily Life," Parneet Pal, Carley Hauck, Elisha Goldstein, Kyra Bobinet, and Cara Bradley (2018) explore five daily practices for bringing more mindfulness into your life.

- **Start each day with a mindful wake-up.** Sit in your bed or chair in a relaxed position but with a straight spine. Take three deep, long nourishing breaths in through your nose and out through your mouth. Ask your brain what its intention is for the day and set that intention as a goal. Throughout the day, stop, breathe, and check in with yourself and your intentions.

- **Enjoy mindful eating.** Before you begin a meal, close your eyes and begin to breathe slowly in and out of your stomach eight to ten times. This allows you to slow down and transition to your meal. After breathing, pay attention to the physical sensations in the belly to determine just how hungry you actually are and then eat accordingly. Slow down and breathe deeply as you eat so that you can savor and digest your food. Take the first three bites and mindfully experience the flavor, taste, and textures of the food. If you don't love it, don't continue eating it.

- **Rewire your brain with a mindful pause.** Slow down your fast brain that operates on autopilot in favor of your slow, more effective brain by putting obstacles in the fast brain's way. Try writing new notes reminding yourself to take a deep breath before proceeding.

- **Engage in a mindful workout of your mind and muscles.** Whatever the physical activity in which you engage, move in a way that not only gets the blood pumping but also shifts the thinking from feeling busy and distracted to feeling capable and strong. When working out, be clear of your aim, warm up (five minutes), settle into a rhythm (ten to fifteen minutes), challenge yourself (ten to fifteen minutes), cool down (five minutes), and rest (five minutes).

- **Drive yourself calm instead of crazy.** The following behind-the-wheel strategies will help you practice mindfulness while driving. When stressed, take a deep breath, ask yourself what you need (for example, to feel safe), give yourself what you need (for example, saying "I feel safe"), recognize the other drivers who are experiencing the same things you are, and then take another deep breath.

Meditate or Pray

Both prayer and meditation can increase mindfulness and prevent excessive worry. Spend ten to fifteen minutes daily engaged in some form of meditation. As you inhale, invite spiritual power into your life. As you exhale, offer your loving kindness out to human beings everywhere. Prayer has been associated with a sense of optimism, gratitude, calmness, and increased concentration and focus and can reduce feelings of isolation, anxiety, and fear as well (Ted, n.d.). My church has a hotline that members can call every morning to hear a word of prayer that sets a positive tone for the entire day.

Engage in a Walking Meditation

This strategy kills two birds with one stone. Combine the principle in chapter 5: Movement (page 50) with the principle of spirituality by taking a walking meditation. Adding a meditative element to your walk can boost your mood, clear your head, and even help you sleep better.

In your walking meditation, you will engage in guided imagery. As you begin your walk, concentrate on yourself personally. Be sure that your arms are in a comfortable position. Notice the steps you are taking and the way your legs move. After a few minutes, begin to notice the sounds around you. Are there birds chirping? Are there cars driving by? Consider sounds that are both pleasant and unpleasant. Now concentrate on smells. Perhaps there is a person burning wood in a fireplace, or you can smell the fresh earth around you. Now, move to vision. Take in all the colors, objects, and scenery around you. Notice any changes in the neighborhood that come to mind. In the final minutes of your walk, bring your awareness back from the environment around you and become aware once more of your body (Bertin, 2017).

Practice Gratitude

Begin a gratitude journal and spend five or ten minutes at the end of every day writing down those things for which you are grateful. Scott (2020b) says that this can be a great reminder of those things that are most important to you and what makes your life worthwhile. Gratitude amplifies the positive experiences, people, and things in your life and reminds you how blessed you truly are. It can also remind you not to take the simple things or important people in your life for granted.

Volunteer Your Time

Volunteer your time for someone who is in need. One of the best ways to demonstrate your spirituality is to make a difference in someone else's life. This act of kindness will increase your sense of purpose and meaning on the earth as well as assist you in putting things into perspective when dealing with personal challenges. One of the best gifts that you can give to anyone is your time.

Practice Forgiveness

Virginia Commonwealth University psychologist Everett Worthington (2021) has developed a research-based model of forgiveness called REACH. REACH is an acronym that enables you to forgive people who have caused you hurt. Unfortunately,

Worthington was personally able to test this model when, during a home invasion, his mother was murdered and he chose to forgive the perpetrator of this heinous crime. REACH stands for the following (Worthington, 2021).

- *Recall* **the hurt.** In order to heal, you must face the fact that you have been hurt but make the decision not to hold a grudge or pursue payback.

- *Empathize* **with your partner.** Put yourself in the other person's shoes and visualize what the offender might have been feeling.

- **Give an** *altruistic* **gift.** Give the altruistic, unselfish gift of forgiveness to the person who hurt you.

- *Commit* **to the experience of forgiveness**. Write yourself a note about it.

- *Hold* **onto forgiveness.** When doubting whether the forgiveness has actually taken place, reread the note to prove that you really did forgive.

This is a very difficult process in which to engage and takes a strong person to commit to it. However, this process will pay big dividends for improving both the mental and physical health of the person doing the forgiving.

Part 2: Happy Classrooms

One of the most prevalent concepts in the current educational literature is social and emotional learning (SEL). SEL is the process by which children and adults acquire and apply the knowledge, attitudes, and skills essential for understanding and managing their emotions, setting and accomplishing positive goals, feeling and showing empathy for other people, and establishing and maintaining meaningful relationships. Most models consist of a framework that defines five core competencies: (1) self-awareness, (2) self-management, (3) social awareness, (4) responsible decision making, and (5) relationship skills (Collaborative for Academic, Social, and Emotional Learning, 2021).

Many of the precepts inherent in SEL have a spiritual basis. The self-awareness component of SEL enables students to identify emotions, recognize their strengths and needs, and develop a growth mindset. When students are taught the spiritual concept of mindfulness, they are capable of becoming more self-aware of their feelings and emotions.

The concept of empathy is a major precept of SEL and spirituality alike. There is a lack of empathy that exists among school-age children (and adults as well) that seems to be perpetuated by the overreliance on social media and the limited interpersonal contact due to COVID-19 restrictions. By equipping students with the social skills they need to be able to understand what their classmates are experiencing through instructional strategies like discussion and role play, students' empathy is enhanced, and they understand it as a major component of social awareness.

Encouraging students to practice the challenging concept of forgiveness goes a long way when implementing a proactive classroom management plan. Involving students in service-learning projects where they must dedicate time and effort to improving the lives of others while accomplishing curricular objectives is a win-win for students' affective and academic improvement.

Part 3: Action Plan

Recall at the beginning of the chapter the discussion of the song "Amazing Grace," one of the most well-known songs associated with spirituality. While religion and spirituality are not synonymous, both have benefits to the brain and body. Use the following Action Plan for specific ways to incorporate increased spirituality into your daily life.

Action Plan for Incorporating Spirituality

What are my plans for incorporating more spirituality into my life and helping my students do the same?		
Recommendations	**Presently Doing**	**Strive to Do**
Determine the higher power in whom I believe.		
Seek out other people to support me in my spiritual journey.		
Practice mindfulness throughout each day.		
Engage in walking meditation.		
Begin a gratitude journal.		
Volunteer my time to make a difference in the lives of others.		
Teach students the five core competencies of social-emotional learning.		
Encourage students to practice the SEL competencies and recognize them when they do so.		

Goals and Notes:

12

Purpose

"The psychological tendency to derive meaning from life's experiences and to possess intentionality and goal-directedness that guide behavior" (Ryff, as cited in Amen, 2018, p. 179)

"Leader of the Band" is one of my favorite songs. It is Dan Fogelberg's (1981) most personal song and a tribute to his father, who was a band director. One of Fogelberg's fondest memories was his father allowing him at age four to stand in front of him and conduct the band at Bradley University. When Fogelberg grew up and decided to leave college in the middle of a semester, his father disagreed with his decision but allowed his son to pursue his own purpose, which would also be music (Fogelberg.com, n.d.). Fogelberg went on to become one of the top-selling artists of the 1980s. This chapter explores the twelfth and final principle: purpose.

Purpose

Part 1: Healthy Teachers

Purpose: What Should I Do?

We have all heard of people who pass away soon after they retire from a job they spent many years dedicated to, or of a couple who were married for many happy years and then when one passes away, the other also passes soon after. When I ask educators in my classes to stand if they know persons in either one of the aforementioned categories, usually over 70 percent of the class is standing. That is because this phenomenon doesn't happen coincidentally. Oftentimes, when people retire from a job worked for years, or a couple loses a devoted spouse loved for years, they lose their purpose. When some people lose their purpose, they lose their life.

Allow me to elaborate. When Carrie Fisher died, her mother, Debbie Reynolds, lost her purpose. She even commented to her son that she wanted to be with her daughter. One day later, Debbie Reynolds was with her daughter.

When Kate Spade died of suicide, her heartbroken father did not make it to her funeral. He died before he could get there. The question has been asked, Can you die of a broken heart? The answer is yes, absolutely. When the heart feels broken, the brain produces cortisol, a stress hormone, which can help to deplete the immune system. So if one is not sick, the depletion can make them sick. If already ill, it can make one sicker. The syndrome is called takotsubo cardiomyopathy (Harvard Health Publishing, 2020c).

Charles Lazarus, the founder of Toys "R" Us died within one week after learning that the well-respected chain was closing. Former First Lady Barbara Bush died in April of 2018. President George H. W. Bush passed away on November 30, 2018, seven months later. They had been married for seventy-three years. Former New York Mayor David Dinkins lost his wife, Joyce, in October of 2020 at the age of eighty-nine. Mayor Dinkins followed her one month later in November of 2020 at the age of ninety-three, following sixty-seven years of wedded bliss. There are many additional examples, but I think you get the point.

According to the *New York Times* (Khullar, 2018), only approximately 25 percent of adult Americans cite a clear purpose for a meaningful life, while 40 percent either claimed they were neutral on the subject or that they didn't have a purpose at all (cited in Morin, 2020).

For those who are deeply spiritual, purpose involves serving their faith. But having a purpose is applicable to all of us, whether spiritual or not. In the very broadest terms, it's the message you want to give. It's the song you want to sing or the mark you want to leave. It's the way people find meaning in their family, work, or community.

For this chapter, I use Carol Ryff's definition of purpose. The University of Wisconsin psychologist defines *purpose* as "the psychological tendency to derive meaning from life's experiences and to possess intentionality and goal-directedness that guide behavior" (Amen, 2018, p. 179).

When I teach *The 7 Habits of Highly Effective People* (Covey, 2020), I open the class with the following statement.

> At one time, there was a commercial on television that asked the question, What do you want on your tombstone? They were talking about pizza, but I am not.

We then engage in an activity where participants write an epithet for their tombstones. Once they have done this, they can "live life backward" to accomplish daily those things for which they want to be remembered.

Before my mother, Eurica, died in 2016, she asked me to speak at her funeral. I ended my comments with one of Mom's favorite poems, "The Dash" by Linda Ellis (2014). It talks about how we should live the time and space between the year we are born and the year we die—in other words, how we should live our purpose.

What the Brain Research Says: Why Should I Do It?

In 2009, a study of over 73,000 Japanese men and women found that those who had a strong connection to their sense of purpose (which they call *ikigai* in Japanese) tended to live longer than those who did not (Leonard & Kreitzer, 2016). Author Dan Buettner (2012) studied communities throughout the world in which people were more likely to live past one hundred. He found that one of the factors that most centenarians share is a strong sense of purpose. In 2014, researchers used data that tracked adults over a fourteen-year period and found that having a purpose in life appears to widely buffer against mortality risks (Hill & Turiano, 2014).

Having purpose in life gives the brain a constant, never-ending drip of dopamine, a positive neurotransmitter (Amen, 2018).

A 2010 study published in *Applied Psychology* (Kobau, Sniezek, Zack, Lucas, & Burns, 2010) found that people with high levels of well-being, which included a sense of control over life, a feeling that what they do matters, and a sense of purpose, tended to live longer (Morin, 2020).

In her research, Ryff (Amen, 2018) found that people who lived their lives with a higher sense of purpose experienced a number of advantages, including the following.

- Better mental health
- Decreased depression
- Increased happiness
- Increased personal growth and acceptance of self
- Improved quality of sleep
- Longer life

People who have a sense of purpose also appear to have a greater sense of resilience and well-being. Extensive research on the science of well-being has found that people with a strong sense of purpose are better able to handle the ups and downs of life since that purpose acts as a psychological buffer against obstacles. These people remain satisfied with life even if they are experiencing a difficult day (Amen, 2018).

According to Amen (2018), people with a sense of purpose in life also experience a lower risk of stroke and cardiovascular disease, increased immunity, and a better quality of sleep. They are also less likely to be affected by negative social media issues, such as not getting an adequate number of likes.

 A lack of purpose has been associated with higher levels of cortisol (the stress hormone), lower HDL cholesterol, increased markers of inflammation, and larger amounts of abdominal fat (Amen, 2018).

Purpose even appears to prevent Alzheimer's disease. In studies of thousands of elderly subjects, Patricia Boyle, a neuropsychologist at the Rush Alzheimer's Disease

Center in Chicago (as cited in Amen, 2018), finds that people with a low sense of life purpose were 2.4 times more likely to get Alzheimer's disease than those with a strong purpose. Boyle and other researchers from Chicago's Rush University studied more than 900 people who had higher scores on a *purpose* scale. They also had a reduced risk of acquiring Alzheimer's disease, a slower rate of cognitive decline during aging, and a lessening of mild cognitive impairment (Amen, 2018).

New evidence is suggesting that a sense of meaning in life can mitigate the symptoms of Alzheimer's disease. This phenomenon occurred even when the plaque had already begun accumulation in the brain (Wallace, 2012).

We appear to be hardwired for purpose: to believe in purpose, to find purpose, and to live purpose. Having a purpose affects our minds, our hearts, and our happiness. It's a part of our biological makeup.

Action Steps: How Should I Do It?

Answer Questions to Find Your Purpose

A TEDx Talk by Adam Leipzig (2013), CEO of Entertainment Media Partners, has more than ten million views. It helps people find their life's purpose in five minutes by answering the following five questions:

1. Who are you? What is your name?
2. What do you love to do? What is the one thing you do where you feel supremely qualified to teach others?
3. Whom do you do it for? How does your work connect to others?
4. What do those people want or need from you?
5. How do they change as a result of what you do? (cited in Amen, 2018, p. 194)

I responded to Leipzig's (2013) questions. Here are my personal answers regarding purpose.

1. My name is Marcia.

2. I love conducting workshops and writing about the strategies that should be used if we want to take advantage of the way all brains learn best.

3. I do it for teachers, administrators, parents, business and community leaders, or anyone who teaches anyone anything.

4. These people want to be more successful at imparting content to their students, children, and employees so that the learning sticks, regardless of the content or the age or grade level of the person.

5. Over two thousand emails from educators have let me know that since using the brain-compatible strategies I teach, their students' academic

achievement has increased, behavior problems have been reduced, and teaching and learning have become so much more fun!

Respond honestly to Leipzig's (2013) questions to determine your own personal purpose. Notice that since three of the questions deal with others, it might be that a person's happiness is found not in selfish pursuits but in helping other people.

Determine Your Purpose

Jeremy Smith (2018), author and editor, relates that the goals that give us the gift of purpose are the ones that can influence the lives of other people. As stated earlier in this chapter, these goals have been associated with improved mental and physical health and help both individuals and the species as a whole to survive. He suggests six ways to determine purpose.

1. **Read to examine the lives of others as you seek your purpose.** Reading connects us to others across time and space.

2. **Turn hurts into healing for others.** Oftentimes purpose can grow out of both our own suffering and the suffering of others.

3. **Cultivate awe, gratitude, and altruism.** Being appreciative of our lives and seeking to help others foster purpose.

4. **Listen to what other people appreciate about you.** Pay attention to what people thank you for.

5. **Find and build community.** Take a look at the family and friends around you in finding your purpose.

6. **Tell your story.** Make a narrative out of your own life.

Select Additional Tips for Finding Purpose

Amy Morin's (2020) article, sanctioned by medical doctor Carly Snyder and titled "7 Tips for Finding Your Purpose in Life," includes the following tips.

1. Donate time, money, or talent to help other people.

2. Listen to the feedback that others give you.

3. Surround yourself with people who are making positive changes.

4. Start conversations with people who may not be in your social circle.

5. Explore those things that truly interest you or that you share on social media.

6. Consider injustices that truly upset you.

7. Discover what you truly love to do.

Decide which of these aforementioned tips could lead you to discover your purpose and make a SMART plan for acting on them using the steps contained in this chapter.

Write a Personal Mission Statement

In Covey's (2020) *The 7 Habits of Highly Effective People*, habit 2 is "Begin with the end in mind." One of the activities connected to this habit is to write a personal mission statement. This mission statement is based on the principles that guide one's life and operationalize one's purpose. It can be as simple as one sentence or as complicated as one desires. When I teach *7 Habits*, my class members begin to write their personal mission statements. It is not something that can usually be completed in one day since it requires a great deal of thought. One gentleman, however, did complete his in one sentence. He wrote, "I want to be the kind of person that my dog already thinks I am." I thought that said it all! I also share my personal mission statement with the class. It has three parts.

1. To be the best daughter, sister, wife, mother, grandmother, aunt, and friend that I can be and leave this world a better place because I was here

2. To improve the professional and personal lives of the people with whom I come in contact

3. To help educators uncover the gift in every child

Are there days when I am not the best person I could be? Absolutely! But by knowing my mission, I am made aware of my shortcomings and how to correct them. This is similar to a pilot who has a destination but is taken off course by turbulence. Because he has filed a flight plan, he knows how to correct his path and get back on track.

Set SMART Goals

Rick Warren, coauthor of *The Daniel Plan* (Warren et al., 2020) and author of the megahit bestseller *The Purpose-Driven Life* (Warren, 2002), suggests that people write out their goals and purposes in five areas in an effort to lead a more balanced life: "(1) faith, (2) food, (3) fitness, (4) focus, and (5) friends" (Warren et al., 2020, p. 216). He states that it is necessary to set SMART goals in each of the five areas. SMART is a mnemonic device for the following characteristics of effective goals.

- **Specific:** The S in SMART stands for *specific*. Goals need to be very clear and not ambiguous. They should answer the following five questions: What do I want to accomplish? Why do I need to accomplish it? Who besides me will be involved? Where will it take place? and Which requirements and constraints will I have to consider?

- **Measurable:** The M in SMART stands for *measurable*. If goals are not measurable, then you have no idea when they are accomplished. You need to be able to answer questions such as, how much and by when?

- **Attainable:** Although goals can be big and test your faith, they should be realistic and important to you.

- **Relevant:** Your goals should be worthwhile and truly matter to you.

- **Timebound:** Your goals should be accomplished within a specific timeframe or deadline. (Warren et al., 2020)

Part 2: Happy Classrooms

Since you have devoted a major part of your life to education, it is obvious that this may just be part of your purpose. I know it is part of my purpose since I have spent more than forty-eight years in this business and never regretted one day of it. When teaching, I have often stated that we educators belong to a special club. We are the only profession that impacts every other profession. Every doctor, lawyer, writer, scientist, artist, and so on, has at some point had a teacher to help them hone their craft.

Set some SMART goals for your classroom this and every year so that you are continually improving and growing as a teacher. No matter how wonderful we all are, we should never cease to set goals that would help us become better at what we do. Like the grasses in the field, if we are not continually growing, then we are dying.

The concept of purpose also relates to the lessons you teach. The human brain has but one purpose. It is not to make straight As or score high on the Scholastic Aptitude Test. The purpose of the human brain is survival. Therefore, when students cannot see the correlation between the lesson you are teaching and their survival in the world, they will ask you the age-old question, Why do we have to learn this? It is a very legitimate question.

If you don't want to hear that question, then establish a purpose initially so that students know exactly what they are expected to learn and why. In fact, if you wait until you have completed your lesson plan to determine its purpose, you have waited too long. In any lesson, the initial question for planning should be, What should students know, understand, and be able to do? The remainder of the lesson plan should ensure that this question is answered.

When it comes to a curricular objective, be sure to tell students what they should know, understand, or be expected to do. Students cannot live up to your expectations if they do not know what those expectations are. The purpose should not be a well-kept secret. I made good grades in school, but I wasted time trying to guess what was going to be on the upcoming assessment. Tell students the purpose, and academic achievement will improve.

Part 3: Action Plan

Recall at the beginning of the chapter the discussion of "Leader of the Band" by Dan Fogelberg. Like his father, Fogelberg found his purpose in his music. Each individual must find their own purpose. Mine is educating students and adults. Use the following Action Plan to decide what that all-important purpose is in your life. Taking this step alone can enrich and lengthen your life.

Action Plan for Determining Purpose

What are my plans for determining the purpose in my life?		
Recommendations	Presently Doing	Strive to Do
Answer Leipzig's (2013) five questions to help find my initial purpose. 1. Who are you? What is your name? 2. What do you love to do? What is the one thing you do where you feel supremely qualified to teach others? 3. Whom do you do it for? How does your work connect to others? 4. What do those people want or need from you? 5. How do they change as a result of what you do?		
Select additional tips for determining my purpose.		
Write a personal mission statement.		
Set SMART life goals.		
Determine the purpose of my lesson prior to planning it.		
Communicate the purpose of each lesson to students.		
Assess student learning to determine if the purpose has been achieved.		
Goals and Notes:		

Source for five questions: Leipzig, A. (2013, February 1). How to know your life purpose in 5 minutes *[Video file]. Accessed at www.youtube.com/watch?v=vVsXO9brK7M on October 7, 2021.*

Epilogue

Julia Sanders rises at 5:30 a.m. To begin her morning ritual, she asks Alexa to play some relaxing smooth jazz as she begins fixing a healthy breakfast for herself and her children. Her focus on healthy eating for herself and the children has given her more energy in the morning, which she really needs with the stress of the COVID-19 pandemic and the chaotic school year that has resulted. An alarm wakes her children. It used to be more difficult to wake them up in the morning; it's not perfect now, but they awake much easier since they all began going to bed an hour earlier, having made a house rule to not have any electronic device on at bedtime.

Once Aunt Peggie arrives to stay with the children while Julia works, Julia can leave for her commute to school. She knows Aunt Peggie can't keep up with the kids' work. Thankfully, Julia made some changes at home that seem to be helping her children focus on their work: she makes sure to open all the blinds to increase the natural light, for example, and Aunt Peggie takes the children outside when the weather is nice for a change of scenery and fresh air. Julia knows this is helpful because she herself has started taking a thirty-minute walk around the parking lot when her kids are at sports practice after school.

Teaching her eighth-grade students both in person and in virtual classes is challenging. Julia still finds her students have trouble focusing, and she feels easily overwhelmed. Things have been better, though, since she started using music in her classroom at different points in the day to both increase energy and focus and help students and herself relax. She has also sought to build relationships with her students—especially those who are learning virtually. She has noticed this has helped increase their engagement in the class.

Evenings at home are still hectic—how can they not be with three kids, a full-time job, and a household to run? Fortunately, Julia has taken steps to connect with her spirituality by meditating and being mindful of those things that are going well. This helps her to relax despite the constant pressure. She knows that even though things are difficult, teaching is her purpose in life and her passion.

We are in a profession that greatly impacts every other profession. Every doctor, scientist, or engineer came by way of a teacher. Teaching today, however, is far more challenging than it was when I began almost a half-century ago. Yet there are teachers today who, despite all the challenges, are making a discernible difference in the lives of students on a daily basis.

As teachers increase their knowledge on how to remain both mentally and physically healthy, they will be better equipped to deliver the quality instruction so essential for having a classroom of happy and successful students. I trust that this book will become an integral part of that endeavor.

References and Resources

Algozzine, B., Campbell, P., & Wang, A. (2009). *63 tactics for teaching diverse learners: Grades 6–12.* Thousand Oaks, CA: Corwin Press.

Allen, R. (2008). *Green light classrooms: Teaching techniques that accelerate learning.* Melbourne, Victoria, Australia: Hawker Brownlow Education.

Allen, R., & Currie, J. (2012). *U-turn teaching: Strategies to accelerate learning and transform middle school achievement.* Thousand Oaks, CA: Corwin Press.

Amen, D. G. (2003). *Healing anxiety and depression.* New York: Berkley Books.

Amen, D. G. (2015). *Change your brain, change your life.* New York: Harmony Books.

Amen, D. G. (2018). *Feel better fast and make it last.* Carol Stream, IL: Tyndale House Publishers.

American Heart Association News. (2018, October 26). *Can daylight saving time hurt the heart? Prepare now for spring.* Accessed at www.heart.org/en/news/2018/10/26/can-daylight-saving-time-hurt-the -heart-prepare-now-for-spring on July 20, 2021.

Augustin, S. (2018, March 16). *Looking out the window: What should you see?* Accessed at www.psychology today.com/us/blog/people-places-and-things/201803/looking-out-the-window-what-should-you-see on July 20, 2021.

Banner, B., & Hamilton, J. (1967–1978). The Carol Burnett show [Television broadcast].

Basak, C., Boot, W. R., Voss, M. W., & Kramer, A. F. (2008). *Can training in a real-time strategy video game attenuate cognitive decline in older adults? Psychology and Aging, 23*(4), 765-777. Accessed at www.pubmed.ncbi.nlm.nih.gov/19140648 on July 20, 2021.

Bauer, P. (n.d.). *Pharrell Williams: American musician and producer.* Accessed at www.britannica.com /biography/Pharrell-Williams on October 21, 2021.

Baylor College of Medicine. (2020). *A perfect match: The health benefits of jigsaw puzzles* [Blog post]. Accessed at www.blogs.bcm.edu/2020/10/29/a-perfect-match-the-health-benefits-of-jigsaw-puzzles on September 25, 2021.

BBC. (n.d.). *Sold on song top 100: Annie's song.* Accessed at www.bbc.co.uk/radio2/soldonsong/song library/anniessong.shtml on October 21, 2021.

Bertin, M. (2017). *A daily mindful walking practice.* Accessed at www.mindful.org/daily-mindful -walking-practice on October 2, 2021.

Better Health. (n.d.). *Running and jogging—health benefits.* Accessed at www.betterhealth.vic.gov.au /health/healthyliving/running-and-jogging-health-benefits on July 20, 2021.

Bhanoo, S. N. (2013, November 11). Long-term benefits of music lessons. *The New York Times.* Accessed at www.nytimes.com/2013/11/12/science/long-term-benefits-of-music-lessons.html on July 20, 2021.

Berman, M. G., Jonides, & Kaplan, S. (2008). The cognitive benefits of interacting with nature. *Psychological Science, 19*(12), 1207–1212.

Billboard. (n.d.). *Hot 100 60th anniversary interactive chart.* Accessed at www.billboard.com/charts/hot-100-60th-anniversary/ on October 21, 2021.

BrainyQuote. (n.d.). *George Bernard Shaw quotes.* Accessed at www.brainyquote.com/authors/george-bernard-shaw-quotes on July 20, 2021.

Bratman, G. N., Hamilton, J. P., Hahn, K. S., Daily, G. C., & Gross, J. J. (2015). *Nature experience reduces rumination and subgenual prefrontal cortex activation.* Accessed at www.pnas.org/content/112/28/8567 on July 20, 2021.

Brennan, D. (2020, November 17). *Health benefits of essential oils.* Accessed at www.webmd.com/diet/health-benefits-essential-oils on September 21, 2021.

Buettner, D. (2010). *The blue zones: 9 lessons for living longer from the people who lived the longest* (2nd ed.). Washington, DC: National Geographic.

Bullock, G. (2017, January 31). *Photosensitive epilepsy: How light can trigger seizures.* Accessed at www.theraspecs.com/blog/photosensitive-epilepsy-how-different-types-of-light-can-trigger-seizures/#:~:text=Photosensitive%20epilepsy%20is%20a%20condition,stimuli%2C%20predominantly%20related%20to%20light.&text=Photosensitivity%20is%20more%20common%20with,patients%20with%20this%20particular%20condition on July 20, 2021.

Bullock, G. (2018, April 18). *Fluorescent light sensitivity: Causes, symptoms & solutions.* Accessed at www.theraspecs.com/blog/fluorescent-light-sensitivity-causes-symptoms-solutions/ on July 20, 2021.

Burke, D. (2020). *He was a COVID-19 patient. She cleaned his hospital room. Their unexpected bond saved his life.* Accessed at www.cnn.com/2020/06/11/health/orlando-hospital-coronavirus-patient-housekeeper-wellness/index.html on October 21, 2021.

Calm. (n.d.). In *Merriam-Webster's online dictionary.* Accessed at www.merriam-webster.com/dictionary/calm on October 30, 2021.

Cancer Treatment Centers of America. (2019, December 26). *The power of laughter for cancer patients.* Accessed at www.cancercenter.com/community/blog/2019/12/power-of-laughter-for-cancer-patients on July 20, 2021.

Cancer Treatment Centers of America. (2020, December 18). *7 ways to help feel good when you don't feel well.* Accessed at www.cancercenter.com/community/blog/2020/12/feeling-good on July 20, 2021.

Carskadon, M. A. (2011). Sleep in adolescents: The perfect storm. *Pediatric Clinics of North America, 58*(3), 637–647. Accessed at www.ncbi.nlm.nih.gov/pmc/articles/PMC3130594 on July 20, 2021.

Cassata, C. (2016, April 8). *Can you really die of a broken heart?* Accessed at www.healthline.com/health-news/can-you-die-of-broken-heart on July 20, 2021.

Centers for Disease Control and Prevention. (2019, April 15). *Healthy pets, healthy people.* Accessed at www.cdc.gov/healthypets/index.html on July 20, 2021.

Centers for Disease Control and Prevention. (2020). *Sleep in middle and high school students.* Accessed at www.cdc.gov/healthyschools/features/students-sleep.htm on September 23, 2021.

Centre for Optimism. (2019, August 27). *Health and optimism.* Accessed at www.centreforoptimism.com/health on February 6, 2021.

Charmaine. (2018). *10 health benefits of yoga.* Accessed at www.facty.com/lifestyle/fitness/10-health-benefits-of-yoga/3/?da=true&daInit=8 on July 20, 2021.

Cherry, K. (2020, April 29). *What is the negativity bias?* Accessed at www.verywellmind.com/negative-bias-4589618 on September 29, 2021.

Chowdhry, A. (2013, October 5). *Lessons learned from 4 Steve Jobs quotes.* Accessed at www.forbes.com/sites/amitchowdhry/2013/10/05/lessons-learned-from-4-steve-jobs-quotes/?sh=2905757a4f69 on July 20, 2021.

Cleveland Clinic. (2020, February 28). *Daylight saving time: 4 tips to help your body adjust.* Accessed at www.health.clevelandclinic.org/daylight-savings-time-change-4-tips-to-help-your-body-adjust on October 5, 2021.

Colbert, D. (2009). *Eat this and live! Simple food choices that can help you feel better, look younger, and live longer!* Lake Mary, FL: Siloam Press.

Collaborative for Academic, Social, and Emotional Learning. (2021). *SEL is . . .* Accessed at www.casel .org/what-is-sel on July 20, 2021.

Connor, A. (2018). *The lion sleeps tonight—Written by a Zulu migrant worker, made famous by Disney.* Accessed at https://ig.ft.com/life-of-a-song/the-lion-sleeps-tonight.html on October 21, 2021.

Consult QD. (2017, January 17). *A room with a view: Do hospital window views affect clinical outcomes?* Accessed at www.consultqd.clevelandclinic.org/room-view-hospital-window-views-affect-clinical -outcomes/#:~:text=%E2%80%9CWhen%20patients%20are%20medically%20ill,emotional%20 health%20and%20clinical%20outcomes on July 20, 2021.

Cooper, N., & Garner, B. K. (2012). *Developing a learning classroom: Moving beyond management through relationships, relevance, and rigor.* Thousand Oaks, CA: Corwin Press.

Costa, A. L. (2008). *The school as a home for the mind: Creating mindful curriculum, instruction, and dialogue* (2nd ed.). Melbourne, Victoria, Australia: Hawker Brownlow Education.

Covey, S. R. (2020). *The 7 habits of highly effective people: Powerful lessons in personal change* (30th anniversary ed.). Salt Lake City, UT: Covey Leadership Center.

David., L., Shapiro, G., Scheinman, A., Seinfeld, J., Berg, A., & Schaffer, J. (1989–1998). Seinfeld [Television broadcast].

Denver, J. (1974). Annie's song [Song]. On *Back home again.* RCA.

Dodd, J., & Young, S. (2020, July 20). Her kind words helped save his life. *People.* July 20, 2020. Accessed at https://people.com/human-interest/man-beat-coronavirus-bond-hospital-staffer on October 21, 2021.

Edmondson, A. C. (2003). Framing for learning: Lessons in successful technology implementation. *California Management Review, 45*(2). Accessed at https://doi.org/10.2307/41166164 on July 21, 2021.

Edward, B., & Rodgers, N. (1979). We are family [Recorded by Sister Sledge]. On *We are family.* Cotillion.

Ellis, L. (2014). *Live your dash: Make every moment matter.* New York: Sterling Ethos.

Eren, B. (2015). The use of music interventions to improve social skills in adolescents with autism spectrum disorders in integrated group music therapy sessions. *Procedia–Social and Behavioral Sciences, 197,* 207–213.

ESA. (2020). 2020 *Essential facts about the video game industry.* Accessed at www.theesa.com/wp -content/uploads/2020/07/2020-ESA_Essential_facts_070820_Final_lowres.pdf on December 6, 2021.

Ferguson, S. (2019, February 1). *Catastrophizing: What you need to know to stop worrying.* Accessed at www.healthline.com/health/anxiety/catastrophizing#:~:text=Catastrophizing%3A%20What%20 You%20Need%20to%20Know%20to%20Stop%20Worrying&text=Catastrophizing%20is%20 when%20someone%20assumes,they'll%20fail%20an%20exam on July 20, 2021.

Flaherty, D. (n.d.). *1979 Pittsburgh Pirates: Don't ever take sides against the family . . . ever.* Accessed at https://thesportsnotebook.com/1979-pittsburgh-pirates-sports-history-articles on October 21, 2021.

Fogelberg, D. (1981). Leader of the band [Song]. On *The innocent age.* Full Moon/Epic.

Fogelberg.com. (n.d.). *FAQs.* Accessed at www.danfogelberg.com/faqs on October 21, 2021.

Frothingham, S. (2019). *How long does it take for a new behavior to become automatic?* Accessed at www.healthline.com/health/how-long-does-it-take-to-form-a-habit on September 25, 2021.

Game. (n.d.). In *Merriam-Webster's online dictionary*. Accessed at www.merriam-webster.com/dictionary /game on October 31, 2021.

Garone, S. (2020). *The health benefits of natural light (and 7 ways to get more of it)*. Accessed at www.healthline.com/health/natural-light-benefits on July 20, 2021.

Garrison, M. A., & Severino, S. K. (2016). *Wellness in mind: Your brain's surprising secrets to gaining health from the inside out*. Morrisville, NC: Lulu Press.

George, E. M., & Coch, D. (2011). Music training and working memory: An ERP study. *Neuropsychologist, 49*(5), 1083–1094.

Glasser, W. (1999). *Choice theory: A new psychology of personal freedom*. New York: HarperCollins.

Godman, H. (2021, March 29). *Simple, low-cost, low-tech brain training*. Accessed at www.health.harvard .edu/blog/low-cost-low-tech-brain-training-2021032922247 on October 8, 2021.

Gooding, L. F. (2010). Using music therapy protocols in the treatment of premature infants: An introduction to current practices. *Arts in Psychotherapy, 37*(3), 211–214.

Goodreads. (n.d.). *Robert Fulgham*. Accessed at www.goodreads.com/author/show/19630 on September 22, 2021.

Grandner, M., Seixas, A., Shetty, S., & Shenoy, S. (2016). Sleep duration and diabetes risk: Population trends and potential mechanisms. *Current Diabetes Reports, 16*(11), 106. Accessed at www.ncbi.nlm .nih.gov/pmc/articles/PMC5070477 on October 31, 2021.

Greater Good Science Center. (n.d.). *Mindfulness: What is mindfulness?* Accessed at www.greatergood .berkeley.edu/topic/mindfulness/definition on September 25, 2021.

Gregory, G. H., & Chapman, C. (2013). *Differentiated instructional strategies: One size doesn't fit all* (3rd ed.). Thousand Oaks, CA: Corwin Press.

Griffin, M., Friedman, H., Richards, M., Rhinehart, J., Jones, N., Friedman, H., Griffith, K., & Schwartz, S. (1975–present). Wheel of fortune (Television broadcast].

Gump, B. B., & Matthews, K. A. (2000). Are vacations good for your health? The 9-year mortality experience after the multiple risk factor intervention trial. *Psychosomatic Medicine, 62*(5), 608–612. Accessed at www.pubmed.ncbi.nlm.nih.gov/11020089 on July 20, 2021.

Gunnars, K. (2020, November 5). *How much water should you drink per day?* Accessed at www.health line.com/nutrition/how-much-water-should-you-drink-per-day on July 20, 2021.

Hannaford, C. (2005). *Smart moves: Why learning is not all in your head*. Arlington, VA: Great River Books.

Hansen, L. (2002). *Amazing grace: A new book traces the history of a beloved hymn*. Accessed at www.npr .org/2002/12/29/894060/amazing-grace on October 21, 2021.

Harvard Health Publishing. (2020a, July 7). *Blue light has a dark side*. Accessed at www.health.harvard .edu/staying-healthy/blue-light-has-a-dark-side on September 27, 2021.

Harvard Health Publishing. (2020b, June 17). *In the journals: Sitting can shorten your life*. Accessed at www.health.harvard.edu/newsletter_article/sitting-can-shorten-your-life on July 20, 2021.

Harvard Health Publishing. (2020c, January 29). *Takotsubo cardiomyopathy (broken heart syndrome)*. Accessed at www.health.harvard.edu/heart-health/takotsubo-cardiomyopathy-broken-heart-syndrome on October 1, 2021.

Harvard Health Publishing. (2021, March 29). *Simple, low-cost, low-tech brain training*. Accessed at www.health.harvard.edu/blog/low-cost-low-tech-brain-training-2021032922247 on October 10, 2021.

Harvard Men's Health Watch. (2019, October). *The thinking on brain games*. Accessed at www.health .harvard.edu/mind-and-mood/the-thinking-on-brain-games on July 20, 2021.

Harvard Men's Health Watch. (2020, October 13). *Walking: Your steps to health*. Accessed at www.healthharvard.edu on November 18, 2020.

Harvard Women's Health Watch. (2019, August 6). *The health benefits of strong relationships*. Accessed at www.health.harvard.edu/newsletter_article/the-health-benefits-of-strong-relationships on July 20, 2021.

Harvey, S., Felsher, H., Dawson, C, & Dawson, G. (1976–present). Family feud [Television broadcast].

Hayward, J. (2020). *Covering ground with these benefits of walking*. Accessed at www.activebeat.com/fitness/covering-ground-with-these-7-benefits-of-walking on July 20, 2021.

Hazzard, R. (1983). Girls just want to have fun [Recorded by Cyndi Lauper]. On *She's so unusual*. Portrait.

HealthyPlace.com Staff Writer. (2016, March 31). *Why pessimism shuts down our immune system*. Accessed at www.healthyplace.com/self-help/self-help-stuff-that-works/why-pessimism-shuts-down-our-immune-system#:~:text=PESSIMISM%20PRODUCES%20DEPRESSION.,activity%20of%20the%20immune%20system on July 20, 2021.

Hill, P. L., & Turiano, N. A. (2014, May 8). Purpose in life as a predictor of mortality across adulthood. *Psychological Science*, 25(7), 1482–1486. Accessed at www.ncbi.nlm.nih.gov/pmc/articles/PMC4224 996 on July 20, 2021.

IMDb. (n.d.a). *Cyndi Lauper: Girls just want to have fun*. Accessed at www.imdb.com/title/tt4649250/awards/?ref_=tt_awd on October 21, 2021.

IMDb. (n.d.b). *OutKast: Awards*. Accessed at www.imdb.com/name/nm1642036/awards on October 21, 2021.

Ingersoll, R., Merrill, L., & Stuckey, D. (2018). *The changing face of teaching*. Accessed at www.ascd.org/el/articles/the-changing-face-of-teaching on July 20, 2021.

Integris Health. (2019, April 3). *Laughter yoga: Why laughter really is the best medicine*. Accessed at https://integrisok.com/resources/on-your-health/2019/april/laughter-is-the-best-medicine on July 20, 2021.

Javanbakht, A., & Saab, L. (2017, October 27). What happens in the brain when we feel fear. *Smithsonian Magazine*. Accessed at www.smithsonianmag.com/science-nature/what-happens-brain-feel-fear-180966992 on September 24, 2021.

Jensen, E. (2005). *Top tunes for teaching: 977 song titles and practical tools for choosing the right music every time*. Thousand Oaks, CA: Corwin Press.

Jensen, E. (2007). *Brain-compatible strategies* (2nd ed.). Melbourne, Victoria, Australia: Hawker Brownlow Education.

Jensen, E. (2008). *Brain-based learning: The new paradigm of teaching*. Thousand Oaks, CA: Corwin Press.

Jensen, E. (2019). *Poor students, rich teaching: Seven high-impact mindsets for students from poverty*. Bloomington, IN: Solution Tree Press.

Johnston, T. (1972). Listen to the music [Recorded by the Doobie Brothers]. On *Toulouse Street*. Warner Bros.

Kaplan, R., & Kaplan S. (1989). *The experience of nature: A psychological perspective*, London: Cambridge University Press.

Kaplan, R., & Kaplan, S. (1995). The restorative benefits of nature: Toward an integrative framework. *Journal of Environmental Psychology* 15, 169–182.

Karoshi. (n.d.). In *Wikipedia*. Accessed at https://en.wikipedia.org/wiki/Karoshi on July 21, 2021.

Khullar D. (2018). Finding purpose for a good life. But also a healthy one. *The New York Times*. Accessed at www.nytimes.com/2018/01/01/upshot/finding-purpose-for-a-good-life-but-also-a-healthy-one.html on October 21, 2021.

Kobau, R, Sniezek, J, Zack, M. M., Lucas, R. E., & Burns, A. (2010). Well-being assessment: An evaluation of well-being scales for public health and population estimates of well-being among US adults. *Applied Psychology*, 2, 272–297.

Laugh. (n.d.). In *Merriam-Webster's online dictionary*. Accessed at www.merriam-webster.com /dictionary/laugh#:~:text=1a%20%3A%20to%20show%20emotion,The%20audience%20was%20 laughing%20hysterically on October 31, 2021.

Leonard, B., & Kreitzer, M. J. (2016). *Why is life purpose important?* Accessed at www.takingcharge.csh .umn.edu/why-life-purpose-important on July 20, 2021.

Leonette, J. (2018, October 15). *The best and worst light bulbs for your health*. Accessed at www.alpha emerged.com/journal/2018/10/12/light-bulb-and-health on October 10, 2021.

Leipzig, A. (2013, February 1). *How to know your life purpose in 5 minutes* [Video file]. Accessed at www.youtube.com/watch?v=vVsXO9brK7M on October 7, 2021.

Lightstone, N. (2021, February 11). *10 signs you are enjoying your work*. Accessed at www.lifehack.org /articles/work/10-signs-you-are-enjoying-your-work.html on July 20, 2021.

Linda, S., Peretti, H., Creatore, L., Weiss, G. D., & Stanton, A. (1961). The lion sleeps tonight [Recorded by The Tokens]. On *The lion sleeps tonight*. RCA Victor.

Lipka, M., & Gecewicz, C. (2017, September 6). *More Americans now say they're spiritual but not religious*. Accessed at www.pewresearch.org/fact-tank/2017/09/06/more-americans-now-say-theyre -spiritual-but-not-religious on July 20, 2021.

Live Your Legend. (2021, May 7). *Surprising science: Medical proof that doing work you love could save your life*. Accessed at https://liveyourlegend.net/wake-up-call-doing-work-you-love-could-save-your -life on July 20, 2021.

Locke, R. (n.d.). *You will remember information longer if you hand write notes*. Accessed at www.lifehack .org/articles/productivity/you-will-remember-information-longer-you-hand-write-notes.html on September 30, 2021.

Malamut, M. (2018, October 30). Why holding hands might help to reduce pain. *New York Post*. Accessed at https://nypost.com/2019/10/30/why-holding-hands-might-help-to-reduce-pain on July 20, 2021.

Manohar, S. (2020, July). *Laughter clubs continue to be popular in India despite there being nothing to laugh about*. Accessed at www.vice.com/en/article/xg84z3/laughter-clubs-comedy-india-pandemic on July 20, 2021.

Marchal, J. (n.d.). *Learning new words everyday can make you much smarter, study finds*. Accessed at www.lifehack.org/516631/learning-new-words-every-day-can-make-you-much-smarter-study-finds on September 30, 2021.

Markowitz, K., & Jensen, E. (2007). *The great memory book*. Melbourne, Victoria, Australia: Hawker Brownlow Education.

MasterClass Staff. (2020, November 8). *A guide to the 5 levels of Maslow's hierarchy of needs*. Accessed at www.masterclass.com/articles/a-guide-to-the-5-levels-of-maslows-hierarchy-of-needs on July 20, 2021.

Mastropolo, F. (2012). Doobie Brothers' Tom Johnston reflects on "Listen to the Music" at 40. Accessed at https://ultimateclassicrock.com/doobie-brothers-tom-johnston-reflects-listen-to-the -music-at-40 on October 21, 2021.

Mayo Clinic. (2020a). *Getting a good night's sleep* (S. S. Faubion, Ed.). New York: Meredith Corporation.

Mayo Clinic. (2020b). *Finding balance and happiness* (S. S. Faubion, Ed.). *New York:* Meredith Corporation.

Mayo Clinic Staff. (2019, April 5). *Stress relief from laughter? It's no joke*. Accessed at www.mayoclinic.org /healthy-lifestyle/stress-management/in-depth/stress-relief/art-20044456 on July 20, 2021.

Mayo Clinic Staff. (2020, October 14). *Water: How much should you drink every day?* Accessed at www .mayoclinic.org/healthy-lifestyle/nutrition-and-healthy-eating/in-depth/water/art-20044256 on July 20, 2021.

McFerrin, B. (1988). Don't worry, be happy [Song]. On *Simple pleasures*. EMI-Manhattan.

McGauran, D. (2015, October 14). *The 6 health benefits of laughter.* Accessed at www.activebeat.com /your-health/the-6-health-benefits-of-laughter on September 26, 2021.

Medina, J. (2008). *Brain rules: 12 principles for surviving and thriving at work, home, and school.* Seattle, WA: Pear Press.

Medina, J. (2014). *Brain rules: 12 principles for surviving and thriving at work, home, and school* (2nd Ed.). Seattle, WA: Pear Press.

Menken, A., & Ashman, H. (1991). Be our guest [Recorded by Angela Lansbury and Jerry Orbach]. On *Beauty and the Beast original movie soundtrack*. Walt Disney.

Michel, A. (2016, January 29). *Burnout and the brain.* Accessed at www.psychologicalscience.org /observer/burnout-and-the-brain on July 20, 2021.

Miranda, L.-M. (2015–present). Hamilton: An American musical.

Morin, A. (2020, July 13). *7 tips for finding your purpose in life.* Accessed at www.verywellmind.com /tips-for-finding-your-purpose-in-life-4164689 on July 20, 2021.

Movement. (n.d.). *In Merriam-Webster's online dictionary.* Accessed at www.merriam-webster.com /dictionary/movement on October 31, 2021.

Music. (n.d.). *In Dictionary.com online dictionary.* Accessed at www.merriam-webster.com/dictionary /music on October 21, 2021.

National Institutes of Health. (2013, October 28). *How sleep clears the brain.* Accessed at www.nih.gov /news-events/nih-research-matters/how-sleep-clears-brain on July 20, 2021.

Norton, A., Zipse, L., Marchina, S., & Schlaug, G. (2009). Melodic intonation therapy: Shared insights on how it is done and why it might help. *Annals of the New York Academy of Sciences, 1169*, 431–436.

Nutrition. (n.d.). In *Merriam-Webster's online dictionary.* Accessed at www.merriam-webster.com /dictionary/nutrition on October 31, 2021.

Pacheco, D., & Wright, H. (2021, June 24). *The best temperature for sleep.* Accessed at www.sleep foundation.org/bedroom-environment/best-temperature-for-sleep on October 2, 2021.

Pal, P., Hauck, C., Goldstein, E., Bobinet, K., & Bradley, C. (2018). *5 simple mindfulness practices for daily life.* Accessed at www.mindful.org/take-a-mindful-moment-5-simple-practices-for-daily-life on July 20, 2021.

Parker-Pope, T. (2020, December 30). How to get a better night's sleep. *The New York Times.* Accessed at www.nytimes.com/guides/well/how-to-sleep on July 20, 2021.

Passion. (n.d.). *In Merriam-Webster's online dictionary.* Accessed at www.merriam-webster.com/dictionary /passion#:~:text=1%20%3A%20a%20strong%20feeling%20or,has%20a%20passion%20for%20 music on October 31, 2021.

Patton, A., Mahone, C., & Brown, P. (2003). I like the way you move [Recorded by OutKast.] On *Speakerboxxx/The love below*. LaFace; Arista.

Paturel, A. (2014, June/July). *Game theory: The effects of video games on the brain.* Accessed at www.brain andlife.org/articles/how-do-video-games-affect-the-developing-brains-of-children on September 25, 2021.

Peale, N. V. (1993, December 6). *Quotes from the tough-minded optimist.* Accessed at www.centrefor optimism.com/Quotes-from-The-Tough-Minded-Optimist-Peale-by-Dr-Norman-Vincent#:~:text =%22When%20you%20have%20what%20it,%2Dminded%20optimists%20are%20made.%22 on July 20, 2021.

Pennisi, E. (2019). Gut bacteria linked to mental well-being and depression. *Science, 363*(6427), 569. Accessed at www.science.org/doi/abs/10.1126/science.363.6427.569 on October 21, 2021.

Pentland, A. (2010, July 5). *Better living through imitation?* Accessed at www.psychologytoday.com/us/blog/reality-mining/201007/better-living-through-imitation on July 20, 2021.

Premier Health. (2018, May 2). *5 ways mother nature can lift your mood.* Accessed at www.premier health.com/your-health/articles/women-wisdom-wellness-/5-Ways-Mother-Nature-Can-Lift-Your -Mood on July 20, 2021.

Pullen, C. (2017, June 6). *7 ways sleep can help you lose weight.* Accessed at www.healthline.com /nutrition/sleep-and-weight-loss on July 20, 2021.

Rampton, J. (2017, August 21). *The benefits of playing music help your brain more than any other activity.* Accessed at www.inc.com/john-rampton/the-benefits-of-playing-music-help-your-brain-more.html on July 20, 2021.

Recording Academy. (n.d.). *Artist Bobby McFerrin Grammy Awards.* Accessed at www.grammy.com /grammys/artists/bobby-mcferrin/12014 on October 21, 2021.

Relationship. (n.d.). In *Merriam-Webster's online dictionary.* Accessed at www.merriam-webster.com /dictionary/relationship on October 30, 2021.

Rettner, R. (2017, October 21). Regular walking may help older adults live longer. *The Washington Post.* Accessed at www.washingtonpost.com/national/health-science/regular-walking-may-help-older-adults -live-longer/2017/10/20/89363c4a-b4df-11e7-be94-fabb0f1e9ffb_story.html on September 29, 2021.

Reynolds, G. (2016, March 17). *Greenery (or even photos of trees) can make us happier* [Blog post]. Accessed at https://well.blogs.nytimes.com/2016/03/17/the-picture-of-health on July 20, 2021.

Ritvo, E. (2014, April 24). *The neuroscience of giving: Proof that helping others helps you.* Accessed at www.psychologytoday.com/us/blog/vitality/201404/the-neuroscience-giving on July 20, 2021.

Robinson, L., Smith, M., Segal, J., & Shubin, J. (2021). *The benefits of play for adults.* Accessed at www.helpguide.org/articles/mental-health/benefits-of-play-for-adults.htm# on July 20, 2021.

Rodriguez, T. (2016, September 1). Laugh lots, live longer. Scientific American. Accessed at www.scientificamerican.com/article/laugh-lots-live-longer on October 4, 2021.

Rogers, G. B., Keating, D. J., Young, R. L., Wong, M.-L., Licinio, J., & Wesselingh, S. (2016). From gut dysbiosis to altered brain function and mental illness: mechanisms and pathways. *Mol Psychiatry* 21, 738–748. Accessed at https://doi.org/10.1038/mp.2016.50 on October 21, 2021.

Rosengren, C. (2011). *How loving your job helps you succeed.* Accessed at https://money.usnews.com /money/blogs/outside-voices-careers/2011/03/03/how-loving-your-job-helps-you-succeed on July 20, 2021.

Rubin, R., Griffin, M., Friedman, H., Richards, M., & Davies, M. (1964–present). Jeopardy [Television broadcast].

Schlemmer, L. (2018, December 21). *Duke researchers: Life expectancy down for Gen-Xers and Millennials.* Accessed at www.wunc.org/health/2018-12-21/duke-researchers-life-expectancy-down -for-gen-xers-and-millennials on October 1, 2021.

Schlaug, G. (2015). Musicians and music making as a model for the study of brain plasticity. *Progress in Brain Research, 217,* 37–55.

ScienceDaily. (2018, November 5). *Sitting is NOT the new smoking, contrary to popular myth.* Accessed at www.sciencedaily.com/releases/2018/11/181105105419.htm on July 20, 2021.

Scott, E. (2020a, June 26). *Aromatherapy scents for stress relief.* Accessed at www.verywellmind.com /aromatherapy-scents-for-stress-relief-3144599 on October 3, 2021.

Scott, E. (2020b, November 27). *What is spirituality?* Accessed at www.verywellmind.com/how-spirituality -can-benefit-mental-and-physical-health-3144807 on July 20, 2021.

Silver, D., Berckemeyer, J. C., & Baenen, J. (2015). *Deliberate optimism: Reclaiming the joy in education.* Thousand Oaks, CA: Corwin Press.

Sleep. (n.d.). In *Merriam-Webster's online dictionary*. Accessed at www.merriam-webster.com/dictionary /sleep on October 30, 2021.

Smith, D. (2020, February 18). *Nonverbal communication: How body language & nonverbal cues are key.* Accessed at www.lifesize.com/en/blog/speaking-without-words on July 20, 2021.

Smith, S. (1998). *Catering to the stars.* Accessed at www.latimes.com/archives/la-xpm-1998-may-11-ca -48492-story.html on October 21, 2021.

Smith, J. A. (2018, January 10). *How to find your purpose in life.* Accessed at https://greatergood.berkeley .edu/article/item/how_to_find_your_purpose_in_life on July 20, 2021.

Sousa, D. A. (2011). *How the brain learns* (4th ed.). Thousand Oaks, CA: Corwin Press.

Sousa, D. A. (2012). *Brainwork: The neuroscience behind how we lead others.* Bloomington, IN: Triple Nickel Press.

Sousa, D. A. (2017). *How the brain learns* (5th ed.). Thousand Oaks, CA: Corwin Press.

Sowndhararajan, K., & Kim, S. (2016). Influence of fragrances on human psychophysiological activity: With special reference to human electroencephalographic response. *Scientia Pharmaceutica, 84*(4), 724–752. Accessed at www.ncbi.nlm.nih.gov/pmc/articles/PMC5198031 on July 20, 2021.

Sprenger, M. (2008). *The developing brain: Birth to age eight.* Thousand Oaks, CA: Corwin Press.

Star, K. (2020, May 25). *How to overcome all-or-nothing thinking.* Accessed at www.verywellmind.com /all-or-nothing-thinking-2584173 on July 20, 2021.

Stibich, M. (2021, April 2). *Top reasons to smile every day.* Accessed at www.verywellmind.com/top -reasons-to-smile-every-day-2223755 on September 22, 2021.

Stobbe, M. (2020). *For 1st time in 4 years, US life expectancy rises—a little.* Accessed at https://apnews .com/article/health-us-news-ap-top-news-united-states-new-york-72a0edc70c1797d95706743624 45574f#:~:text=NEW%20YORK%20(AP)%20%E2%80%94%20Life,for%20cancer%20and%20 drug%20overdoses on January 26, 2020.

Summer, D., & Omartian, M. (1983). She works hard for the money [Recorded by D. Summer]. On *She works hard for the money.* Mercury.

Tate, M. L. (2011). *Preparing children for success in school and life: 20 ways to increase your child's brain power.* Thousand Oaks, CA: Corwin Press.

Tate, M. L. (2014). *Shouting won't grow dendrites: 20 techniques to detour around the danger zones* (2nd ed.). Thousand Oaks, CA: Corwin Press.

Tate, M. L. (2016). *Worksheets don't grow dendrites: 20 instructional strategies that engage the brain* (3rd ed.). Thousand Oaks, CA: Corwin Press.

Ted. (n.d.). *11 amazing emotional and psychological effects of prayer.* Accessed at www.sunnyray.org/11 -amazing-effects-of-prayer.htm on October 10, 2021.

Terrell, K. (2019, December 16). *Video games score big with older adults.* Accessed at www.aarp.org /home-family/personal-technology/info-2019/report-video-games.html#:~:text=For%20adults%20 age%2060%2D69,37%20percent%20to%2039%20percent on July 20, 2021.

Torres, F. (2020, October). *Seasonal affective disorder (SAD).* Accessed at www.psychiatry.org/patients -families/depression/seasonal-affective-disorder on July 20, 2021.

Trappe, H. J. (2010). The effects of music on the cardiovascular system and cardiovascular health. *Heart, 96*(23), 1868–1871.

Trousdale, G., & Wise, K. (1991). *Beauty and the Beast.* Buena Vista Pictures.

University Hospitals. (2015, July 2). *The top 5 most stressful life events and how to handle them* [Blog post]. Accessed at www.uhhospitals.org/Healthy-at-UH/articles/2015/07/the-top-5-most-stressful -life-events on July 20, 2021.

Underwood, A. (2005, October 3). The good heart. *Newsweek,* pp. 48–55.

U.S. Preventive Medicine. (2017, March 31). *Does a laugh per day keep the doctor away?* Accessed at www.uspm.com/does-a-laugh-per-day-keep-the-doctor-away on September 30, 2021.

Van Overwalle, F., & Mariën, P. (2016). Functional connectivity between the cerebrum and cerebellum in social cognition: A multi-study analysis. *NeuroImage, 124*, 248–255.

Van Toller, S. (1988). Odors and the brain. In S. Van Toller & G. Dodd (Eds.), *Perfumery: The psychology and biology of fragrance* (pp. 121–146). London: Chapman and Hall.

Vaughn, K. (2000). Music and mathematics: Modest support for the oft-claimed relationship. *Journal of Aesthetic Education, 34*(3–4), 149–166.

Ventrella, S. W. (2001). *The power of positive thinking in business: Ten traits for maximum results.* New York: Fireside.

Visible Learning. (n.d.). *Collective teacher efficacy (CTE) according to John Hattie.* Accessed at https://visible-learning.org/2018/03/collective-teacher-efficacy-hattie on July 20, 2021.

Wallace, L. (2012, May 9). Can a sense of purpose slow Alzheimer's? *The Atlantic.* Accessed at www.theatlantic.com/health/archive/2012/05/can-a-sense-of-purpose-slow-alzheimers/256856 on July 20, 2021.

Wallace, M. (1957). *Mike Wallace interview: Frank Lloyd Wright.* Accessed at https://hrc.contentdm.oclc.org/digital/collection/p15878coll90/id/23/rec/1 on October 21, 2021.

Warren, R. (2002). *The purpose-driven life: What on earth am I here for?.* Grand Rapids, MI: Zondervan.

Warren, R., Amen, D., & Hyman, M. (2020). *The Daniel plan: 40 days to a healthier life.* Grand Rapids, MI: Zondervan Books.

WebMD. (2020, July 18). *Sleep more, weigh less.* Accessed at www.webmd.com/diet/sleep-and-weight-loss#1 on July 20, 2021.

Wells, K. (2019, September 27). *How much social media is a healthy amount?* Accessed at www.kykernel.com/opinion/how-much-social-media-is-a-healthy-amount/article_d64f20d8-d48f-11e9-9d17-cbef58285792.html on September 30, 2021.

Whitaker, L. E. (2018, May 16). *Stress: What happens to a teacher's brain when it reaches burnout?* Accessed at https://meteoreducation.com/stress-part-4/#:~:text=When%20teachers%20report%20feeling%20emotionally,beginning%20to%20burn%20itself%20out on July 20, 2021.

Wiley-Blackwell, (2009, February 11). *Adolescents involved with music do better in school.* Accessed at www.sciencedaily.com/releases/2009/02/090210110043.htm on July 20, 2021.

Williams, P. (2013). Happy [Song]. On *Despicable Me 2: Original motion picture soundtrack.* Back Lot Music; I Am Other; Columbia.

Williams, R. (2019, July 19). *5 physical health benefits of spirituality.* Accessed at https://chopra.com/articles/5-physical-health-benefits-of-spirituality on July 20, 2021.

Willis, J. (2007). *Brain-friendly strategies for the inclusion classroom.* Alexandria, VA: Association for Supervision and Curriculum Development.

Wong, H. K., & Wong, R. T. (1998). *The first days of school: How to be an effective teacher.* Mountain View, CA: Author.

Worthington, E. (2021). *REACH forgiveness of others.* Accessed at www.evworthington-forgiveness.com/reach-forgiveness-of-others on July 20, 2021.

Yoga. (2018). *In Encyclopedia.com online encyclopedia.* Accessed at www.encyclopedia.com/philosophy-and-religion/eastern-religions/hinduism/yoga on October 21, 2021.

Young, K. (n.d.). *The science of gratitude—How it changes people, relationships (and brains!) and how to make it work for you.* Accessed at www.heysigmund.com/the-science-of-gratitude on September 30, 2021.

Index

CASEMATE | ILLUSTRATED

THE WINTER WAR
1939–40

PHILIP JOWETT

☾ CASEMATE | ILLUSTRATED

CIS0028

Print Edition: ISBN 978-1-63624-238-5
Digital Edition: ISBN 978-1-63624-239-2

Aircraft profiles © Vincent Dhorne 2023
Tank profiles © Battlefield Design 2023

Design and cartography by Battlefield Design
Printed and bound in the Czech Republic by FINIDR s.r.o.

CASEMATE PUBLISHERS (US)
Telephone (610) 853-9131
Fax (610) 853-9146
Email: casemate@casematepublishers.com
www.casematepublishers.com

CASEMATE PUBLISHERS (UK)
Telephone (0)1226 734350
Email: casemate-uk@casematepublishers.co.uk
www.casematepublishers.co.uk

Half-title page image: A Finnish soldier in a defensive position in the Karelian Isthmus during the final fighting of the war. Over his standard woolen uniform, he wears a white cloth snow suit and covering over his headgear. In November 1939, 144,372 sets of snow camouflage suits were available. During the winter, production was stepped up: a total of 31 factories were to produce enough for the 300,000 or so Finnish troops under arms. (Author's collection)

Page 2 image: A young Finnish ski soldier. Hanging from his belt are spare 70-round magazines for his Suomi KP/-31 sub-machine gun. (Author's collection)

Title page image: Soviet 203mm tracked howitzers move to the Red Square parade ground during the 1939 May Day parade. Known as the B-4, this large howitzer with an 11-mile range was widely used during the Winter War. During the Red Army offensive of March 1940, 142 of these guns and their 15-man crews laid down devastating fire on the Finnish lines in Karelia. (Author's collection)

Contents page: December 22, 1939: a Finnish soldier takes aim at an enemy plane with a captured 7.62mm DA aircraft machine gun stripped from a Soviet SB-2 bomber and attached to a fence post to provide stability. (Author's collection)

Contents page Map: Winter War: terrain and communications (Wikimedia Commons: www.ibiblio.org/hyperwar/ETO/Winter/USMA-Finnish/index.html)

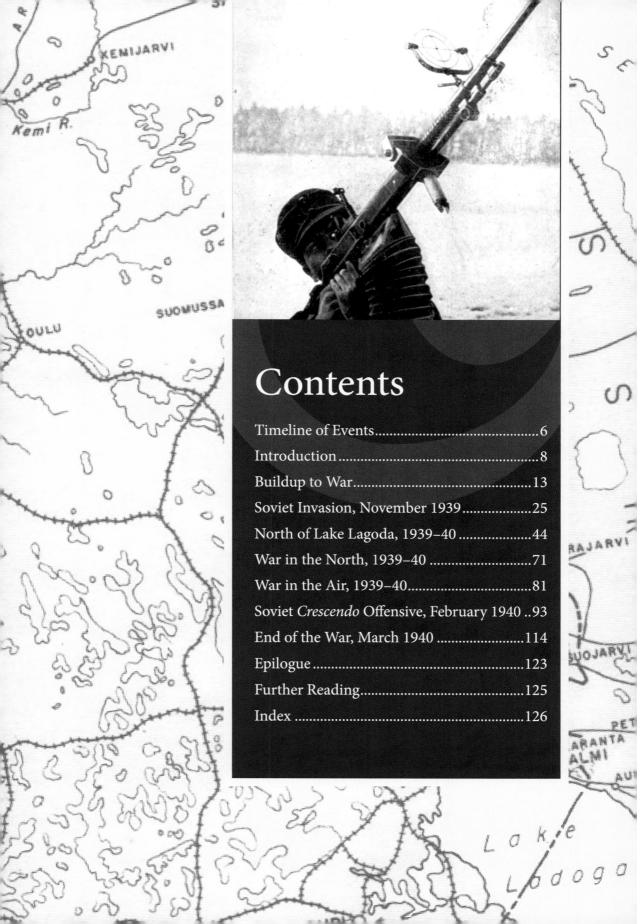

Contents

| Timeline of Events

Following futile negotiations between Helsinki and Moscow, on November 30, 1939, 600,000 Red Army troops crossed the border into Finland, while the Red Air Force unleashed bombing raids on Helsinki and other key cities. With the Soviet invasion, so commenced the bitter three-and-a-half-month war that came to be known as the Winter War, a classic David and Goliath struggle that ultimately witnessed some 70,000 Finnish casualties and upward of half a million Soviet casualties, most of whom were sacrificed in massed infantry charges or perished from hypothermia, frostbite, and starvation. When the guns finally fell silent on March 13, 1940, the Finns had been subjugated and surrendered 16,000 square miles of territory to Stalin.

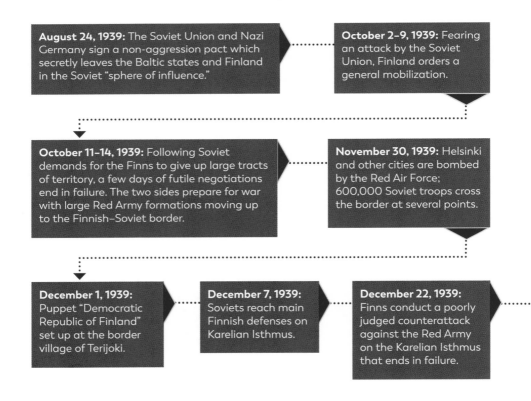

August 24, 1939: The Soviet Union and Nazi Germany sign a non-aggression pact which secretly leaves the Baltic states and Finland in the Soviet "sphere of influence."

October 2–9, 1939: Fearing an attack by the Soviet Union, Finland orders a general mobilization.

October 11–14, 1939: Following Soviet demands for the Finns to give up large tracts of territory, a few days of futile negotiations end in failure. The two sides prepare for war with large Red Army formations moving up to the Finnish–Soviet border.

November 30, 1939: Helsinki and other cities are bombed by the Red Air Force; 600,000 Soviet troops cross the border at several points.

December 1, 1939: Puppet "Democratic Republic of Finland" set up at the border village of Terijoki.

December 7, 1939: Soviets reach main Finnish defenses on Karelian Isthmus.

December 22, 1939: Finns conduct a poorly judged counterattack against the Red Army on the Karelian Isthmus that ends in failure.

The crew of a Soviet 122mm Model 1910/30 prepare for action. This model was the mainstay of the heavy howitzers of the Red Army in the 1930s and into the post-1941 period. Their replacement, the 122mm Model 38, was in limited service during the Winter War. (Author's collection)

December 1939–January 1940: Red Army advances are stopped, with many Soviet formations surrounded in the forests of eastern Finland.

January 9, 1940: Finns win a spectacular victory at Suomussalmi, destroying the Soviet 163rd and 44th Divisions.

February 1, 1940: Soviets launch their February offensive, Operation *Crescendo*, concentrating primarily on the Karelian Isthmus.

February 11, 1940: Red Army penetrates Mannerheim Line on Karelian Isthmus and advances north, pressing Finnish troops back to secondary-line defenses.

March 1–9, 1940: Fighting for the strategic Finnish port of Viipuri begins and the last Finnish reserves are deployed to this strategic city. On the 9th, exhausted Finns withdraw from Viipuri but fight on until peace is negotiated.

March 12–13, 1940: Negotiations take place between the two combatants. A peace agreement is signed: Finland loses 16,000 square miles of territory while maintaining its independence.

| Introduction

In the mid- to late 1930s, on the brink of a major conflict, Europe was divided between often precarious democracies and dictatorships. The Soviet Union in the late 1930s was a totalitarian state led by the brutal dictator Joseph Stalin who had risen to power in the early 1920s. Stalin's Machiavellian ascent involved betrayal of many of his former revolutionary comrades with whom he had worked alongside since before the 1917 Revolution.

Because of the way he had risen to the top of the Soviet Union's leadership, he was to remain paranoid about plots against him until his death in 1953. After dealing with several of his former comrades in a series of show trials from the late 1920s, the 1930s saw his suspicions turning to the Soviet Union's military leadership: the Red Army's ranks were decimated by

One of the reasons for the Soviet Union's hostility to Finland was the 1918 Civil War between the Finnish Whites and Reds. The victory of the Whites saw the creation of an independent Finland and heavy defeat for the Bolsheviks' Finnish protégés. White forces were aided by German troops and during the conflict a large number of Red troops, including several hundred women, were executed by firing squad. Here a column of Red prisoners is guarded by White guards and German soldiers, April 1918. (Author's collection)

This candid 1939 photograph features two of the most powerful men in the Soviet Union in the 1930s: Joseph Stalin and his military Commander-in-Chief, Marshal Kliment Voroshilov, share a hearty joke for the propaganda camera. Voroshilov, one of the "survivors" of the purges of the 1930s, was an expert at keeping onside with the paranoid Stalin. His failures during the Winter War did not result in a bullet in the back of the head like so many of his counterparts. He did, however, lose command of the Red Army in Finland to General Timoshenko in January 1940, but went on to other commands and lived a rare full life in the world of Stalin's "court," dying aged 88 in 1969. (Author's collection)

his purges with thousands of innocent officers being shot or sent to the gulags of Siberia. While Stalin dealt with the "threats" from inside the Soviet Union, he harbored ambitions to restore former Soviet territories to his control. His perverse non-aggression pact with Hitler's Germany in August 1939 allowed him to make plans to let loose the Red Army against neighboring states. The first part of his plan was to take advantage of the German invasion of Poland in September 1939 by invading, with Hitler's agreement, the eastern part of the country. Stalin's next victims were to be the three Baltic states of Estonia, Lithuania, and Latvia which had been independent since the end of World War I. Stalin was to absorb the Baltic states by a mixture of threats, false promises, and aggressive politics. Between 1939 and 1940 the three Baltic states were to become republics of the Union of Soviet Socialist Republics.

Stalin also had his eye on the former Soviet province of Finland which had gained its independence in 1917. Finland was a sparsely populated country of 3,700,000 people scattered over 130,000 square miles. The country was covered in forests, lakes, and swamps. Most people lived in villages and small towns. There are an estimated 60,000 lakes in Finland which cover 15 percent of the country's land mass. Forests dominated the country and the

The Soviet Union's aggression in 1939 was portrayed by their propaganda machine as a war of liberation for the oppressed peoples of Poland, Estonia, Lithuania, Latvia, and Finland. During 1939 and 1940 the Red Army invaded eastern Poland and "liberated" the Baltic states which had been independent for 20 years. Here a Red Army soldier embraces a "persecuted" peasant who is happy to be "liberated" by the Red Army. (Author's collection)

Two smartly turned-out Finnish machine-gunners with their Maxim M/32-33 heavy machine gun in a prewar exercise. Before the conflict broke out, Soviet news agencies claimed that many Finnish reservists had little or no uniform and many had no shoes. Although there were shortages on the Finnish side, it was the poor Soviet soldiers who were often sent to war with inadequate clothing for the coming winter. (Author's collection)

Finnish cavalry during the Winter War was made up of a single brigade, comprising the "Haimeen" Cavalry Regiment, the "Undenmaa Dragoon" Regiment, and the 1st Mounted Rifle Battalion. Each infantry division was provided with a light squadron that included cavalry and a motorcycle company. Most cavalry fought in the infantry role. The total number of cavalrymen in 1939 was 8,000. (Author's collection)

timber produced from them was the country's main export. In the late 1930s, about half the population were involved in one way or another with the timber industry. The Soviet Union in comparison had a population of 180 million and its industrial base had developed steadily since the 1917 Revolution. It had a large munitions industry which was responsible for producing the 3,200 tanks and 2,500 aircraft that could be committed to defeating Finland. Stalin was also prepared to commit as many of his 100 infantry divisions as necessary.

Stalin's main concern was the proximity to the Soviet city of Leningrad and the major naval base at Kronstadt to the Finnish border. He demanded, in 1939, that Finland cede the Bjorko region and its islands to the Soviet Union. Finland was also requested to give the Soviets a lease on the Hanko Peninsula to prevent any German access to the Gulf of Finland. In return the Soviets would cede to Finland a nondescript piece of wooded land close to Lake Onega. These demands were quickly refused by the Finns and it became obvious that war would follow. On November 26 a Soviet "provocation" was created with Soviet claims that Finnish artillery had fired on a village on the border between the two countries. Four days later the Red Army began a major offensive against the Finns in the Karelian Isthmus.

| Buildup to War

Attempts at solving the dispute between the Soviet Union and Finland were proving futile and it was only a matter of days, or weeks at the most, before the Red Army invaded.

Finnish intelligence already knew that Soviet plans for an invasion of their country were at an advanced stage. Red Air Force reconnaissance planes had mapped out the 800-mile-long border and photographed all the important Finnish cities, ports, industrial centers, and fortifications.

The reconnaissance flights had concentrated on the Karelian Isthmus, the obvious target for the initial attack. The Isthmus was the primary route of the Red Army into Finland and attempts at fortifying it had been attempted during the 1920s and 1930s. Soviet intelligence had quickly concluded that Finland, regardless of its defensive measures, was hopelessly ill-equipped to defend itself against their invasion. As the last weeks and days of peace ebbed away, it became obvious that making comparisons between the might of the Soviet Union

During a prewar exercise, a Finnish Army heavy howitzer is brought into action under camouflage netting. The gun is a 15.2cm H/17 howitzer, which was basically the French-made Mk 1917 155mm Schneider. During the 1920s, a few of these guns were purchased by the Finns to utilize the large numbers of captured Soviet shells from the civil war. Due to a tight military budget, a total of eight were bought, arriving in 1923, 1926, and 1929. (Author's collection)

13

and a small state like Finland was farcical; it was almost a pointless exercise to compare the Soviet armed forces with the Finnish army and its tiny air force and navy. During the late 1920s and 1930s, the Soviet Union had built up its military into one of the largest forces in the world. In comparison, the Finns had cut their military budget as most European countries had due to the worldwide recession of the early 1930s. The Red Army was 10 times stronger than the Finnish Army even though it was spread across the vast Soviet empire. In 1937, the official strength of the Red Army was 1,500,000; by 1939, this had doubled to 3 million.

The Red Army had deployed five armies from the Leningrad garrison along the long Finnish–Soviet border for the invasion of Finland. The 14th Army with three weak rifle divisions, the 88th, 104th and 122nd, were to invade northern Finland. These rifle divisions were below strength but they were given the easiest task of the five armies, with their main objective being the poorly defended port of Petsamo.

The 9th Army was responsible for taking sparsely populated central Finland with three divisions in the middle of the country and two positioned just above the Arctic Circle, opposite the Finnish village of Salla. The rifle divisions attached to the 9th Army were the 44th, 54th, 88th, and 122nd and their objective was to advance west across the "waist" of Finland, to cut the country in half and hasten the defeat of the Finns.

A Finnish Army M1929 field kitchen feeds troops taking part in a prewar exercise, October 1939. These small field kitchens were more transportable than the Red Army's and did not give away their position as easily as the enemy's. The kitchens supplied hot food that literally kept Finnish soldiers alive in the winter of 1939/40. (Sa-Kuva-111734)

In a prewar exercise these Finnish troops are fully kitted out with the German M16 steel helmet. During the 1930s, the Finns used the M16 plus another distinctive Finnish model that was introduced during the war. The telephone operator's rifle propped against the rock is an M27 Mosin–Nagant which was the shortened version of the M1891. Some 150,000 ex-Imperial Russian M1891s were found in stores when Finland declared its independence in 1917. In 1927, the Finns improved the M1891 with a stronger barrel which improved the rifle's accuracy. (Author's collection)

Delivered in 1939, a pair of Finnish Army Vickers 6-ton light tanks during a prewar exercise. Some 27 of these tanks had arrived in Finland and were fitted with Swedish-made turrets armed with Bofors 37mm guns. These tanks were on a par with the T-26 light tanks in Red Army service but the Finns had to use them sparingly during the Winter War. (Author's collection)

The 8th Army was positioned on the border to the north of the vast Lake Lagoda and had the dual objectives of, firstly, to draw Finnish units away from the decisive Karelian Isthmus sector, and then to advance as deeply as possible into southern–central Finland to take territory and frustrate the Finnish defense. The 8th Army was comprised of the 18th, 56th, 139th, 155th, and 168th Rifle Divisions with each division given its own objective along the northern shore of Lake Lagoda.

Massing south of the lake was the 7th Army, ready to strike across the Karelian Isthmus. The 7th Army, tasked with breaking the Finnish defenses on the Isthmus, was the largest and most powerful Red Army formation in 1939 and boasted between 12 and 14 divisions in the field at the start of the offensive, including the 24th, 43rd, 50th, 70th, 123rd, and 142nd Rifle Divisions. In support of the initial assault would be several tank brigades. Other divisions could be added as necessary: the main reserve was made up of the 138th Rifle Division and the 10th Tank Corps.

Finland, fully aware of the threat from its powerful neighbor, had introduced compulsory military service in 1932 as the army underwent reorganization. Finland's regular army stood at 33,000 officers and men organized into nine infantry, two cavalry, four field

A crewman of a Soviet T-26 light tank poses beside his vehicle in the summer of 1939 wearing double-breasted overalls. These cloth overalls appear to have come in double- and single-breasted versions with both worn with leather crash helmet and goggles. He also wears a pair of leather gauntlets and has a pair of binoculars in the brown leather case around his neck. (Author's collection)

artillery, one antiaircraft, and three coastal artillery regiments. Upon mobilization, this force could be expanded to six divisions with 127,000 men who had all served at least one year under the compulsory military service regime. In addition, there was a 100,000-strong force of reservists plus another 100,000 paramilitary civil guards, under the command of regular army General Kurt Wallenius who had been head of the Finnish Army before 1930. This 400,000-strong regular and paramilitary armed force was supported by the female volunteer organization "Lotta Svärd", that took up rear-echelon roles.

Finland's air force was made up of just over 100 aircraft with many of its planes on the verge of obsolescence. The army had a handful of tanks. Its artillery was made up of a wide variety of medium types, a few heavy guns, and 100 mostly modern antitank guns. Fortunately, the Finns had already begun mobilization when the Soviets attacked; in fact, the Finns had called up the reserves in October for refresher training in the expectation that they would be needed.

The crew of a T-35 multiturreted medium tank examine a map with their commander in the weeks leading up to the Winter War. This huge 45-ton tank had a main turret with a 75mm gun and two turrets fore and aft with 45mm guns and five machine guns. Several countries had developed similar multiturreted tanks but the Soviet Union was the only one to produce them in any quantity. They were to prove ineffective during the Winter War and several were put out of action and used by the Finns in the subsequent 1941–4 Continuation War. (Author's collection)

ORDER OF BATTLE, NOVEMBER 1939

RED ARMY

7th Army

Karelian Isthmus: Commander V. F. Jakolev

19th Corps

24th Rifle Division

43rd Rifle Division

70th Rifle Division

123rd Rifle Division

40th Tank Brigade

50th Corps

40th Rifle Division

90th Rifle Division

142nd Rifle Division

35th Tank Brigade

10th Tank Corps*

1st Tank Brigade

13th Tank Brigade

7th Army Reserve

138th Rifle Division

13th Tank Brigade

8th Army

North of Lake Lagoda, Lagoda Karelia: Commander I. N. Habarov

1st Corps

139th Rifle Division

155th Rifle Division

56th Corps

18th Rifle Division

56th Rifle Division

168th Rifle Division

8th Army Reserve

75th Rifle Division

34th Tank Brigade

9th Army

Central Finland: Commander M. P. Duhanov

47th Corps

122nd Rifle Division

163rd Rifle Division

Special Corps

54th Rifle Division

44th Rifle Division[†]

97th Tank Battalion

14th Army

Murmansk, Northern Front: Commander V. A. Frolov

14th Rifle Division

52nd Rifle Division

104th Mountain Division

* withdrawn from the front by December 20 due to poor performance

† in transit in November 1939

FINNISH ARMY

Army of the Isthmus

General Hugo Österman

II Corps

4th Infantry Division

5th Infantry Division

11th Infantry Division

U-Group

M-Group

L-Group

III Corps

8th Infantry Division

10th Infantry Division

R-Group

Reserve

1st Infantry Division

IV Corps

Lagoda, Karelia and mid- and northern Finland: General J. Hagglund

12th Infantry Division

13th Infantry Division

North Finland Group

General Wiljo Toumpo

Comprising border guards, reservists, civil guards, home guards

Marshal Mannerheim (1867–1951)

Carl Gustaf Emil Mannerheim (in the center-foreground of the photograph) belonged to the Finnish aristocracy which had its roots in Sweden. This "foreign" influence over the Finnish elite largely ended when Finland was brought under the control of Imperial Russia in 1809. His great-grandfather, Count Carl Mannerheim, became the first head of the executive of the newly created Duchy of Finland in the mid-1800s. Carl Gustaf joined the Imperial Russian Army and served in the Chevalier Guard until 1905. He fought in the Russo-Japanese War of 1904–5 and during World War I was commander of a cavalry brigade. From December 1917, when Finland broke away from the rest of the Russian empire, he took command of the anti-Communist White forces. His forces were victorious during the 1918 civil war against Finnish Communists, making him the only successful White commander in the Soviet Civil War of 1918–22. He retired from front-line service in the 1920s when in his mid-50s, but remained extremely influential with the Finnish military, arranging to send young officers to training academies in France and Germany. In 1931, he was made President of the Council of Defense and was able to have more influence over the future of the Finnish Armed Forces. When war with the Soviet Union threatened, the 72-year-old demanded to be made Commander-in-Chief and he led Finland from November 1939 until the end of Continuation War in 1944. He became Finnish President in August 1944 and managed to maintain Finland's independence even after his country's defeat by the Soviet Union.

Red Army machine-gunners undergo training with their Degtyaryov DP-27 light machine gun, 1939. The DP-27 was to serve the Red Army from 1928 until the end of World War II. These men wear the standard winter uniform. The greatcoat and woolen *budenovka* winter hat were to prove inadequate in the extreme temperatures during the winter of 1939/40. (Author's collection)

21

The Lotta Svärd

Formed in 1918 during the Finnish Civil War, the Women's Auxiliary Service was given the name "Lotta Svärd" (LS) in 1920, after a poem about a woman volunteer who provided food to troops during the Finnish War of 1808–9. During the 1920s, the LS had 60,000 members and by 1939, 100,000 women were involved. The Finnish LS was associated with the men's Civil Guard and was trained to perform duties such as drivers, radio operators, air-raid defense, clerks, cooks, laundry workers, and nurses. During the Winter War, their rear-echelon roles allowed more men to be assigned to combat units.

These two young girls are members of Lotte Svärd, the Finnish female volunteer organization raised during the 1918 civil war. (Author's collection)

Two members of Lotta Svärd are part of the early warning system during a Red Air Force bombing raid. From a wooden platform on the outskirts of a Finnish city, they telephone in to the antiaircraft defense coordinator. Both girls are well wrapped up against the winter weather with warm hats and luxuriant-looking fur coats. (Author's collection)

Red Army recruits take their oath of allegiance. Many troops were stationed in the Soviet Far East in 1939 but those stationed near the Finnish border were deemed capable of dealing with the "small" nation. (Author's collection)

Red Army soldiers practice their water-crossing skills, inflating a rubber dinghy. Preparations for the coming war with Finland were haphazard and this kind of equipment would see little or no service in the 1939–40 fighting. Most Soviet troops had seen no combat. (Author's collection)

The Finnish Civil Guard

The Finnish Civil Guard—"Suojeluskunta" or SK—was a paramilitary organization made up largely of ex-fighters of the irregular White forces who had fought in the 1918 civil war. Many of these fighters had joined the regular army post-1918 while other pro-Whites joined the newly formed SK. Members of the regular armed forces were often in the SK as well, although their front-line service took priority. During the interwar period, the Suojeluskunta acted as a training organization for the youth of Finland and organized athletic events and cross-country skiing. Volunteers were given shooting practice and were also trained in heavier weaponry like machine guns and mortars. When the Winter War began, there were about 120,000 members of the SK with 65,000 immediately absorbed into the regular army. The other 55,000 were either too old, too young, or worked in reserved occupations and these men continued to serve in the SK. With their own rifles and uniforms in most cases, this second-line force was a useful addition to the regular army throughout the war. Although they were meant to serve in support roles, on many occasions, they were drafted into the front lines to fight alongside their regular comrades. A strong motivation for SK volunteers to fight to the end was the knowledge that any who fell into Red Army hands would be regarded as "class enemies" and severely treated, even executed, if Finland was occupied.

Soviet Invasion, November 1939

Large Soviet forces had been building up against the Finnish border in the southeast of the country only 20 miles from the Soviet city of Leningrad. The Red Army then crossed the Finnish border at several points, from the far north in Lapland to the Karelian Isthmus in the south. While all the attacks were large scale involving several divisions, the main offensive was against the Karelian Isthmus.

The war began with the artillery of the 7th, 8th, 9th, and 14th Armies unleashing a bombardment all along the 800-mile border between Finland and the Soviet Union. The

Red Army artillerymen in training in the buildup to the war. They are wearing the new type of fur-lined winter coat that was in short supply during the Winter War. Other winter clothing worn by these troops include felt over-boots over the top of the standard leather boots. The artillery pieces are 76mm M1909 mountain guns, a French design used during the war by both the Soviets and the Finns. Some 40 percent of Red Army units sent into Finland had been given little or no training. (Author's collection)

Finland, November 1939

Russian attacks,
30 November 1939–
31 January 1940

Finnish counterattacks,
27 December 1939–
5 January 1940

Finnish dispositions in 1939:

1 'Army of Isthmus', 6 divisions
III Army Corps, left flank
II Army Corps, right flank

2 IV Army Corps, 2 divisions

3 North Finland Group,
home guard units

Tana

Petsamo

104 DIV.

14TH ARMY

Murmansk

Varzino

Ivalo

3

KOLA PENINSULA

122 DIV.

Kandalaksha

88 DIV.

ARCTIC CIRCLE

WHITE SEA

Rovaniemi

Boden

Kemi

Kuusamo

163 DIV.

Kem

9TH ARMY

Oulu

Raate

Raahe

Soumussalmi

44 DIV.

Nadvoitsy

Kuhmo

54 DIV.

Reploa

GULF OF BOTHNIA

Kokkola

Medvezhyegorsk
(Karhumäki)

155 DIV.

Vaasa

FINLAND

2

139 DIV.

8TH ARMY

Vartsila

56 DIV.

Petrozavodsk
(Äänislinna)

18 DIV.

15TH ARMY

168 DIV.

Podporozhye

Tampere

1

LAKE LADOGA

U.S.S.R.

Viipuri
(Vyborg)

MANNERHEIM
LINE

Turku

Koivisto

13TH ARMY

HELSINKI

Volkhov

7TH ARMY

LENINGRAD

Hanko

GULF OF FINLAND

N

0   50   100   250
Kilometres

shelling was followed by the advance of hundreds of thousands of Red Army troops, thousands of armored vehicles, and the bombing of Finnish cities, towns, and villages by hundreds of Red Air Force bombers. Armored columns of tanks and armored cars advanced into Finnish territory up to a depth of 25 miles, as small units of Finns withdrew before them into the forests of eastern Finland. Before long, the narrow forest roads were crammed with wall-to-wall columns of tightly packed armor and trucks. It was then that the highly mobile Finnish troops, usually on skis, attacked the columns in a series of deadly ambushes. This was the pattern of combat in the early days of the war that was repeated up and down the border with isolated Soviet units surrounded, and suffering from the intense cold during the worst Finnish winter since 1878. The flank units guarding the columns were incapable of providing the necessary protection.

The commander of a Red Army tank unit briefs his men before going into action. Soviet officers were constantly under the scrutiny of political commissars and were afraid to make independent decisions as it was just too dangerous. Any defeats were blamed on officers even when they had simply obeyed orders. These crewmen are standing in front of a white-painted T-26 light tank and wear a mixture of clothing including leather crash helmets and *budenovka* winter hats. (Author's collection)

Red Army radio operators use their transceiver to receive instructions from their command headquarters during a 1939 exercise a few months before the invasion of Finland. During the Winter War signalers had great difficulty trying to maintain contact between headquarters and the front-line units who often received confusing instructions via radio and field telephones. As with other aspects of the Red Army's performance in November and December 1939, a shortage of well-trained technicians caused major issues. (Author's collection)

Red Army tankers gather around a T-26 light tank as they prepare to invade Finland. They share out food-parcel treats and one man has a Soviet newspaper. Many Red Army units had had to endure a 200-mile trek from the northwest of Russia to assembly points along the Finnish border. (Author's collection)

This poor-quality photograph issued by the Soviet propaganda agency shows a column of STZ Komsomolets armored tractors moving through deep snow. The Komsomolets was based on the tracked artillery tractors produced by the British Army in the 1920s and 1930s. The STZ, first produced in 1937, had a machine gun in the driver's compartment and could carry six troops in exposed seats behind. (Author's collection)

Red Army advances through the eastern Karelian Isthmus were soon held up by several factors, including the natural obstacles created by the myriad lakes in the region. Gaps between the lakes were sown with mines and tank traps prepared during the buildup to the war. Machine-gun emplacements also covered the corridors that the Red Army had to advance through. When they could not hold their positions any longer, the Finns withdrew to prepared positions.

The fighting around the port of Taipale turned into one of the most decisive battles of the first phase of the war. Taipale, at the eastern end of the Mannerheim Line, was held by the Finnish 10th Division. The Soviet attack on Taipale was led by the 4th, 49th, 142nd, and 150th Rifle Divisions, and the 39th Tank Brigade. Fighting began on December 6 and lasted until the 27th and ended with the Finns still in control of their defensive positions. During the assaults on the Taipale defenses, wave after wave of Soviet troops were killed in front of the Finnish machine guns. A great deal of Soviet military materiel was also lost with 18 of the 39th Tank Brigade's 50 tanks destroyed. Troop losses on both sides were heavy with 10,000 Soviets killed while the Finns suffered over 2,000 casualties. The resulting stalemate in the battle for Taipale led to the Red Army switching its main attack to the opposite end of the Mannerheim Line. Finnish forces now held their positions until the fighting on the Karelian Isthmus resumed two months later.

To the west of Taipale along the Mannerheim Line was the village of Summa which was held by the Finnish 3rd Division. With its surrounding defenses of 41 concrete bunkers, Summa was one of the strongest defensive positions in the Mannerheim Line. The fortified village was on the road to the port of Viipuri and stopping the Soviet advance here was vital to Finland's survival. In the first assault 20 Soviet tanks broke through Finnish defenses but then drove around aimlessly without infantry support. The Finns had allowed the tanks to penetrate their lines to then hit the following Red Army infantry hard. Poor communications between Soviet units meant that the Finns could deal with the frontal attacks of the Soviet troops first and once these had been repelled, they could then deal with the enemy tanks which were now isolated and vulnerable. Poor planning for the attack against Summa was demonstrated by the 138th Division tanks all running out of fuel. With few antitank weapons at this stage of the war, Finnish troops attacked the tanks with whatever they could, including the homemade Molotov cocktails.

A pair of whitewashed T-26 light tanks move across rough country on the first day of the invasion, November 30, 1939. One tank is the standard model while the rear tank has a frame aerial mounted around the turret. By the late 1930s, the Soviet Union boasted the largest armored force in the world, with 10,000 of these tanks produced up to 1939. (Author's collection)

In Profile:
BT-5 Light Tank and &
BA-10 Armored Car

Soviet BT-5 Model 1934 Light Tank, 34th Light Tank Brigade, Lemetti South, February 1940. This light tank's suspension is based on the US Christie system. It is well armed with a 45mm main gun in its early-pattern turret. It has arrived at the front in the standard factory green and has been hastily camouflaged with a coat of whitewash which is already fading.

Soviet BA-10 Armored Car, 163rd Rifle Division, Soumussalmi, January 1940. This heavy BA-10 armored car of the doomed 163rd Rifle Division has, like many other armored vehicles in the Winter War, had a mottled white camouflage scheme applied over the original factory green finish.

Red Army BA-10 heavy armored cars advance in column along a wide forest road on the approaches to the Finnish border in late November 1939. Once they crossed into Finland, most roads would be much smaller and these vehicles would have to travel single file with forests all around them. The BA-10 was a new vehicle developed in 1938 and was well armed with a 45mm 20-K main gun in the turret. The vehicles have been given a good covering of white paint to cover the standard green paintwork before moving towards the front. (Author's collection)

A Red Army machine-gunner pushes a heavy Maxim M1910 through the snow on a sledge made from a pair of skis. Some machine guns were mounted on a more substantial sledge that was usually towed by its crew rather than pushed along. (Author's collection)

General Kirill Meretskov (1897–1968)

A 20-year-old Kirill Meretskov joined the Bolshevik Party in 1917 and served in the Red Army from 1920. Like many officers who fought in the Russian Civil War of 1918–22, he rose through the ranks over the next 20 years. In 1939, he was in command of the Leningrad Military District and was given responsibility for the early operations against Finland. By December 9, 1939 Meretskov was deemed to have failed and his command fell to the General Staff under Marshal Kliment Voroshilov. He was given command of the 7th Army on the southern sector of the Finnish–Soviet border in January 1940, in charge of Soviet forces trying to penetrate the Finns' Mannerheim Line. The overwhelming forces available to Meretskov meant that his troops were able to breach the Finnish defenses and take their objective, the port of Viiborg. Meretskov's earlier failures were forgotten and he was awarded the Hero of the Soviet Union and promoted to army general, the second-highest rank in the Red Army, in 1940.

A volunteer of the Finnish "People's" Army wearing his Finnish Army M27 brown woolen tunic and a Red Army winter hat. According to the limited evidence about this "puppet" army of Communist Finns living in the Soviet Union, its members were armed with standard Mosin–Nagant M1891 rifles and many were issued with Polish Army greatcoats captured by the Red Army in September 1939. (Author's collection)

In the early stages of the war the Soviets used the time-honored strategy of creating a "puppet" Terijoki government led by friendly Finnish politicians. Here the Soviet Foreign Minister Molotov signs the "Mutual Assistance and Friendship" agreement on behalf of his country in the captured Finnish village of Terijoki, just across the Soviet–Finnish border. Signing on behalf of the pro-Soviet Finns and was Otto Kuusinen (standing at right), a renegade Communist during the 1918 civil war. Looking on are Voroshilov and Stalin. (Author's collection)

The Mannerheim Line

The strategic Karelian Isthmus had long been seen as the obvious route into Finland, especially in the case of Imperial Russia and now the Soviet Union. Blocking the Karelian Isthmus was the 88-mile-long Finnish defense line named after the country's leader, the Mannerheim Line. It was compared to far more substantial European fortifications like the French Maginot Line and the German Siegfried Line but it was not at the same level. It was constructed with the help of Belgian engineer officer General Badout, beginning in 1927. This line was not really a continuous line but was made up of a belt of defenses which included trenches, antitank traps, barriers, and strongpoints. In some sections the line was reinforced by neat lines of large boulders which had been dragged from the forests on carts. Its 66 machine-gun posts included 44 which had been built in the 1920s and were of poor construction. The Mannerheim Line ran from Taipale at the mouth of the Vuoski River on Lake Lagoda to the Baltic Sea near the fortress of Koivosto. A third of the defensive belt was made up of the Vuoski River with land defenses linking two lakes, the Ayranaan and Muolaan. Then came the exposed Summa sector which was defended by some larger concrete gun emplacements. Although these defensive works were substantial compared to those on other sections of the line, none was capable of sustaining heavy artillery fire. Another lake formed a small length of the line before its defenses came under the protection of the guns of Koivosto Fortress. Along with the physical defense works that had been built along the line, marshes, rivers, and lakes formed a formidable barrier of themselves. Marshal Mannerheim was quoted as saying that the real Mannerheim Line was really a "Finnish soldier standing in the snow."

A Finnish soldier armed only with his rifle defends a snow-covered trench along the Mannerheim Line, December 1939. During the conflict, it suited the Red Army leadership to exaggerate the strength of the Mannerheim Line. At the same time the Finns underplayed the significance of the defensive system and said it was the bravery of the Finnish soldier holding back the Reds. The most formidable defenses were north of Summa where the trenches and fortifications protected the vital Lahde Road. (Author's collection)

The 67-year-old Finnish President, Kyosti Kallio, visits a front-line machine-gun post on the Mannerheim Line in early November 1939. He took a keen interest in the performance of the Finnish armed forces and was seen at the front on several occasions during the war. Kallio served as president from March 1937 until a few weeks before his death on December 19, 1940. (Author's collection)

December 22, 1939: Finnish troops clamber over a disabled T-26 light tank destroyed during the Soviet offensive into the Karelian Isthmus. A large number of Soviet tanks were put out of action and many were later repaired and added to the Finnish armory post-1940. (Author's collection)

This Finnish crew of a Maxim M1932 7.62mm heavy machine gun operating in South Karelia are well camouflaged in their white coveralls over their gray woolen uniforms. The M1932 was a slightly modified version of the original German M1910 developed by Aimo Lahti, a Finnish armaments manufacturer who changed the feed mechanism on the gun to take metal ammunition belts instead of the original cloth belts. (Author's collection)

Soviet Bombing Campaign

The world had seen the effect of bombing campaigns during prewar conflicts in Ethiopia and Spain. It had also seen the effect of the Luftwaffe's bombing campaign during the September 1939 invasion of Poland. Red Army Air Force theorists strongly believed that bombing civilian targets would cause a loss of morale amongst the Finns. So as soon as the war began, on November 30, Red Air Force bombers from Soviet bases in Estonia bombed the Finnish capital at 1430 hours. Although the targets were Helsinki's railway station, docks, and the airport, some bombs fell on residential areas and hit schools, houses, and apartment blocks:

This Finnish air raid protection poster of 1938 says "*Ilmasta! Uhkaa! Vaara!*" that translates as "Danger Threatens from the Sky!" ("All Citizens to Civil Defense Work!"). The symbolic VSS Civil Defense Force member is protecting the Finnish population from the Red Air Force air raids. (Author's collection)

These Finnish antiaircraft guns—Swedish 75mm Bofors M29s—are positioned on the outskirts of Helsinki in the months leading up to the war. Helsinki was protected from the autumn of 1939 by the 1st Antiaircraft Regiment that had four heavy batteries with three to four guns each, assisted by a light antiaircraft battery armed with machine guns, with gunners trained to operate against aircraft. (Author's collection)

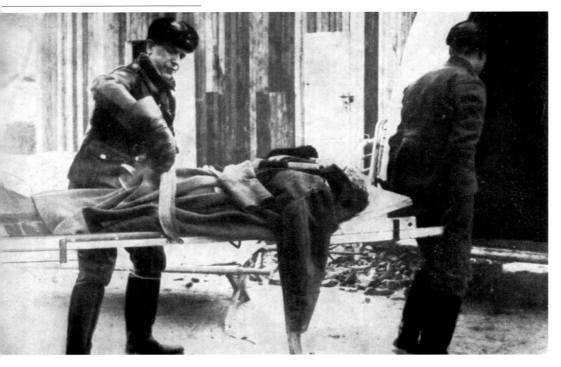

A female patient at a Finnish Red Cross hospital wounded during a Red Air Force bombing raid. The original caption says that the hospital was bombed even though it was clearly marked with red crosses. It was reported after the war that 957 civilians were killed during the regular Red Air Force raids on Finnish cities and towns. (Author's collection)

65 Finns were killed and 130 were wounded. Other raids were taking place over the towns Viipuri, Korka, and Hanko. Over the two days of bombing at least 80 civilians were killed but the human losses and material damage only served to make the Finns more determined to resist, according to eyewitnesses. The Finnish weather now came to some extent to the rescue of the population with the shortness of daylight hours at the height of winter hampering raids.

The first snows fell on December 2 with two days of blizzards following that saw many potential bombing targets obscured by the drifts. Regardless of the conditions, the Red Air Force was to continue its raids against civilian targets although some attacks against Helsinki had to be canceled. This gave the emergency services time to try and repair some of the damage caused during the first two days of heavy bombing. Incendiary bombs were put out and important roads were cleared of rubble to allow vehicles to pass. Many women and children fled to the shelter of the forests during the early raids and most were properly evacuated during the lull in bombing. Other measures taken included the removal of patients who could be moved out of the main hospitals. Better air raid shelters were prepared and firefighting volunteers were formed into groups to fight the fires. The Red Army Air Force was continually frustrated by the lack of military targets during the war so instead continued to target towns and cities. Some military targets were hit on the Karelian Isthmus and around Lake Lagoda, but did little damage to the dispersed Finnish units. Finnish communications were also targeted by Soviet bombers with mixed results, while the Finns became adept at repairing any damage. Field Marshal Mannerheim claimed that 150,000 bombs weighing 7,500 tons fell on Finland during the war.

During the initial bombing campaign, the Finns suffered 700 civilian dead and 1,400 wounded. The Finnish leader complimented the behavior of the Finnish people, saying: "Total air war in our country was met by a calm and intelligent population whom danger merely steeled and united more strongly." Soviet records show that they claimed to have mounted 2,075 bombing raids on 516 targets during the war. Viipuri, the strategic port, came in for particularly heavy treatment with 12,000 bombs falling on it according to the Soviets. Soviet propaganda never mentioned the bombing of civilian targets although the relative lack of Finnish military targets shows that the bombs they claimed to have dropped had to land somewhere. The relative failure of the Red Air Force bombing campaign led Soviet theorists to conclude that strategic bombing was not a good idea. In reality, the lack of major targets was an issue and the Soviets decided to reduce the number of bombers sent on raids. Previously there had been between 40 to 50 bombers on each raid and this was reduced to 25 to 30. At the same time, the number of fighter escorts was increased to make the bombing formations a harder target for the Finnish pilots, and the bombers could concentrate on the accuracy of their bombing rather than worrying about enemy fighter attacks.

A Finnish mother and her two young children saying goodbye to their family as they travel by train to the safety of Sweden, November 1939. Bombs had fallen on Helsinki on the first day of the war and many who could went into temporary exile for the duration of the conflict. Pictures like this went around the world and sympathies grew for Finland in the western press. (Author's collection)

Finnish Counteroffensive

There were discussions amongst the Finnish commanders of taking advantage of the Red Army's failures by launching a counteroffensive in the Karelian Isthmus. General Hugo Österman proposed an offensive on December 11 but he was rebuffed by Mannerheim. The Finnish leader was, however, persuaded to support the idea of an attack and plans were hastily prepared as from the 20th. It was decided to commit the untested 6th Division, the Finns' reserve formation, in the Isthmus. When the offensive began at 0630 on December 23, the objectives were to attack Soviet-held territory in the Isthmus from two directions and envelop the demoralized Red Army divisions. The 6th Division would attack first from the northwest and would then be joined by units of the 4th Division striking to the south, with the 1st and 5th Divisions attacking from the north.

This well-known poster issued by the British aid organization, the Finland Fund, cannot be any clearer in its support for Finland. At the bottom of the original poster is a panel which asks for donations: "To Arms Against Tyranny!" The Finnish cause—a David and Goliath struggle—was popular with most of the western world and many volunteers went to fight for the Finns. (Author's collection)

As soon as the offensive began, problems surfaced, with the initial artillery bombardment lasting only 10 minutes. The few Finnish artillery pieces did not have the range to properly support the offensive and mortars sent to supplement the field guns arrived with the wrong ammunition, and Finnish units did not have much idea where the concentrations of enemy troops were due to a total lack of reconnaissance. With the Red Air Force dominating the skies, the Finns did not want to waste their precious aircraft trying to find the Soviet positions. Further confusion was caused by the lack of telephone communication, with lines cut and the Finns having to rely on messages carried from unit to unit by runners. When the Finns did advance toward Soviet positions, they were faced by enemy tanks with no weapons to counter them. General Österman had been ordered to call off the attack if no substantial gains were made and he did so in the late afternoon of the first day. Some units had even managed to advance two and half miles but the Finns had suffered 1,300 casualties, with 200 men suffering frostbite. The 6th Division returned to their lines and the "disappointing" and costly offensive came to an inglorious and abrupt end.

A patrol of Finnish troops wearing the standard steel helmet of the Finnish Army in 1939, the M16 German model. Their white coats are worn over the top of their M/36 overcoats and only one soldier has the usual white helmet cover. Boots appear to be the curled-up-toe type worn by the Laps in the far north of the country. (Author's collection)

North of Lake Lagoda, 1939–40

To weaken the Finnish defenses on the Karelian Isthmus, the Soviet 8th Army crossed the Finnish–Soviet border on December 7 from various points to the north of Lake Lagoda. Lake Lagoda, north of the Karelian Isthmus, provided a natural obstacle to the Red Army. However, the territory above the lake could provide an opportunity for the Soviets to outflank the Finns holding out on the isthmus.

The Red Army command estimated that any attack might yield several possibilities, including the drawing off of Finnish troops from defending the isthmus to the south of Lake Lagoda. Secondly, if the Finns did not reinforce their defenses around the lake, then the advancing Red Army could trap the defenders in the isthmus in a deadly pincer movement. A third, far more optimistic scenario, would see the six Soviet divisions launching an offensive to reach the Finnish capital, Helsinki.

One of the more colorful Finnish officers to serve during the Winter War was Captain Aarne Edward Juutilainen, "The Terror of Morocco," who had joined the French Foreign Legion in 1930. After five years in North Africa, he returned to Finland and fought in the battle of Kollaa which lasted from December 7, 1939 until March 13, 1940. He used his anti-guerrilla experience from Morocco to good effect, training a special unit that was given the title of "The Moroccan Company." During the battle a single Finnish division, the 12th, fought off Red Army infantry divisions and a tank brigade. He became a national hero and went on to fight in the Continuation War of 1941–4 and was wounded three times. (Author's collection)

This Finnish sniper is using a captured Soviet Mosin–Nagant M1931 rifle with telescopic sights. The Finns had their own sniper rifle, the M28/30 which was itself an adaptation of the Soviet Mosin–Nagant. Here the sniper has not donned his white coveralls but would not go into action without them. (Author's collection)

Finnish Sergeant Pekka Niemi, a former world ski-running champion, served in one of the Finnish "suicide squads" which operated behind enemy lines. His rifle appears to be a captured Soviet AVS-36 automatic rifle, the forerunner of the SVT, that entered service with the Red Army in 1938. (Author's collection)

Thirty-four-year-old Simo Hayha, known as "White Death," was the most prolific Finnish sniper of the war with a total of over 500 kills to his name. He served under Lieutenant Juutilainen in the 6th Company, 34th Infantry Regiment, and chalked up this tally in 100 days of fighting. His sniper rifle was a standard Finnish-produced Mosin–Nagant M28/30. He used iron sights rather than the conventional telescopic sights, which meant raising his head slightly. He was also armed with a Suomi KP/-31 sub-machine gun—many of his kills were achieved with this close-quarter weapon. On December 21 he achieved his highest daily count with 25 kills entered in his journal that night. His career was ended on March 13, 1940 when he was hit by an explosive bullet that took away much of the lower left side of his face. Although left for dead, he survived his horrific injury but took 14 months to recover with 26 operations. In total, he was credited with 542 kills and rightly became a legend in Finland and in the international press. (Author's collection)

Finnish troops well camouflaged in their white coveralls. The machine-gunner has acquired a Soviet Degtyaryov DP-27 light machine gun while his comrade is armed with a Finnish-made Suomi KP/-31 (Suomi-konepistooli m/31), regarded as one of the best sub-machine guns in the world and which were issued in large numbers to the Finnish Army. (Author's collection)

Finnish troops during the battle for the Ilomantsi region, December 10–16. The 400 Finns defending Ilomantsi to the north of Lake Lagoda were attacked by 14,000 Soviets supported by 140 field guns and 45 tanks. Reinforcements were sent to aid the Finns with the newly raised "Tavela Group" under Colonel Paavo Talvela. The fighting around Ilomantsi gained the nickname of the "Sausage War" when starving Soviet soldiers stopped to eat sausages from a captured field kitchen rather than continuing their attack. (Author's collection)

Finnish infantrymen wearing gasmasks. In late December, poison gas was allegedly used by the Red Army in the Lake Lagoda sector. The Finns were totally unprepared for this mode of warfare and ordered 60,000 gasmasks from Great Britain. According to reports, however, the extreme cold condensed the gas and made it ineffective, leading the Soviets to cease using it. There were 13 reports of gas use by the Red Army in the war, always strongly denied by the Soviet Union. (Author's collection)

The Soviet 155th Division was given the objective of Ilomantsi which it reached after fierce fighting, on December 9. Two divisions, the 18th and the 168th, were to advance to Kitela in separate columns, one taking a northern route and the other a southern route. Both divisions reached the town on December 12 and dug in before moving farther west. The 56th Division had reached its objective at Kollaa on the day it crossed the border but the fighting for the town was to continue for many weeks. Soviet artillery was reported to be firing 40,000 shells a day into the Finnish positions but the Finns could only reply with 1,000 shells. The 12th Finnish Division holding Kollaa was reinforced by a few smaller units and managed to stop any further advances by the 56th until the end of the war. Soviet losses during the fighting around Kollaa were estimated at 8,000 killed and wounded while the Finns lost a proportionately high number of casualties with 1,500 killed or wounded. Finnish units were pushed out of their original positions by the sheer volume of force of the attacking Red Army during the early fighting. However, over the next several weeks, the Finns, with a series of small but effective counterattacks, managed to push the Soviets back. The resolve of the 12th Division to hold their positions surprised the Soviet commanders but not the Finnish. When General Hagglund asked the Finnish commander, Captain Aarne Juutilainen, if his defenses around Kollaa would hold, he received a defiant reply: "Kollaa will hold unless the order is to run away!"

Finnish ski troops look curiously at a disabled OT-26 Soviet flamethrower tank adapted from the double-turreted version of the T-26 light tank. The left turret has been removed and plated over, while the flamethrower turret is positioned where the right turret was. These tanks were used in the chemical tank battalions, with 52 allocated to each mechanized corps. The main weakness of the OT-26 was the short 25-meter range of the flame it produced which meant it had to close with the enemy to be decisive and was often destroyed by the Finns in the process. (Author's collection)

The Red Army's 75th and 139th Rifle Divisions had succeeded in taking the town of Tolvajarvi on December 12 with a powerful force of 45,000 troops, 335 artillery pieces, and 140 tanks, but now they came under fierce attack from a Finnish force made up of seven infantry battalions under Colonel Tavela. His forces were much smaller than the enemy's with only 7,000 to 9,000 men and 20 artillery pieces, but using their well-tested tactics of ambush and envelopment of the static Soviets, the Finns deployed 4,000 troops against a 20,000-strong enemy formation. At the end of the fighting the Soviet forces had been largely destroyed, losing 20 tanks, 39 armored vehicles, and 30 field guns.

The Soviet 168th Rifle Division had crossed the border and advanced along the northern shore of Lake Lagoda. They captured the villages of Salmi and Pitkaranta before reaching the Finnish defenses at Kitela on December 12. Meanwhile, the 18th Division advanced across the frontier to the north of the 168th, taking the town of Uomaa and reaching the Finnish defenses at Kitela at about the same time. The Soviet advance then faltered and the two Red Army divisions began to organize a series of ten defensive positions. These were known by the Finnish troops throughout the Winter War as "*mottis*" which became a familiar term to the outside world. *Motti*, literally "a pile of logs cut ready for use," was a Finnish tactic to immobilize, segment, surround, and destroy an enemy far larger than them; this evolved to mean an enemy "pocket" or the German *kessel* (lit. cauldron). However, the Finns were to find that not all Soviet troops were prepared to give up the fight easily and IV Corps under Major-General Woldemar Hagglund had to fight for every inch of ground.

This abandoned Soviet T-37A light amphibious tank has shed one of its tracks and its two-man crew have either escaped or frozen to death inside it. Temperatures inside tanks fell to −30°C and with no internal heating, they became death traps. Engines also seized up in the cold and keeping the engine running impacted the precious fuel. The T-37A was a 3.2-ton amphibious tank with wooden floats on the side and was armed with a single DT 7.62mm machine gun. During the war, 29 of these tanks were captured with some put into service by the Finns from 1941. (Sa-Kuva-123846)

Abandoned snow-covered Red Army materiel lies at the side of a forest road in the East Lemetti *motti* that includes two field guns and a BT-5 medium tank. Besides the usual horrors faced by Soviet troops trapped in a *motti*, they also had to endure an influenza bug which devastated their ranks. (Author's collection)

The Red Army defensive positions around Kitela, Uomaa, and Lemetti were well organized and included 200 tanks. It was the sheer scale of the Kitela defensive position that set it apart from other Soviet strongpoints as it covered 20 square miles. A big difference between these *mottis* and those in other sectors was the defiance shown by the Soviet soldiers defending them, determined that they would not share the same fate as their comrades at Suomussalmi and other battlefields to the north. Their resistance surprised the Finns who were used to leaving Soviet soldiers stuck in their defenses to starve and freeze before attacking them. However, despite their bravery, the Soviets were soon running out of food and other supplies as all attempts of resupply, except by air, had failed. On February 17 the troops of the 18th Rifle Division in the two Lemetti *mottis* were ordered to break out. The desperate attempt to break Finnish encirclement was partially successful but the Soviets suffered horrendous casualties: more than 3,000 were killed, including some 300 officers, and the HQ unit that included four female typists. The surviving 18th Rifle Division troops surrendered on February 18. The 34th Tank Brigade held out for a few weeks before giving up the fight on the 29th. When the Finns entered the *motti*, they counted 4,300 dead on the battlefield with an unknown number of dead under the snow. War booty taken by the Finns included 128 tanks, 91 artillery pieces, 120 motor vehicles, and 62 field kitchens.

The Soviet 168th Division dug in around the perimeter of the "Great *Motti*" at Kitela was proving an impossible nut for the Finns to crack. This was largely down to the fact that supplies could get through, brought across the frozen Lake Lagoda from the south or by air. Attempts to get ammunition and food to the other *mottis* farther east from across the Soviet border all failed as supply columns were constantly ambushed by the Finns. Desperate Soviet defenders in the Great *Motti* fought each other over the airdropped supplies. Meanwhile, horse-drawn supply wagons were picked off by Finnish troops on the banks of Lake Lagoda. Despite heavy losses in the *motti* and amongst the supply troops, the 168th manage to hold out until the end of war.

A Finnish soldier in full winter gear examines the damaged exhaust of an abandoned Soviet T-26 light tank. Most captured tanks were described as "junk" by the Finns due to their poor servicing. During the Continuation War of 1941–4, the Finns relied heavily on reconditioned tanks captured in the Winter War. (Author's collection)

This close-up of a Finnish soldier about to go on patrol with the ubiquitous Molotov cocktail on the right and a Finnish-designed satchel charge on the left. The satchel charge was developed in 1936 by Captain Kaarlo Tuuma; its 5kg TNT charge could penetrate 12mm of armor plate. It was produced during the Winter War in three sizes—2, 3, and 4 kilograms—which made it difficult to throw any distance. Casualty rates amongst the "suicide squads" using any of the hand-held weapons was high with casualty rates reaching 70 percent. So many Molotov cocktails were produced in 1939 that the supply of locally resourced bottles began to run out. The Finnish State Liquor Board rushed 40,000 unused bottles to the front to keep production going. (Author's collection)

A pair of Soviet "Betka" BT-7 tanks bogged down during the fight for the *mottis* of January and February 1940. The BT-7 was an improvement on the BT-5 with a more powerful engine, an improved gearbox, and slightly improved armor protection. US Christie-designed suspension gave the BT-7 good maneuverability but the even better traction could not save tanks from getting stuck. These tanks have formed into a laager defense with their guns pointing in various directions to repulse Finnish attacks. (Author's collection)

Major-General Paavo Talvela (1897–1973)

One of the romantic figures that emerged during the Winter War was Finnish Major-General Talvela, the "Lawrence of the North" as the British press christened him, after T. E. Lawrence (of Arabia fame). He was a military maverick who had resigned on several occasions during his military career, usually on a point of honor. When war broke out in November 1939, Talvela asked to be removed from his desk job in Helsinki and sent to the front. He was given command of what became the "Group Talvela," formed from a regiment of the 7th Division. Talvela was given the task of defending the Tolvajarvi sector from the Red Army's 139th Division and later the 75th Division. This difficult mission was achieved by a variety of tactics which managed to push back the superior Soviet forces. During the early fighting around Tolvajarvi in December 1939, this former champion ski-runner formed an elite 250-strong unit of ski commandos. His handpicked troops were dressed in white camouflage suits and white-covered steel helmets and armed with machine pistols and 250 rounds of ammunition. With 10 days' rations in their backpacks and lambskin sleeping bags, this unit, commonly called the "Suicide Squad," launched long-range patrols behind enemy lines. Their main target, other than isolated Red Army units, was the Murmansk–Leningrad railway line that brought up troops and supplies into northern Finland. Press reports claimed that the "Suicide Squad" did significant damage to the railway line and reached as far as the Red Army base at Kandalaksha on the White Sea.

A Soviet soldier, his face haggard and gaunt, gobbles down some bread after being taken prisoner. Some Soviet troops were terrified that when they fell into Finnish hands, as their commanders had told them that if captured, they would be flayed alive. In most cases, Red Army soldiers were treated well and had more to fear from a return to their homeland than any treatment they would receive in the prison camps. (Author's collection)

This column of demoralized and exhausted Soviet troops trudge into captivity. The Red Army in Finland in 1939 was a mix of "elite" units like the 44th Division and poorly trained, raw conscripts. While thousands of Soviet troops were in Finnish captivity in December 1939, the Soviet propaganda machine was awarding 2,600 medals to "heroes" of the war. (Author's collection)

This Finnish leaflet/poster was to the point in appealing to Red Army troops to give up the fight—"Through Capture, Freedom!"—and gave the starving Soviet soldier an alternative to dying for the Motherland. One of the main reasons that only 6,000 of the 1.2 million Soviet troops in the war surrendered was fear for their families— fatalistically, it was preferable to die a "hero" than risk the consequences for their families if they surrendered. (Author's collection)

This Finnish mountain gun in a timber casemate ranges on Soviet lines during the battle at the frozen lake of Kiantajärvi near Suomussalmi. A motorized unit of Finns formed from a machine-gun platoon and mounted on five lorries with a single antiaircraft gun defeated a much larger enemy force of 400 men on December 30 at the lake. Although the Finns were outnumbered, they were more heavily armed and annihilated the lightly armed Soviets. (Author's collection)

Battle of Suomussalmi

Suomussalmi is in the center of Finland along the Finnish–Soviet border and was the objective of the Soviet 9th Army at the start of the war. The 163rd Rifle Division was given the task of taking the strategic village and crossed the border on November 30. Just as on other fronts, the powerful Red Army columns faced little initial resistance as the Finns withdrew in front of them.

Finnish machine-gunners well kitted out for cold weather employ twin Degtyaryov DT light machine guns taken from a crashed Soviet plane. The DT was designed for tanks but was also used as the defensive armament of Polikarpov R-5 and R-Z light bombers. (Author's collection)

Finnish artillerymen manhandle their medium artillery piece in a blizzard after their astounding victory over the Red Army at Lake Kiantajärvi near Suomussalmi, to redeploy to a new firing position. Most Finnish artillery pieces were captured by the Whites during the civil war of 1918. Each Finnish regiment supposedly had 36 guns and 1,813 troops on strength, along with 40 motor vehicles and 615 bicycles! (Author's collection)

A Finnish ski soldier checks over a Red Air Force R-5 army cooperation plane abandoned near Suomussalmi, January 1940. Its crew have made a half-hearted attempt to camouflage it before hastily retreating. (Author's collection)

Finnish soldiers examine a disabled Red Army T-20 Komsomolets prime mover which has run into a snowdrift with its tarpaulin cover to provide protection against the freezing weather. Designed in 1936 and entering service in 1937, the T-20 was part of the Red Army motorization program. It towed artillery pieces with the gun crew riding in the row of seats at either side while the drivers protected them with two DT machine guns. The intention was that 60 prime movers would be available to the artillery units in each rifle division. (Author's collection)

Finnish ski troops walk past a line of T-26 light tanks destroyed in the fighting around Suomussalmi on January 7, 1940. The long-running battle of Suomussalmi ran from December 7, 1939 until January 8, 1940. Both the Red Army and the Finns each committed some 20,000 troops with other units in reserve. Photographs of lines of destroyed Soviet armor in the snow were shown all over the world. (Author's collection)

The 163rd advanced southwestward toward Suomussalmi along the Raate Road where it planned to regroup before advancing further into Finland. The ultimate objective was the city of Oulu which would effectively cut Finland in two. Facing the 163rd Division was a single independent battalion of Finns, the Er.P 15, which had been split up into company-sized units. The 163rd Division was soon strung out in a single-file column over five miles of narrow forest road and as the Soviet tanks and trucks advanced deeper into the forest, the Finns, usually on skis, attacked them at various points. The attackers broke from the cover of the forest, shooting up tanks and transport vehicles which then blocked the narrow roads, splitting the column into segments. Many of these isolated segments were overrun before the Finns melted back into the forest. The surviving units found themselves in a desperate situation—surrounded, running out of rations, and freezing to death. Vehicles turned into death traps as the temperatures plummeted, while the Finnish troops waited for the opportune moment to strike: when they finally did, using sub-machine guns, rifles, grenades, and fighting knives, the slaughter was almost total.

Finnish troops examine a captured 76mm M1936 divisional gun or semi-universal gun at Suomussalmi. This modern gun which entered service in 1936 doubled as a field gun and an antiaircraft gun. It could take shells from older 76mm guns which allowed the Red Army to utilize its large stocks of this caliber ammunition. In 1939 every Soviet rifle division had a heavy gun and a light gun battalion with the latter having three batteries of four guns each. (Sa-Kuva-4764)

This BA-10 heavy armored car was captured by the Finns on December 30 in an attack at Lake Kiantajärvi in the vicinity of the Suomussalmi battleground. BA-10s were produced from 1938 and were armed with a main 45mm turret gun and two light machine guns. They were effective and any captured examples were immediately put into action by the Finns. (Author's collection)

On December 20, the commander of the 163rd Division, Andrei Zelentov, requested permission to break out of the Finnish *motti* and withdraw back to the border. Ordinarily such a request would have been a death sentence, but Zelentov wanted to save as many of his men possible. His superiors, however, denied his request and instead proposed to send part of the 44th Division as a relief force to break the siege. This relief force was made up of the 1st Battalion of the 305th Rifle Regiment and the 3rd Battalion of the 662nd Rifle Regiment. However, due to confusion at Red Army headquarters, the entire 44th Division was deployed down the Raate Road on January 1, 1940. It did not take long for the 44th to encounter the same difficulties as the 163rd had: the Finns used their usual tactics to isolate sections of the Soviet column. The 44th managed to make some progress along the Raate Road despite the Finnish attacks but was halted at Haukila, seven miles from Suomussalmi.

Finnish units from the 9th Division were then organized into four squadrons named after their respective commanders to begin coordinated attacks against the 44th, their attacks to concentrate on Haukila where the majority of the 44th forces were digging in in preparation for the expected Finnish offensive. In the meantime, the Soviets were reinforced with the arrival of the 3rd NKVD Regiment. The Finns had laid mines between the isolated units of the 44th to prevent any back-and-forth movement along the road. On the 6th the Finns began their *motti* tactics, firing from the cover of the forest at several points along the enemy column. Although the Soviets did their best to form defensive formations along the narrow road, they never knew where the next attack was coming from. After two days'

This looks like a "grotesque tableau" with a Finnish ski soldier pausing beside a pile of frozen Red Army soldiers. Isolated Soviet units suffered massive casualties from frostbite and hypothermia. Poor-quality uniforms and the often complete lack of shelter resulted in many horrific scenes like this. (Author's collection)

fighting, the Red Army units had suffered heavy casualties and at night temperatures fell to −40°C and many exposed Soviet troops standing to their arms literally froze to death. By the 7th, the 44th was in an equally desperate situation as the 163rd at Suomussalmi: the fate of the two divisions was sealed.

The 163rd was all but destroyed as a fighting force and few of its men ever returned to Soviet lines, with thousands of troops lost. Once the grim body count had been done by the Finns, the sheer scale of their victory over the 44th and 163rd Divisions became obvious. Some 27,000 Red Army troops were dead and their bodies, according to witnesses, "were stacked like cordwood in the forests." The 44th was totally annihilated during its efforts to relieve the 163rd from its death trap. Amongst the war booty taken by the Finns were 102 field guns, 43 tanks, 300 vehicles, and 1,170 horses. The victory was not without cost to the Finns who lost 900 men during the battle. Their losses were harder to bear: the Finns did not see their men as expendable and replacements were in short supply. Whatever the cost to the Finns, the destruction of the two Soviet divisions was seen as a major victory for the embattled country. Helsinki celebrated the victory with church bells ringing out and national flags flying from most buildings.

Colonel Hjalmar J. Siilasvuo who had planned and led the destruction of the Soviet divisions was promoted to general. He was not allowed much time to savor his victory as he was immediately dispatched to the south to help defend Kuhmo, where the Soviet 54th Division's advance had been halted on December 20 and its troops forced to establish a number of defensive positions. From January 28 until the end of the war in mid-March, the 54th came under constant attack from Finnish forces. However, the Finns were short of

This Soviet soldier caught in the open during the fighting around Suomussalmi has frozen to death during the night. Some soldiers tried to ease the discomfort of the freezing conditions by drinking vodka; however, the effects of alcohol led them to believe that they were warmer than they were and thousands fell asleep which meant that they soon froze to death. (Author's collection)

Finnish soldiers stand guard over a large group of Soviet prisoners from the 44th Division, January 1940. The destruction of the "elite" Red Army formation at Suomussalmi was seen as the most important Finnish victory during the Winter War. (Author's collection)

This 1939 Finnish propaganda leaflet was dropped over Red Army lines. The soldier displays a list of rewards for bringing weaponry over to the Finnish lines: a revolver is worth 100 rubles, a rifle 150 rubles, a sub-machine gun 400 rubles, a machine gun 1,500 rubles and, top of the list, a tank 10,000 rubles. In reality, there were enough abandoned tanks and materiel lying around the forests to warrant this offer invalid. (Author's collection)

troops and often had to rely on former border units. General Siilasvuo's 9th Division was one such unit and proved far weaker than the Soviet 54th Division it was attacking, suffering shortages of artillery and ammunition. The Soviet 54th Division was therefore able to hold out until the peace treaty was signed. During the siege of the Kuhmo *motti*, the Red Army tried to relieve the besieged 54th with a newly formed 18,000-strong ski brigade. The 54th's commander had the foresight to build an airstrip at the start of the siege and Red Air Force planes managed to fly in supplies which also assisted the defenders in holding out.

General Hjalmar Siilasvuo, the 47-year-old victor of Suomussalmi, studies a map of the battlefield, January 1940. The veteran commander had seen service in the German military during World War I, in the Finnish Jäger Corps, from 1915. He commanded Finnish forces in the Suomussalmi region when the Red Army invaded and fought them along the Raate Road and then at Suomussalmi where his troops totally destroyed the 163rd and 44th Soviet Divisions. (Author's collection)

General Grigory Kulik (1890–1950)

Born in Ukraine in 1890, Grigory Kulik served in the Russian Imperial Army in World War I as an NCO in the artillery. He became a close confidant of Joseph Stalin during the Russian Civil War and was given the command of the artillery at the battle of Tsaritsyn in 1918. His devoted loyalty to Stalin meant that he was promoted far above his abilities, gaining high command in the Red Army in the 1920s and 1930s. His main problem was that he was an arch traditionalist who saw no merit in any innovations that the Red Army tried to introduce. In 1935, he was appointed chief of the Artillery Directorate even though his critics said he was stuck in 1918. He was opposed to the introduction of the T-34 and KV-1 tanks that were to prove vital to the survival of the Red Army in 1941. He used his influence to try and change the main armament of both tanks in favor of an inferior gun produced by a factory of which he was the patron. Another negative influence was his opposition to the laying of minefields on the Soviet–Polish border. The lack of such defenses smoothed the way for the German Wehrmacht when they invaded the Soviet Union in June 1941. His poor command of the Red Army artillery during the Winter War led to a fall from favor. In 1940, his still-close friendship with Stalin did not save his young bride from arrest and execution because of her aristocratic background. A few months after his bride's "disappearance," he was promoted to the rank of marshal but he continued to be a negative influence. Another weapon he opposed was the Katyusha rocket launcher which proved crucial in the Red Army's victory in May 1945. His poor performance during the Winter War and the wider Patriotic War of 1941–5 ultimately contributed to his arrest and execution in 1950.

Foreign Volunteers for Finland

The worldwide sympathy for the Finnish cause soon materialized into active support from foreign volunteers wanting to fight for the Finns. Many were untrained and Finnish resources could not cope with the arrival of thousands of raw recruits. Some 1,200 Danes volunteered but only 300 had a military background. This lack of available training meant that some Danish volunteers saw no service before the war ended in March 1940. Around 725 Norwegians also volunteered to fight but only 125 were able to make it to the front where they served on the Salla Front. Up to 1,000 Estonians were reported to have volunteered but only about 100 arrived in time to serve. Hungarian volunteers numbered 346 but due to the politics of Europe at the time, they had to travel via a roundabout route, only arriving at their training camp at Lapua just before the end of the war. Amongst the many nationalities who fought for Finland, according to official Finnish figures of March 1940, were 850 Ukrainians, 20 Latvians, 51 Belgians, 18 Germans, 17 Dutch, and 13 Yugoslavs. Smaller numbers came from France 2, Italy 7, Poland 7, Great Britain 13, Switzerland 6, Lithuania 3, and Luxembourg 3. Lone volunteers came from Austria, Czechoslovakia, Yugoslavia, and Portugal while another 15 were from "unknown" countries. Some volunteers just wanted to fight against the Soviet Union like Ukrainians and Poles, while others wanted to fight for Finland. The most numerous group of foreign volunteers were the Swedes who were formed into the Swedish Volunteer Corps—Svenska Frivilligkaren SFK (in Swedish)—with 9,640

volunteers. During the last days of February, the Stridsgruppen SFK (in Finnish), made up of 8,260 Swedish, 600 Danish, and 725 Norwegian volunteers, took over Finnish positions on the Salla Front. Finns living abroad also answered the call with 346 volunteers, including 230 ex-pats from the USA. Some 372 Ingrians from the border area between Finland and the Soviet Union also volunteered to fight as some had Finnish ancestry.

Two Swedish volunteers of the Svenska Frivilligkaren in the forests of Finland with British-made Boyes 14mm Model 37 antitank rifles. Around 100 of these weapons were donated by the British government in January 1940 who specified that 30 should be given to the newly arrived Swedish volunteers. Although these weapons would be soon outdated, they were still capable of penetrating the armor of light tanks like the T-26 and T-37A. (Author's collection)

| War in the North, 1939–40

The Red Army's invasion of northern Finland above the Arctic Circle began with the 14th Army's thrust to take the port of Petsamo on the Arctic Ocean on November 30. 14th Army units were able to overcome light Finnish resistance and take the port on the second day of the invasion. Landing parties from the Soviet Arctic Fleet were assisted by troops moving overland from the Petsamo base as they advanced southward along the Arctic Highway. By December 15, Red Army units had taken the nickel mine at Salmijara and had reached Nautsi on the 19th.

A Finnish ski unit using reindeer as draught animals on the Petsamo Front in Arctic Finland, December 1939. They are fighting the Red Army's 52nd and 104th Divisions which are supported by coastal artillery guns. The Finns belong to the Northern Finland Group responsible for the defense of 400 miles of Finnish territory under Major-General E. Viljo Tuompo. (Author's collection)

A well camouflaged sub-machine-gunner on the Petsamo Front, early 1940. He is armed with an SIG Bergmann M1920, a Swiss license-built copy of the German MP18,1. The Finns had a variety of small arms in service in 1939; this weapon was used alongside the more modern Suomi. (Author's collection)

A Finnish ski patrol moves through deep snow on the Lapland Front in the vicinity of Petsamo in early 1940. It was on this northern front that some units used the abundant reindeer farmed by the Laplanders to carry supplies for them. Lapland was defended by a small Finnish force commanded by Major-General K. M. Wallenius. (Author's collection)

The young Finnish crew of an old-pattern Maxim heavy machine gun during fighting in the Salla sector, late January 1940. They are well camouflaged with their white snow suits with hoods and have white covers for the Maxim when not in action. (Author's collection)

General Martti Wallenius (center, with binoculars) was the Finnish commander of the armies in the north during 1939–40. He was a former journalist who had fought in the Finnish Civil War of 1918 and was a close associate of Marshal Mannerheim. His face was widely featured on the covers of various news magazines during the war: the Marshal was aware of the value of propaganda to the Finnish cause. On December 31, 1939 Wallenius told the press that his troops were now operating on Soviet territory: "We don't let them rest, we don't let them sleep. This war is a war of numbers against brains. We train our men to fight individually and they can do it, whereas the Russian can never rid himself of his natural gregarious instincts." (Author's collection)

The Finns destroyed several Soviet supply convoys in December 1939. This line of trucks has been ambushed along a road on the northern bank of the River Kemi in the Salla region. Some of the cargoes have already been stripped, with ammunition taken immediately to the front. Such war booty helped keep the Finnish Army fighting for several months. (Author's collection)

Soviet propaganda shows an embattled Red Army ski unit fighting off Finnish ski troops. The artist captures the tenseness of the battle as white-camouflaged Finnish soldiers emerge from the trees to attack the beleaguered patrol. He also accurately portrays the mix of uniforms worn by the Red Army during the Winter War. (Author's collection)

The interior of an arctic dugout shows the cluttered but effective shelter that these bunkers provided Finnish troops in the winter of 1939/40. Officers and men huddle together around a stove which heats food and water for washing. Spending the freezing nights in shelters like this allowed Finnish troops to rest and eat a hot meal before spending another day on the front lines. (Photographic Center of the General Headquarters, Helsinki)

The Soviets at Nautsi were forced to withdraw when it proved impossible to get supplies through to the garrison there. They moved temporarily 20 miles north before returning south when they had gathered enough supplies to push onto Nautsi again. It was the weather with its −25°C temperatures that caused the Soviets problems. Finnish military forces in the sector under Captain Antti Pennanen were initially restricted to a single infantry company, the 10th Separate Company, and four old 76mm field guns of the 5th Separate Artillery Battery. The guns dated back to 1887 and were really museum pieces with limited ammunition available. During the fighting the Finns were reinforced by the 11th Separate Company and a small unit known as the Reconnaissance Detachment. These paltry Finnish forces were facing 52,500 troops of the 14th Army with its three divisions, the 14th, 52nd, and 104th. Under the command of General Meretsov, the 52nd and 104th Divisions conducted the campaign, while the 14th was held in reserve. Mannerheim ordered his outnumbered northern forces to fight like the Russians had against Napoleon in the winter of 1812: withdraw when faced with superior numbers and then strike the enemy from the side and rear.

During fighting around Salla, a Finnish ski unit uses a snowdrift for cover. The soldiers have their skis at the ready to escape at speed across the snow. It was the years that Finnish troops had spent living in these conditions that gave them the edge in most encounters with the Red Army. (Author's collection)

Finnish soldiers throwing M32 stick grenades in the Salla sector, January 28, 1940. When this photograph was taken, the Finns were struggling to hold on to the village of Salla and were awaiting reinforcements. The M32 was based on the German stick grenade of World War I. It had a useful clip attachment so it could be clipped onto a belt. The Finns used at least seven types of grenade from various countries, all with differing fuse lengths which could result in fatal errors. (Author's collection)

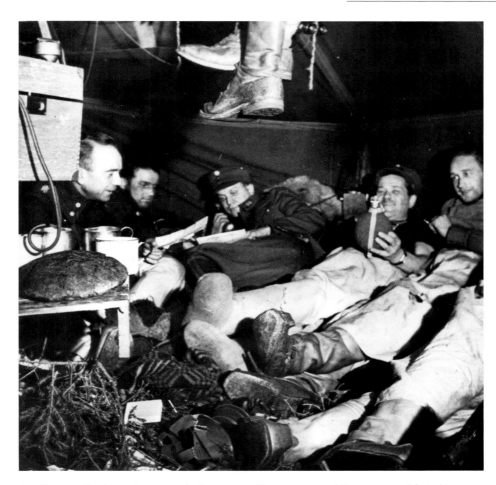

Another arctic dugout as crowded as ever with as many soldiers as possible taking shelter in the heated bunker. The dugout has cooking facilities: a loaf of warm bread is ready to eat. Fir-tree greenery has been brought in for bedding. On the left junior officers are operating a field telephone. (Author's collection)

The Salla Front

On November 30 two divisions of the Soviet 9th Army crossed the Finnish–Soviet border just above the Arctic Circle in Lapland. Made up of the 88th and 122nd Rifle Divisions, this force had the objective of cutting Finland in half along the country's "waist." The initial objective was the capture of the village of Salla, defended by a single Finnish battalion. On December 9 the Soviets reached the village and drove the meager defense force into the forests. With the first objective reached, the two Soviet divisions separated, with the 88th advancing in a northwesterly direction, its objective Pelkosenniemi, while the 122nd moved in southwesterly direction, aiming for the village of Kemijarvi. Once these villages had been taken the Soviets would then move west toward the Finnish–Swedish border. They would then take the border towns of Rovaniemi and Tornio—and Finland would then effectively

Swedish gunners operate a Swedish 40mm Bofors M36 antiaircraft gun on the Salla Front. The main suppliers of this popular antiaircraft gun were Sweden, Hungary, and the United Kingdom. Sweden had promised a total of 76 of these guns, with 53 arriving before the war began, along with 144,000 shells. Hungary was to supply 40 Bofors with 24 guns and 10,000 shells delivered in December 1939 at the height of the fighting. Great Britain supplied 18 of these guns along with 36,000 shells. (Author's collection)

be cut in half along its middle. This separation of the north and south of Finland would, the Soviets hoped, result in a shortening of the war. However, these advances would have to be undertaken across difficult country with the Finns continuously harassing the Red Army columns. In the meantime, the Finns were reinforced by another battalion which encouraged them to take the offensive.

By February 16, the 122nd Division was only 14 miles from Kemijarvi, but two days later the Finns launched several counteroffensives. The Finns attacked both Soviet columns and with the usual combination of severe weather conditions, broke the Soviet resolve. A chaotic withdrawal by the Red Army saw their remaining troops taking up defensive positions around Salla. Both sides were totally exhausted by the weeks of fighting and the Salla Front remained quiet for the rest of the war. The attempt to cut Finland in half had cost the Red Army dearly, with an estimated 4,000 dead, while the Finns lost 650 men. It was decided to send the 9,000 Swedish volunteers of the Svenska Frivilligkaren to the Salla region to relieve the Finnish forces. They were to serve as a major deterrent to any further Red Army advances in the north until the end of the war in March 1940.

A Finnish submarine and coastal defense vessel during a prewar exercise in the Baltic Sea, 1939. The navy was strictly a coastal defense force with two heavy cruisers, four submarines, a few gunships, and a couple of dozen MTBs. As in the ground war, the Finnish Navy was dwarfed by its Soviet opposition. (Author's collection)

Naval Warfare 1939–40

Naval warfare during the Winter War was limited by several factors with neither the Red Navy nor the Finnish Navy playing a major role. Firstly, the Gulf of Finland where any naval clashes would have taken place was largely frozen over by the end of December. Secondly, both the Finnish Navy and the Soviet Baltic Fleet had limited capabilities. Most fighting involved Soviet ships bombarding Finnish coastal batteries. The Finns only had 18 vessels, with some operating on Lake Lagoda when the war began. The Red Navy did manage to capture some outlying islands in the Gulf but failed to take Finnish ports on the mainland. Soviet ships did bombard several Finnish ports, including Porvo, 20 miles to the east of Helsinki.

The Soviets faced determined Finnish coastal guns which inflicted a great deal of damage on their ships. Three destroyers, two submarines, and several auxiliary vessels were damaged as was the battleship *October Revolution* that was also hit by shells from coastal batteries. A Soviet attempt by the cruiser *Kirov* and two escorts to take on the Finnish coastal defenses at Hanko in early December also ended in failure. Stalin's order to deploy submarines against the Finnish port of Turku was called off, after fearful Soviet admirals managed to persuade him that the waters around the harbor were too shallow for submarines. The Baltic Fleet did occupy several disputed islands in the Gulf of Finland but did not have large-scale amphibious capabilities to attack major fortified ports. In early 1940, Soviet ships supported the land offensive up the Karelian Isthmus and landed troops.

Ships of the Soviet Baltic Fleet on operations during the leadup to the Winter War. Neither the Soviet nor Finnish navies would have much influence on the war as the sea was frozen for the duration of the conflict. The Soviet Navy did, however, play a role in the takeover of the Baltic states of Estonia, Latvia, and Lithuania in 1939–40. (Author's collection)

War in the Air, 1939–40

The war in the air above Finland during the 1939–40 conflict saw the same disparity in numbers as on the ground and at sea. With 114 front-line aircraft available in November 1939, the Finnish Air Force was outnumbered 18 to 1 by the Red Air Force, with most of its aircraft on the verge of obsolescence.

Apart from a few dozen Dutch-made Fokker XIII fighters, most Finnish aircraft belonged to the late 1920s and early 1930s. This was particularly telling when aircraft performance was improving at a rapid rate during the mid- to late 1930s. The Finns had 162 aircraft of all types and only 200 trained pilots to fly them, which meant any new planes they acquired would not really expand the air force.

A Dutch-designed fighter, the Fokker XXI, of the Finnish Air Force being prepared for combat at the height of the Winter War. This slightly outdated plane was the best that was available to the Finns in 1939–40 and managed to shoot down 127 Soviet aircraft. Most XXIs had 825hp Twin Wasp engines and were built in Finland before the war. In order to keep their fighters in the air, the Finns drained the oil out of the engine every night and stored it inside warm hangars, which stopped it from freezing in the –20°C to –40°C temperatures—and then poured it back in before takeoff the next morning. (Author's collection)

The British supplied the Finnish Air Force with 18 Bristol Blenheim I light bombers in 1937, joined by 12 improved Blenheim Mk IVs in December. The Blenheim was known in Finnish service as the "Tin Henry" but served them well during the Winter War and the later Continuation War of 1941–4. (SA-Kuva-115380)

Twelve Royal Swedish Air Force Gladiator IIs (J8As) comprised the fighter element of Flygflottilj 19—Flying Regiment 19 of the Swedish Voluntary Air Force—that assisted the Finns. They arrived in January 1940 and fought in Lapland in the far north, along with four Hawker Hart light bombers. The squadron shot down eight Red Air Force fighters and stopped several air raids on northern Finnish towns by chasing off the attacking bombers. (Author's collection)

A Fokker C.V-E army cooperation plane being prepared for takeoff in the months before the Winter War. In 1927, one of these modern (for the times) aircraft was bought from the Netherlands followed by another 13 in 1934. By 1939 the plane was on the verge of obsolescence but saw service throughout the Winter War and into the post-1941 conflict with the Soviet Union. (Author's collection)

The Finnish fighter force had 36 Fokker XIII fighters backed up by some 17 outdated British-made Bristol Bulldog IVA fighters. Light bombers like the Fokker C.V-E and C.X operated as reconnaissance and ground-attack planes. Although the C.X only entered service in 1935, it was still too slow to avoid the Soviet fighters. The C.V-E had been in Dutch service since 1927 and with a top speed of 145mph, it was 67mph slower than the C.X. Finnish bombers were few and far between apart from a force of Bristol Blenheim Is: with a top speed of 285mph, the Blenheim was effectively a light bomber that could outrun some modern fighters. In desperate need of more modern aircraft, the Finns did manage to receive some welcome reinforcements as from January 1940. These included 30 French Morane-Saulnier 406 fighters which was the standard French Air Force fighter. They performed well in Finnish hands and became a vital part of the Finnish air defense, serving effectively until the end of the war. Thirty Gloster Gladiator fighters also arrived from Britain but 18 were lost on the first day of action and the survivors were withdrawn to quieter sectors. They were later handed over to some Swedish volunteer pilots along with two Hawker Hart light bombers. Another foreign aircraft that fought over Finland in the latter stages of the war was the Italian Fiat G.50 Freccia fighter. Thirty-five were ordered by Finland and the 33 that arrived fought during the last weeks of the war and into the Continuation War. Some 44 US-made Brewster F2A Buffalo fighters were sold to Finland toward the end of the war but only five saw any combat. The arrival of new aircraft meant that by the end of the war the strength of the Finnish Air Force was 200 aircraft despite heavy losses during the Winter War.

Lieutenant Jorma Sarvanto was the highest-scoring ace in the Finnish Air Force during the Winter War. Flying a Fokker D.XXI he flew many operations against the Red Air Force from the December 19, 1939 to the end of the war in March 1940, shooting down 13 enemy planes. His greatest feat took place on January 6, 1940 when, on his own, he took on seven Soviet Ilyushin DB-3 bombers and shot down six. The only bomber which got away was later shot down by another Finnish pilot, Lieutenant Per-Erik Sovelius. (Author's collection)

An army officer and an air force officer hold a pre-operation briefing with a Finnish pilot before he undertakes a reconnaissance mission over the front. Most reconnaissance missions were flown by aging Dutch Fokker C.Vs that were mainly license-built at the State Aircraft Factory at Tampere. Finland used two variants of the C.V—the C.V-D and C.V-E with a total of 17; others donated by Norway did not arrive in time to take part in the war. (Author's collection)

Finnish ground crew attach a bomb under the wing of a Fokker C.V-E light bomber before a bombing raid over Soviet lines. The Dutch-designed reconnaissance plane had a secondary role as a bomber and could carry a total bomb load of 440lb. These planes were also armed with a single light machine gun operated by the observer/bomb aimer of the two-man crew. (Author's collection)

A Finnish mechanic inspects the engine of an Italian Fiat G50 fighter. The widespread sympathy for Finland meant that the country was able to buy aircraft from both socialist and fascist governments. (Author's collection)

In Profile:
Bristol Bulldog LLv 26 Fighter
& Fokker D.XXI Fighter

Finnish Bristol Bulldog LLv 26 Fighter, November 1939. The completely out-of-date Bristol Bulldog was in service with one of the two fighter squadrons of the Finnish Air Force in late 1939. Its 17 Bulldogs may have been obsolete but they still managed to shoot down six Soviet aircraft during the war. This aircraft is finished in the usual brown-green paint with the blue-swastika-on-a-white-disc insignia.

Finnish Fokker D.XXI Fighter, January 1940. This iconic fighter of the Winter War was flown by First Lieutenant Jorma Sarvanto, the principal Finnish flying ace of the conflict. At the start of the war the Finns only had a handful of these reasonably modern Dutch fighters. The aircraft was largely responsible for the aerial victories of the Finnish Air Force. Sarvanto shot down several Soviet bombers flying this aircraft. The paintwork is again in the factory brown-green finish with the usual blue-swastika symbol on the fuselage, and upper and lower wings. On the tail is a white 2 and the registration on the fuselage is FR-97.

The Soviet Air Force supported the Red Army during the Winter War with around 2,500 aircraft, including 1,044 fighters and 855 bombers plus transports, organized into four bomber brigades and two fighter brigades in November 1939. Most Red Air Force aircraft operated from newly occupied airbases in Estonia near the Finnish border. Like the Finns, most Soviet aircraft were also aging, especially their three types of fighter—the Polikarkov I-15, I-153, and I-16— but they had several thousand of them in 1939. The I-15 biplane fighter had a top speed of 228mph while the improved I-153 was much faster at 275mph. The I-16 monoplane fighter had a top speed of 323mph and was seen as a ground-breaking aircraft when it entered service in 1935. Polikarkov also made the R-5 and R-Z reconnaissance/light-bombers that were equivalent to the Finns' C.V-E and C.X but the more modern R-Z had a top speed of 180mph against the R-5's 141mph. The three bomber types were the Tupolev SB-2-100 light bomber, the Ilyushin Il-4 (DB-3) medium bomber, and the Tupolev ANT-6 (TB-3) heavy bomber, with top speeds of 280mph, 265mph, and 155mph respectively with the slow ANT-6 being relegated to transport roles post-1940. The SB-2 had a bomb payload of 1,430lb while the Ilyushin Il-4 (DB-3) medium bomber could carry 4,400lb, and the ANT-6 3,300lb.

A Red Air Force I-16 fighter squadron in the last few days of the fighting in 1940. By March the Polikarkov I-16 Type 28 dominated the skies above Finland with 20mm cannons mounted in its wings. With a top speed of 326mph, the small, stubby plane was a lot faster than the Finns' Fokker D.XXI at high altitudes. However, at lower levels where much of the dogfighting took place, the I-16 did not have such a great advantage. (Author's collection)

Crews of a flight of Tupolev SB-2-100 light bombers prepare to take off on an air raid over Finland in the early days of the war. The SB-2 was fast when it first came into service in 1936 and, as used by the Republican Air Force in the Spanish Civil War, it could outpace most enemy fighters. It had a bomb capacity of 1,100lb and a range of 435 miles so they were usually stationed close to the border during the Winter War. (Author's collection)

Another SB-2-100 taxies to take off for an operation over Finland. Large numbers were shot down by enemy fighters or by ground fire. By 1939 the SB-2's speed advantage had been lost as the handful of Fokker D.XXIs of the Finnish Air Force took their toll. The bomber was poorly protected with unarmored fuel tanks behind both engines which made them easy targets for the well-trained Finnish pilots. Heavy losses forced the Soviets to try and improve the bomber and some changes were made before the German invasion of 1941, but they were nevertheless obsolete. (Author's collection)

A flight officer hands what look like propaganda leaflets to the pilot of an I-16 fighter before takeoff. The two main fighters in service in 1939–40 were the I-16 and the I-15 with the former known as the "Ishak" (donkey). This aircraft was the world's first low-wing cantilever monoplane fighter with retractable landing gear. It was difficult to fly and had particularly poor visibility for the pilot. Any captured examples were, nevertheless, taken into service by the Finns who called the aircraft the "Flying Squirrel." (Author's collection)

During the early Soviet air raids, small numbers of Finnish fighters operated against the largely undefended bombers. Finnish pilots would often fly on solo missions and dive into the middle of a formation of Soviet bombers and shoot down one or two before breaking off combat. As one pilot said, they would "charge into the middle of the Soviet bomber formations, causing them to scatter like a flock of starlings and then pick off individual birds."

The air war over Finland saw the employment of two further types of aircraft, with one belonging to the 19th century and the other more modern. In the first instant, several observation balloons were used to direct artillery fire along the Mannerheim Line in early 1940 and operated day and night. The other more modern aircraft employed by the Soviets was a pair of Kamov autogyros[1] which performed reconnaissance duties. Two Kamov autogyros, an An7 and a slightly modified A-7bis were sent to the northwestern Front in mid-December 1939. The A-7 could not be used due to a lack of some crucial spare parts and it was only the A-7bis that saw service. It took part in 20 sorties over several months, sending important intelligence to Red Army artillery units.

During the Soviet February offensive and until the end of the fighting in mid-March, Finnish pilots continued to defiantly operate against mounting odds. During the fierce air

---

1   Autogyros are part helicopter and part plane with rotor blades that provide upward lift and a standard aircraft engine at the front that provides forward thrust.

This Red Air Force Iluyshin 4 (DB-3) medium bomber, *Dalny Bombardirovschick*, has crashed in the forest having been hit by Finnish machine-gun ground fire. Finnish soldiers examine it to see if it is worth adding to their growing stocks of captured Soviet hardware. Five of these DB-3s captured in reparable condition were used during the Continuation War from 1941. Another six DB-3s were sold to the Finns in 1941, captured by the German Wehrmacht during Operation *Barbarossa*. (Author's collection)

battles in February, they shot down 251 Soviet planes and on March 3 they downed 28 enemy aircraft that day. Besides shooting down Soviet aircraft, the Finnish fighters and bombers flew mission after mission against Red Army ground targets. They particularly targeted the Soviet communication system as well as supply lines from Leningrad to the front. As the situation grew more desperate, by early March Finnish pilots were almost constantly in the air. By the time the war ended, all the air crews were totally exhausted and could not possibly have continued to fly at the rate that they had been.

During the war the Red Air Force was reported to have lost between 700 and 900 planes with the majority being bombers. Finnish antiaircraft fire accounted for up to 444 of the Soviet planes shot down while 240 were shot down by fighter pilots. Soviet sources claimed that 400 of their aircraft were lost due to "inclement weather" or lack of fuel and tools. Although Finnish losses of 62 planes shot down was a comparatively low figure, it was high as a percentage of the aircraft involved.

Second Lieutenant Viktor Vasilyevich Talalikhin (1918–41) was one of the aces of the Red Air Force during the Winter War, flying a Polikarpov I-153 fighter. He had joined a Moscow flying club earning a flying license while working in a meat factory before joining the air force. During the Winter War he carried out 47 sorties and shot down four Finnish planes and was awarded the Order of the Red Star. During the German invasion of the Soviet Union, he again proved to be a brave pilot, flying 60 missions in the summer of 1941. In August 1941, he was awarded the Order of the Red Banner for a particularly heroic and almost suicidal heroic act. Having run out of ammunition during an attack on German Heinkel 111 bombers, he rammed his fighter into one of the enemy planes before parachuting to safety. In October 1941, he was jumped by a large number of Messerschmitt Bf 109 fighters and was shot down and killed. (Author's collection)

A smiling senior lieutenant of the Red Air Force during the February offensive which finally overwhelmed the Finns. A large number of Soviet pilots who survived the Winter War were to be swept from the skies during the German invasion of their country just over a year later. (Author's collection)

91

In Profile:
Polikarpov 1-15bis Fighter, Tupolev SB 2M-100 Bomber & Polikarpov I-16 Type 24 Fighter

Soviet Polikarpov 1-15bis Fighter, Leningrad VO-VS, November 1939. The Polikarpov I-15bis was the improved version of the original I-15 which entered service in 1933. I-15bis fighters entered Red Air Force service in 1937. Individual numbers on the fuselage could be in white or yellow on a green color scheme or red or yellow on white paint scheme.

Soviet Tupolev SB 2M-100 Bomber, 41st Bomber Aviation Regiment, December 1939. This light bomber was the mainstay of the Red Air Force bombing effort for much of the Winter War, alongside two other types—the DB-3 medium bomber and the ANT-5 heavy bomber. It has been painted in factory white and has the red stars on both wings and fuselage; the yellow number 9 denotes its aircraft number.

Soviet Polikarpov I-16 Type 24 Fighter, Lake Lagoda Sector, 1940. This Polikarpov fighter operated over the Lake Lagoda sector of the front in the winter of 1939/40. The I-16 was a revolutionary design when it took its first flight in 1933 but was outdated by 1939. It was still, however, the most modern type in service during the Winter War.

Soviet *Crescendo* Offensive, February 1940

After the unexpected and spectacular victories of the Finns from December 1939 to January 1940, the watching world looked on in admiration. Many naïvely believed that the "brave" nation's victory was a complete and final one and that the Soviet Union would back down. In reality, the cost of achieving their victories had exhausted the Finns' resources and tested them to the limit.

Although Stalin was stunned by the defeats of the Red Army in Finland, he was in no mood to withdraw from the conflict. His stubborn, unflinching attitude was to restart the war in earnest in the first months of 1940. Any further attacks on Finland would not begin before making changes to the Red Army command. Marshal Semyon Timoshenko, the 45-year-old victor of the wars against the Japanese in the Far East in 1938 and 1939, was chosen to take command of the campaign against Finland. One of the first decisions that the new commander made was to concentrate the coming offensive against the Karelian Isthmus. There was a stalemate in the fighting in central and northern Finland and it made sense to use the superior firepower of the Red Army to blast the Finns from the isthmus. Once the isthmus had fallen and the Mannerheim Line was breached, the strategic port of Viipuri in northeastern Karelia would fall.

General Semyon Timoshenko was given command of the newly designated North-Western Front during the Winter War. He took over command in January 1940 and managed to reorganize his forces for the coming offensive against the Finns. One of his first tasks was to weed out incompetent officers who had failed to perform in the earlier fighting. At the end of the war, he was appointed by Stalin to assess the weaknesses shown by the Red Army during the Winter War. His role as Defense Minister was interrupted by the German invasion in June 1941 and he was given command of the Western–Central Front. He was one of the few high-ranking officers to survive the disaster of Operation *Barbarossa* and managed to stabilize the front before the first Soviet counteroffensive. He is seen here after his promotion to marshal in May 1940 and wears the new ranks introduced in that year. (Author's collection)

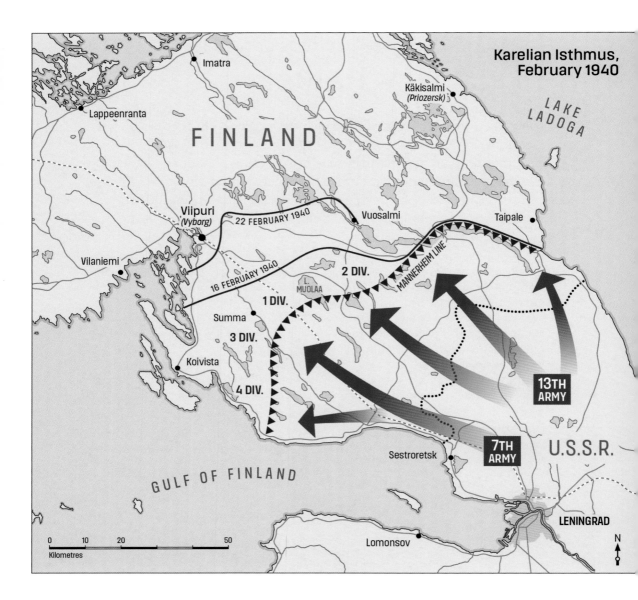

Karelian Isthmus,
February 1940

Imatra

Käkisalmi
(Priozersk)

LAKE
LADOGA

Lappeenranta

FINLAND

Viipuri
(Vyborg)

22 FEBRUARY 1940

Vuosalmi

Taipale

Vilaniemi

16 FEBRUARY 1940

L.
MUOLAA

2 DIV.

MANNERHEIM LINE

1 DIV.

Summa

3 DIV.

13TH
ARMY

Koivista

4 DIV.

U.S.S.R.

Sestroretsk

7TH
ARMY

GULF OF FINLAND

LENINGRAD

0   10   20   50
Kilometres

Lomonsov

N

In an effort to counter the Finnish ski troops who caused so much havoc in late 1939, a new Soviet unit was formed. The 2,000-strong Siberian Ski Brigade was raised exclusively from Siberians, being made up of the men in three "independent ski battalions." This group of enthusiastic ski troops in the middle of their training will soon be going into action. However, they were later found to not have been given proper instruction in the care of their weapons. Their rifles and sub-machine guns had not been cleaned and lubricated properly and many jammed due to frozen oil. (Author's collection)

Happy Red Army ski troops of the Siberian Ski Brigade pose for the propaganda camera in the days leading up to the February 1940 offensive. The brigade was said to have high morale and was well equipped when it went into action. Some units received ski manuals which provided only the briefest of basic instructions with line drawings to assist the user. Truckloads of these manuals arrived at the invasion embarkation points where the men were supposed to give themselves a crash course in the art of skiing. When they did go into action, their advance was hampered by poor maps and by the death of their popular commander in the first skirmish. However, they did fight well and helped draw Finnish troops away from their sieges of the isolated *mottis*. (Author's collection)

Timoshenko spent January 1940 in careful preparation for his new offensive with a major shakeup of the Red Army on the North-Western Front. He got rid of inefficient officers who had genuinely failed during the December fighting. But some scapegoats had to pay for the embarrassing defeats in Finland and several high-ranking officers were shot. Amongst those blamed for the defeats along the Raate Road and at Suomussalmi was General Alexei Vinogradov, the 40-year-old commander of the 44th Division, who was shot on January 11. He was reported to have withdrawn from the battlefield along with two of his officers, Volkov and Pahomov, who were also shot in the aftermath of the fighting. Other officers and commissars were also shot. The Finns reported that prisoners of war returned to the Soviet Union in the aftermath of the war were also shot later, in the summer of 1940. Although Timoshenko was seen as a more enlightened commander, he was still ruthless and more than willing to send thousands of Soviet soldiers to their deaths. His new tactics were not intended to cut down on casualties as long as the end result was a victory for Stalin and his regime. The Soviets introduced new drills and new tactics, including the use of flamethrower tanks and even radio-controlled tanks to force breakthroughs in Finnish

By the end of January the Finns had succeeded in thwarting the Red Army invasion but were exhausted. Even after defeating the Soviets in early January and killing thousands of their troops, they knew that the war was not won. It would have been a foolish Finn who didn't think that the Red Army would regroup and come back in greater numbers. This Finnish ski patrol moves through a town near the front on January 8, expecting within weeks to have to face a force that even their bravery and enterprise could not overcome. (Author's collection)

defenses. Timoshenko tried to install better morale into his troops and made a great show of presenting 2,600 bravery awards to veterans of the earlier fighting. He had brought into the theater a large number of Ukrainian troops who were well regarded. These seasoned troops were needed to fill the gaps in the ranks after weeks of wasteful frontal attacks on well-prepared Finnish positions. In mid-January a conservative estimate was that the Red Army had suffered 100,000 casualties since November. Half of these were troops who had been killed in action or had frozen to death. The other half were the wounded with a large number being incapacitated from frostbite and the loss of fingers or limbs. At the same time, it was estimated that Finnish losses were 6,000 with 1,200 of these as deaths.

The hard core of the Red Army opposing Finland was a 24-division force with a further three divisions in reserve on the Karelian Front. This new force had 13 more divisions than that which had attacked Finland in November 1939. In support of the offensive was a 720-strong artillery force in 20 artillery regiments and seven armored brigades with 455 tanks. Air support was to be provided by 15 new air regiments with 450 bombers and fighters.

The Soviet officer in charge of an antiaircraft machine gun quad scans the skies for any sign of Finnish air activity, February 1940. The gunners are poised to fire at any low-flying planes that appear over the forest looking for ground targets. When an enemy aircraft appeared, they would only have a couple of seconds to fire off a few rounds. The "Quadruple Maxim Antiaircraft System Model 1931" had been improved in 1931 when optical sights were fitted. (Author's collection)

Although it was rushed, Timoshenko's reorganization and massive reinforcement of the Red Army on the North-Western Front was finished by the end of January 1940. This second offensive was to involve up to 1.2 million troops in five armies and was to be supported by 3,000 aircraft. Timoshenko would concentrate his efforts on the Karelian Isthmus using 460,000 men with 3,000 tanks, 3,350 guns, and 1,300 aircraft.

They were facing 150,000 exhausted Finns whose only hope of holding the Red Army back was if by some miracle the defenses of the Mannerheim Line held. Regardless of the skill and courage demonstrated by the Finns in late 1939, they now faced odds that were overwhelming. Overstretched Finnish forces were only going to get weaker from now on, while at the same time more Red Army reinforcements were being pushed forward to the attack. The Soviet 7th Army which had attacked the Karelian Isthmus in November 1939 had been re-organized and split into two with a new 13th Army being formed in December. This heavily reinforced two-army force was to lead the attack on the isthmus with more units in reserve if needed.

This propaganda photograph from early 1940 shows a group of Soviet troops listening intently to their officer who reads the *Pravda* newspaper to them. When the new offensive against Finland was launched in February 1940, the Soviet armed forces were much better prepared. These men have been issued with the new type of winter fur hat in place of the largely ineffective *budenovka* hat. (Author's collection)

Red Army artillery spotters in the deep snow of the Finnish countryside check the fall of shot on Finnish positions using a range finder on a tripod and binoculars, early 1940. During the 1939 fighting, the accuracy of the artillery was poor with massed artillery saturating an area rather than targeting specific targets; as a result, commanders could not call on artillery support but most of these problems had been resolved by early 1940. (Author's collection)

The offensive opened on February 1 at 1245 when a large-scale artillery bombardment targeted the strategic village of Summa. Over 300,000 shells fell on Finnish positions on the first day with the Red Army guns lined up virtually "wheel to wheel." At the same time Soviet planes were targeting the Finnish lines of communication to sow confusion, as well as attacking their supply facilities farther back from the front. These opening bombardments were followed by a week of Red Army infantry attacks interspersed with a series of smaller-scale artillery strikes. The massed Soviets infantry attacks were testing the Finnish defenders to their limits but were costly for the attackers.

On the 11th an artillery duel took place between the outmatched Finnish artillery and the Soviets. It was reported that the Red Army officers were not just shocked but were also infuriated by the accuracy of the Finns' artillery. They believed that the enemy artillery had been neutralized by 10 days of incessant shelling. A total of 104 Red Army batteries were soon involved in the counterbattery fire against the desperate Finns with at least 400 guns taking part. The systematic destruction of the Finnish defenses was now underway while the defenders hunkered down in their bunkers during the day. At night they emerged and tried to repair the damaged trenches and defensive positions. At the same time, they had to

A group of Red Army officers pose outside their headquarters tent. They display the cross-section of uniform worn by most Soviet soldiers during the Winter War. All wear various woolen *budenovka* winter hats which were renowned for providing little or no protection from the cold. Coats and other cold-weather clothing include the sheepskin coat worn by the man on the left, and woolen overcoats. The wadded cotton jacket and trousers worn by the man in the center of the group were intended to be worn in light winter weather, not in the conditions in Finland. (Author's collection)

Junior Red Army officers pose in the forests of southern Finland during the offensive of February 1940. The role of a lower-ranking Red Army officer was a thankless task with threats coming from various directions. Besides the usual danger of being killed when they were required to lead from the front, they were also under the scrutiny of the "*Politruks*," the political commissars who were constantly on the lookout for any "unpatriotic" behavior. Although the main purges against the army had slowed down by 1939, many still fell victim to an unsatisfactory report. (Author's collection)

Soviet troops firing Maxim M1910 heavy machine guns during the February offensive. The Imperial Russian Army had used this sturdy but heavy machine gun since 1910 and it served the Red Army from 1914 until 1945 and beyond. In 1930, several modifications were introduced to the machine guns in service, including the addition of a safety catch, a valve to allow easier emptying of the water jacket, and better sights. Earlier modifications in the 1920s included the introduction of grooves in the water jacket which helped keep the barrel cooler. (Author's collection)

The crew of this Soviet heavy howitzer have camouflaged their gun and limber with white sheets in the snow-covered terrain of Finland. They are going through the gun drill with their pre-1914 122mm Model 1910/30 which was an updated version of the Model 1910 Schneider. (Author's collection)

fight off nightly attacks by Soviet tanks that were supported by infantry pulled behind them on sledges. With their medium or light guns, there was no way for the Finns to reply to the long-range enemy artillery. Soviet artillery officers were so confident of their superiority that they often did not bother to camouflage their positions.

On February 11 the much-vaunted Mannerheim Line was penetrated by Red Army assault forces, divided into four "assault echelons" with each being approximately the size of half an army. As the Soviets broke through, the Finns withdrew in front of their advance. On February 17, Marshal Mannerheim ordered the withdrawal of his weary and battered men to the secondary defenses of the Mannerheim Line, 10 miles to the north—a risky maneuver. The Finns had resisted the Red Army offensive for 16 days under a storm of cannon fire and bombs, yet there was little they could do but survive in their trenches and pillboxes amongst fast-rising casualties. Some regiments lost two-thirds of their men with most units now full of raw recruits and Civil Guard veterans. Many simply disappeared, buried under the sheer weight of the enemy bombardment.

Timoshenko had cleverly chosen to concentrate his attack in the Summa area where the forests opened up into fields, which allowed him to use his tanks to better effect than in 1939. The Soviet troops were now better trained than a few weeks before and were proving to be "hardy and brave." The Finns still managed to keep most of their units in good order and fought several rearguard actions as they withdrew to the new defensive line farther north but their resources were now dangerously stretched with reinforcements and ammunition running low. Morale was still surprisingly high, although most knew that they could only resist for so long.

Colonel-General Terenty Shtykov of the Soviet 7th Army inspects troops who have arrived from Leningrad for the February offensive. The 33-year-old commissar was a party loyalist and had had a role in the 1938 purge of military officers. He had a political mentor, First Secretary Andrei Zhdanov, whose position in the Soviet regime gave Shtykov a certain amount of security in the paranoid world of the Red Army. As a political commissar he could only rise to the junior general rank of colonel-general. (Author's collection)

This Soviet propaganda photograph from early 1940 shows the well-uniformed crew of a Maxim M1910 machine gun going into action. The original caption says that they are skillfully moving into position to assault the Mannerheim Line. Although the training, equipment, and tactics of the Red Army in early 1940 had improved, their commanders still committed them to costly frontal attacks. (Author's collection)

The Soviets were still taking heavy casualties: 800 were killed between February 20–22, for example. However, these were far less than the losses suffered in late 1939; in any event, the Red Army leadership was unconcerned at the number of casualties they were suffering. Tank losses were also high with between 10 and 30 being destroyed every day of the campaign, mostly victims of the Finns' "secret weapon," the Molotov cocktail—a dangerous way to destroy a tank. A spokesman for the Finnish General Staff said: "There are enormous heaps of Soviet dead in front of the Finnish positions. Yet, despite these losses, we always feel that there are tens of thousands of Soviets available to be sent in. We need men and materiel, especially planes. So far, the Finnish Army has been able to hold its own but we need the civilized world to aid us to the utmost."

A Finnish 81mm mortar crew in action from their log bunker. The medium mortar was a vital weapon in the Finnish Army during the war with 292 available in November 1939. France sent 100 mortars with 200,000 bombs, while Italy sent the same number with 75,000 bombs. Hungary did not send any mortars but did send 32,500 bombs for the French and Italian mortars. By March 1940 a total of 691 mortars were in service with the Finnish Army. (Author's collection)

A Finnish soldier takes aims with his Finnish-made Suomi KP/-31 sub-machine during the fighting in February 1940. The Suomi was a robust weapon, inaccurate over 100 yards but deadly at close range. Its drum magazine held 70 rounds of 9mm ammunition that really packed a punch. Initially, it was only issued to squad leaders and junior NCOs but as more became available it was issued more widely. (Author's collection)

As they emerge from a trench system on the Mannerheim Line, a patrol of Finnish soldiers check their rifles. This photograph taken in February 1940 shows that the fighting spirit of the Finnish Army was still in evidence. (Author's collection)

Finnish troops prepare to tow a captured flamethrower tank from the battlefield after it had been disabled during the fighting on the Mannerheim Line. This is the newer type T-26, the OT-130, which fired its flame out of the adapted turret. Many Soviet tanks were left stranded when their engines seized up with temperatures falling to −10°C and lower. (Author's collection)

During the February fighting on the Karelian Isthmus, two female Soviet medical officers smile for the camera. Both are lieutenants while the officer on the right has the brass symbol of the Medical Corps above the two red-square-jewel rank insignia. The red cloth star on their *budenovka* winter hats would be backed by a larger cloth star in the Medical Corps color, dark green. (Author's collection)

A Soviet officer examines a wine crate full of Molotov cocktails captured from the Finns. These homemade weapons were full of what was described as a "mixed cocktail" of crude kerosene, tar, and gasoline. Earlier versions were ignited by the gasoline-soaked rag wrapped around the neck of the bottle and then lit. Later versions had a sulfuric-acid ampule attached to the top of the bottle and when smashed against the side of a tank, the contents ignited. (Author's collection)

These ski troops are wearing newly issued snow overalls and the standard Red Army balaclava worn rolled up. The semi-automatic rifles carried by all three are World War I-era 6.5mm Fedorov Avtomat M1916s. These were issued to the Russian Imperial Army in small numbers and then seem to been put into storage. With the new Soviet semi-automatic rifle, the SVT-40, still awaiting issue, these rare weapons were issued to ski scouts during the Winter War. (Author's collection)

Soviet troops carry a wounded comrade to an aid station during the fighting in the Karelian Isthmus. In such freezing conditions even a minor wound could prove fatal and the incidence of gangrene amongst the wounded was appalling. This casualty is fortunate that he has been wounded near the end of the war instead of at the height of the severe winter of 1939/40. (Author's collection)

In Profile:
Vickers Mk E Type B Light Tank & T-26 Model 1933 Light Tank

Finnish Vickers 6-ton Mk E Type B Light Tank, 4th Company, Tank Battalion, Honkaniemi, February 1940. This British-made light tank was imported by the Finns in small numbers; some, like this type, were converted with an Oerlikon 20mm main gun. This Vickers which took part in the only armored clash of the Winter War has been hastily whitewashed with the original paintwork showing through. In order to distinguish their tanks from the similar-looking Soviet T-26 light tanks, its crew have painted a tricolor band of white–blue–white on the turret, the Finnish national colors.

Soviet T-26 Model 1933 Light Tank, 35th Light Tank Brigade, Honkaniemi, February 1940. This T-26 light tank was taken from the same British design as the Finnish Vickers 6-ton it faced in battle. The paintwork is in the standard factory green with a hastily applied whitewash over the top.

The Battle of Honkaniemi

On February 26, 1940 the only tank battle of the Winter War took place when six Finnish 6-ton Vickers light tanks faced off against three Red Army T-26 light tanks. The Finnish tanks were from the 4th Tank Company while the Soviet tanks were from the 35th Light Tank Brigade. The Soviet tanks were taking part in a reconnaissance mission and were approaching Honkaniemi. In a one-sided clash the Finns lost all their tanks: one tank was destroyed by a grenade attack while the other five were destroyed by the Soviet T-26s under the command of Captain V. S. Arkhipov. During the buildup to the encounter, the 4th Tank Company had already lost seven of their original 13 tanks due to engine problems. This poor showing by the Finns was largely a result of their lack of experience in using tanks in formations.

One of the new tactics used by the Red Army in early 1940 was the employment of metal sledges towed by a light tank to transport troops into battle. This touched-up photo shows a sledge with five soldiers hunkered down being towed into action. The idea was that the troops would be provided protection by the steel casemate around the sledge and then leap into action when they got close to Finnish lines. General F. D. Gorolenko's 50th Rifle Corps was issued with some of these sledges. Another innovation was an armored shield fitted with skis that could be pushed or pulled into action to give the men manning them some protection from enemy fire. (Author's collection)

111

Two elderly Finnish Home Guard volunteer skiers move up to the front wearing their own "Model Cajander" civilian clothes. (Aimo Cajander was the Finnish prime minister up until the Winter War.) Most Finns learned to ski almost before they could walk and used the Finnish ski designed for cross-country skiing, the "*Lapika,*" that was thinner and narrower than the more common Norwegian ski. It was fastened by a simple strap held in position by the turned-up toe of the Finnish boots. During the Soviet February offensive, the Finns were obliged to draw on the often untrained or poorly trained Home Guard. When the volunteers arrived at the front, they were rushed into the lines where many were soon killed due to their lack of combat training. (Author's collection)

Amongst the large volumes of Red Army equipment captured by the Finns in late 1939 and early 1940 were 16 of these trucks mounted with antiaircraft quad Maxim M1910 machine guns. Although having a limited range, these quads forced enemy aircraft to fly at a higher altitude, thus reducing their accuracy in bombing or strafing runs. (Author's collection)

In another example of the Finnish Army using captured weaponry, this antitank crew man a Soviet 37mm antitank gun, based on the German 30 L/45. A number of these effective weapons were put into service by the Finns alongside their own Swedish Bofors 37mm antitank guns. (Author's collection)

Lieutenant M. Sipovich waves the Red Flag in triumph, Karelian Isthmus, February 1940. He single-handedly neutralized the concrete bunker he is sitting on. Captain Korovin looks on. (Author's collection)

113

End of the War, March 1940

By late February the war was virtually over: the Finnish people knew that they could not resist for much longer. Although their soldiers still held their positions and the Finnish pilots still flew mission after mission, they knew the game was up. The best that Finland could hope for was, unlike the Baltic states and Poland, to maintain their independence. While Finnish diplomats began the process of trying to negotiate a peace deal with the unforgiving Soviet Union, they had to fight on to earn this last freedom with their blood.

Finnish ski troops withdraw from their positions on the Karelian Isthmus in March 1940 as the Red Army moves to take over the ceded territories lost to the Soviet Union. The original caption says that these "heroic" troops moving into Finnish territory will not receive the usual "fanfare" they might have expected. (Author's collection)

A Home Guard officer serving on the Northern Front in the closing stages of the war wears the M1927 brown woolen uniform, a pair of reindeer gloves and has the three gold rank devices that show he is a captain. As the war drew to a close, reserve units had to fill gaps. (Author's collection)

Finnish soldiers resisting the Red Army offensive in March 1940 pore over a map. They hold positions at Viipuri, one of the main centers of resistance. (Author's collection)

The Final Battle—Viipuri

After the defeat of the Finns at the second battle of Summa, Mannerheim ordered a northward retreat to a secondary defensive line on February 15. This second line was soon broken and the Finnish troops had to withdraw again to positions around the port of Viipuri, arriving on February 27. The morale of the remaining Finnish forces on the Karelian Isthmus had been badly affected by the sheer volume of force of the Soviet February offensive. Finnish soldiers were now at the end of their tether with many of the best troops killed since the fighting began again in February: half of the Finnish Army's 150,000 men were either dead or wounded.

Finnish communications had largely broken down and individual units were now fighting their own localized battles. For the first time during the war, some Finnish units were choosing to surrender rather than stand and face the increasing numbers of Soviet tanks, the constant artillery bombardment, and heavy aerial bombing. By March 12, both sides were totally exhausted, particularly the Finns. Casualty rates on both sides were horrendous though the Red Army had the advantage of being able to call on almost unlimited reinforcements. They also had the advantage of copious amounts of shells and small-arms ammunition which had arrived before the offensive began. On the Finnish side ammunition was running low and this was especially the case when it came to the ex-Soviet weaponry they were now using.

The desperate defense of the city of Viipuri took place in March 1940. This is one of the few guns that took part in the battle for the vital port. It is a 76mm 76K/02 which was one of the most common types of ex-Soviet field guns in Finnish service during the Winter War. (Author's collection)

The commander of the Soviet 7th Army, General Meretskov, was then ordered to attack the port of Viipuri. His 10th and 28th Corps were to advance to the western side of the port. The Soviet 19th Corps was to attack to the east while two corps, the 34th and 50th, were to make a frontal attack on the port's defenses. Situated on the Gulf of Finland, Viipuri was defended by two Finnish divisions, the 3rd and 5th of the II Army Corps. These two divisions were hastily reinforced by ad-hoc units made up largely of rear-echelon personnel: cooks, clerks, and other administrative staff now had to take up arms in the most vital battle of the war. Troops were also moved from so-called "quiet" sectors of the front as the coming battle was seen by both sides as the deciding encounter of the war. In desperation, the Finns had raised a last-minute battalion of boys and old men who had up until now been deemed too old to fight. This unit was sent to join the newly formed Coast Group under Chief of General Staff, Lieutenant-General K. L. Oesch, responsible for defending the northern shore of the Gulf of Finland and Viipuri Bay. Also in his force was the 4th Division as well as several ad-hoc units including some Laplanders who had arrived from the far north in February. With few field guns and predominantly only partially trained soldiers, the experienced Oesch knew his mission was doomed. Finnish formations held in reserve during the early fighting were the 1st and 23rd Divisions of I Army Corps.

General Harald Öhquist (1891–1971) joined the Russian Army's 27th Jäger Battalion in the days before Finnish independence in 1917. During the Winter War he was given command of the Finnish force defending the vital city of Viipuri. His II Corps was stationed on the Karelian Isthmus during the early stages of the Red Army invasion. Although Öhquist was regarded as one of Mannerheim's most trusted officers, he and the Finnish leader had an uneasy relationship. When the Continuation War with the Soviet Union began in 1941, he was not given a "responsible" role due to this poor relationship.

A large Finnish coastal gun mounted in an armored turret is aimed out into the Gulf of Viipuri. The Finns had several coastal batteries mounting guns from 152mm to 305mm which largely kept the Soviet Navy at bay during the Winter War. This gun was one of the coastal guns that helped to break the ice in the Gulf of Viipuri while the Red Army were crossing to access the port in March 1940. (Author's collection)

Fighting for the port began in earnest on March 2 and was to continue to the end of the war. Both sides were exhausted by the fierceness of the fighting and the desperation of the Finnish defense. Soviet forces took several islands in the inlet around Viipuri after heavy resistance by the Finns. By March 8 the Soviet troops attacking across the inlet had established themselves at Vilaniemi and Haranpaa to the west of Viipuri. Most of the islands in the Gulf of Viipuri had now fallen to the Red Army and Finnish defenders had fallen back into the port. These islands were defended sometimes to the last man by the Finns who knew what their fall meant to the defense of Viipuri. On the 9th, it was reported that a nine-mile column of Soviet troops well supported by tanks was moving up to finish off the defenders. At the same time the Soviets captured the defenses around the city of Tali before crossing the Tali River. Soviet troops of the 28th Corps managed to gain a several-mile-wide bridgehead at Vilajoki on the northwestern shore of the Gulf on March 10. It was not just the Finnish defenders who were holding up the Red Army advances but the terrain also had a major effect: swamps and flooded areas stopped supplies getting through. For the next few days, the Finns held out, while in Moscow peace negotiations continued. Fighting continued until the last minute of the war and soldiers on both sides were still being killed when the official ceasefire came into force on March 13.

Wounded Finnish regulars and civilian volunteers detrain at Helsinki station after returning from the front. The Finns suffered heavy casualties during the conflict with the official figure of 43,557 wounded. Although these casualties were dwarfed by those suffered by the Red Army, the Finns could simply not replace the experienced soldiers they had lost. (Author's collection)

The Peace

By the end of February 1940, Marshal Mannerheim, a pragmatist, had decided that his troops and the country as a whole could not resist for much longer. He advised his government that they would have to sue for peace with the hope that their resistance would guarantee some level of independence from the Soviet Union. By early March the Finns were in danger of being totally overwhelmed by the Red Army in the Karelian Isthmus. It was now time to make the decision to sue for peace as the Soviet ultimatum for acceptance of the final peace terms had run out on March 1. To push the Finns along the Soviets launched a devastating attack on the city of Viipuri on the 3rd. On the 6th a Finnish delegation led by the Prime Minister Risto Ryti traveled to Moscow where they tried to ask for some concessions from Stalin. They were dealing with the unsympathetic Soviet Foreign Minister, Vyacheslav Molotov, who coldly replied to their pleas with a simple, "*Nyet.*" Ryti meanwhile was in constant touch with the government back in Finland where the news from the front was getting worse. Before putting the treaty to his ministers, Ryti had spoken with them, saying: "Finland and the rest of Western civilization is still in the greatest danger and no one can say what tomorrow may bring. We believe that by choosing peace we have acted in the best way for the moment."

The vote for acceptance of the terms was passed by 145 votes to 5 and the Treaty of Moscow was signed on March 12, 1940 with Finland ceding 16,000 square miles of its territory to the Soviet Union. The new frontier saw the majority of Karelia handed over to the Soviets, with Finland open to further aggression by Stalin. Because of the redrawing of

The original caption to this photograph says: "Reading the Harsh Terms of Peace" as the people of Helsinki digest the news of the peace agreement. The boarded-up windows of high street shops in the Finnish capital are used to display newspapers and official documents which lay out the Soviet Union's humiliating terms. (Author's collection)

Finnish refugees prepare to leave the ceded territories as the Red Army moves into its newly won territorial gains. A total of 470,000 Finns now became homeless and were evacuated in trucks requisitioned by their government. Many of these refugees had been farmers: 40,000 farms were lost to the Soviet Union. In late June the Finnish government introduced an Emergency Resettlement Act to provide for the desperate refugees. (Sa-Kuva-109394)

Soviet politician M. I. Kalinin (third from right) presenting awards on March 31 to senior officers who had fought with distinction during the Winter War. Kalinin was the Chairman of the Presidium of the Supreme Soviet of the USSR and one of Stalin's right-hand men. The officers are, from left: Brigade Commander A. Khrenov, Corps Commander S. Denisov, Army Commander G. Kulik, Army Commander S. Timoshenko, and Army Commander K. Meretskov. (Author's collection)

the map, a total of 470,000 Finns had to be evacuated from eastern Finland. This meant that 1 in 8 of the prewar Finnish population were now homeless unless they were willing to live under Soviet rule. All available transport was employed to relocate the refugees and their possessions and livestock to the west. For the Soviet Union and Stalin, the recent successes in Poland, the Baltic states, and now Finland were cause for great celebration. As one commentator noted, the border was now more or less where it had been drawn by Peter the Great in 1721.

Under a headline of "Finns Evacuate their Gibraltar," this photograph highlights a tense moment on the new border at Hanko. Besides losing Viipuri which was Finland's most important port, the Finns were forced to lease to the USSR the Hanko Peninsula which was the key to access the Gulf of Finland. The lease on the peninsula was to run for 30 years at an annual rent of £30,000. When Hanko was evacuated by the Finns, 11,000 refugees had to relocate to unoccupied parts of Finland. Here a single Finnish sentry peers from behind a barbed-wire fence as Soviet border guards come to check him out. (Author's collection)

| Epilogue

A 1990 study claimed that the Red Army suffered 53,522 dead, 16,028 missing, 163,722 wounded, and 12,064 frostbitten. In 1999, a Finnish study of the conflict estimated Red Army losses at 84,994 dead or prisoners, 186,584 wounded or disabled, 51,892 sick, and 9,614 frostbitten.

Another more severe Soviet study calculated 126,875 Red Army dead and 264,908 wounded. The Soviet authorities published their own figures for Red Army losses with 48,745 dead and 150,863 wounded. In the closed society that pervaded the Soviet Union these highly optimistic numbers were accepted by the people. However, Nikita Khrushchev, the Soviet leader from 1958 to 1964, candidly said that 1.5 million Soviets had gone to Finland and 1 million did not return. He also admitted that 1,000 aircraft, 2,300 armored vehicles, and enormous amounts of military equipment had been left on the battlefields. This equipment and weaponry lost by the Red Army during the Winter War would have been useful when the Germans launched Operation *Barbarossa* in June 1941. However, the majority of tanks and aircraft were on the verge of obsolescence by 1941 and new models were in production before the Germans invaded. Marshal Mannerheim issued his own estimate of the losses and put the Red Army dead at 200,000. He claimed that thousands of the Soviet wounded had died needlessly due to the almost total lack of Red Army medical attention in 1939. Finland's losses were estimated at 24,904 dead and 43,557 wounded with better medical attention and treatment for the dreaded frostbite. Finnish estimates of the materiel losses for the Red Army were 1,600 tanks and for the Red Air Force between 684 and 975 aircraft.

The caption for this dramatically stylized image from an Italian magazine states: "The tenacious Finnish resistance to the Soviet invasion." Finnish fighters are described as "Ghosts that rise from the forest and the snow using their traditional curved swords to decimate the Red Army." (Author's collection)

| Further Reading

Coates, William Peyton & Zelda, K. Coates. *The Soviet-Finnish Campaign 1939–1940*. London UK: Eldon Press 1941

Condon, Richard. W. *The Winter War: Russia Against Finland*. London UK: Pan/Ballantine 1972

Dittmar, K. *The Red Army in the Finnish War*. New York 1956

Edwards, Robert. *White Death: Russia's War on Finland 1939–40*. London UK: Weidenfeld & Nicolson 2006

Engle, Eloise & Lauri Paananen. *The Winter War: The Russo-Finnish Conflict, 1939–40*. London UK: The Military Book Society 1973

Erickson, John. *The Soviet High Command 1918–1941*. London UK: Macmillan & Co. 1962

Hooper, Arthur Sanderson. *The Soviet Finnish Campaign*. London UK: Self-published 1940

Irincheev, Bair. *War of the White Death: Finland Against the Soviet Union*. Mechanicsburg PA: Stackpole 2016

Johansen, Claes. *Hitler's Nordic Ally?: Finland and the Total War 1939–45*. Barnsley UK: Pen & Sword 2016

Jowett, Philip & Brent Snodgrass. *Finland at War 1939–1945*. Oxford UK: Osprey 2006

Kulju, Mika. *Raatteen tie: Talvissodan phonier sankaritarina*. Helsinki, Finland: Ajatus kirjat 2007

Moynahan, Brian. *The Claws of the Bear: A History of the Soviet Armed Forces From 1917 to the Present*. London UK: Hutchinson 1989

Sander, Gordon F. *The Hundred Day Winter War: Finland's Gallant Stand Against the Soviet Army*. Austin TX: University Press of Texas 2013

Seaton, Albert & Joan Seaton. *The Soviet Army: 1918 to the Present*. London UK: The Bodley Head 1986

Spencer, Malcom L. G. *Stalinism and the Soviet-Finnish War 1939–40*. London UK: Palgrave Macmillan 2018

Trotter, William. R. *The Winter War: The Russo-Finnish War 1939–40*. London UK: Aurum Press 1991

Tuunainen, Pasi. *Finnish Military Effectiveness in the Winter War, 1939–1940*. London UK: Palgrave Macmillan 2018

Vesa, Nenye. *Finland at War: The Winter War 1939–40*. Oxford UK: Osprey 2018

The frozen corpse of a Soviet soldier. Soviet soldiers trapped in the various *mottis* often received as little as 400 calories a day when they really needed 4,000 as a minimum in the freezing weather. (Author's collection)

| Index